INSTITUTE OF ACTUARIES'

TEXT-BOOK

OF THE

PRINCIPLES OF INTEREST,

LIFE ANNUITIES, AND ASSURANCES,

AND THEIR PRACTICAL APPLICATION.

This is a volume in the
Arno Press collection

DIMENSIONS OF ACCOUNTING THEORY AND PRACTICE

Advisory Editor
Richard P. Brief

See last pages of this volume
for a complete list of titles

INSTITUTE OF ACTUARIES'

TEXT-BOOK

OF THE

PRINCIPLES OF INTEREST,

LIFE ANNUITIES, AND ASSURANCES,

AND THEIR PRACTICAL APPLICATION.

PART I.

INTEREST (INCLUDING ANNUITIES-CERTAIN).

RALPH TODHUNTER

ARNO PRESS
A New York Times Company
New York • 1980

Editorial Supervision: Brian Quinn

Reprint Edition 1980 by Arno Press Inc.
Reprinted from a copy in the Haverford College Library

DIMENSIONS OF ACCOUNTING THEORY AND PRACTICE
ISBN for complete set: 0-405-13475-4
See last pages of this volume for titles.

Manufactured in the United States of America

Library of Congress Cataloging in Publication Data

Institute of Actuaries, London.
Institute of Actuaries' textbook of the principles of interest, life annuities, and assurances, and their practical application, part I, Interest (including annuities-certain)

(Dimensions of accounting theory and practice)
Reprint of v. 1 of the author's New ed. published in 1901 by C. & E. Layton, London.
1. Insurance, Life. 2. Interest and usury. 3. Annuities. I. Todhunter, Ralph. II. Title. III. Series.
HG8781.I5 1980 332.8'2 80-1529
ISBN 0-405-13550-5

INSTITUTE OF ACTUARIES'

TEXT-BOOK

OF THE

PRINCIPLES OF INTEREST, LIFE ANNUITIES, AND ASSURANCES,

AND THEIR PRACTICAL APPLICATION.

PART I.

INTEREST (INCLUDING ANNUITIES-CERTAIN).

NEW EDITION.

BY

RALPH TODHUNTER, M.A.,
FORMERLY FELLOW OF CLARE COLLEGE, CAMBRIDGE,
FELLOW OF THE INSTITUTE OF ACTUARIES,
ACTUARY AND SECRETARY OF THE UNIVERSITY LIFE ASSURANCE SOCIETY.

Published by the Authority, and under the Superintendence, of the Institute.

LONDON:
CHARLES & EDWIN LAYTON, FARRINGDON STREET, E.C.

1901.

PREFACE.

The Council of the Institute of Actuaries, while recognizing the skill with which the first Text-Book, Part I., on Interest, had been written, felt that in some ways it might be made more suitable for the students for whom it was intended. When, therefore, a new edition was needed, they laid the matter before Mr. Todhunter, requesting him to consider it from this point of view, giving him full liberty to act as he might think best. He found it desirable to re-write the volume, and has accordingly done so.

It is hoped that the following pages, including in due proportion theoretical explanation and practical example, will prove increasingly useful to all whose duty or pleasure it may be to apply themselves to this important subject, and that Mr. Todhunter's ability and care will earn the gratitude which they surely merit.

C. D. H.

24 *June* 1901.

INTRODUCTION BY THE AUTHOR.

In the preparation of a New Edition of the Text-Book, Part I., it has been found necessary to re-write the work. The general Theory of Compound Interest has been presented in a form which will, it is hoped, afford a comprehensive view of the subject, and special attention has been given to the applications of the Theory to practical financial problems. For the convenience of those students who have no previous knowledge of the methods of the Infinitesimal Calculus, a chapter on the elements of this subject has been included.

In the compilation of the volume assistance has been derived from numerous papers and notes in the *Journal*, and from various treatises on Compound Interest—more especially from Mr. George King's *Theory of Finance*, to which no subsequent writer could fail to be greatly indebted—but, in accordance with precedent, references to authorities have not been given.

The author takes this opportunity of acknowledging his indebtedness to the Council of the Institute for the critical examination which they have given to the work during its progress, while according him entire liberty in the treatment of the subject. He also offers his best thanks to Mr. J. E. FAULKS, B.A., for many valuable suggestions, and to Mr. A. LEVINE, M.A., for assistance in the revision of the earlier proof-sheets of the two concluding chapters and other parts of the work.

R. T.

London, 12 *June* 1901.

TABLE OF CONTENTS.

CHAPTER I.

DEFINITIONS AND ELEMENTARY PROPOSITIONS.

CHAPTER II.

ON THE SOLUTION OF PROBLEMS IN COMPOUND INTEREST—PRACTICAL EXAMPLES—EQUATION OF PAYMENTS.

CHAPTER III.

On the Valuation of Annuities-Certain.

CHAPTER IV.

Analysis of the Annuity.

CHAPTER V.

On the Valuation of Debentures and other Securities—Miscellaneous Problems.

CHAPTER VI.

On the Determination of the Rate of Interest involved in a given Transaction.

CHAPTER VII.

Capital Redemption Assurances.

CHAPTER VIII.

Interest Tables.

CHAPTER IX.

FORMULAS OF THE INFINITESIMAL CALCULUS.

CHAPTER X.

APPLICATIONS OF THE CALCULUS OF FINITE DIFFERENCES AND THE INFINITESIMAL CALCULUS.

TABLES.

INSTITUTE OF ACTUARIES' TEXT-BOOK.

PART I.

THE THEORY OF COMPOUND INTEREST AND ANNUITIES-CERTAIN.

CHAPTER I.

DEFINITIONS AND ELEMENTARY PROPOSITIONS.

1. INTEREST may be defined as the consideration for the use of capital, or as that which is earned by the productive investment of capital. In theory, it is not necessary that the invested capital and the consideration for the use of it should be expressed in terms of one or the same commodity, but in practice it is usual and convenient to express both in terms of some one unit; in the investigations that follow, it will be assumed that both are expressed in terms of a unit of money, without specification of the particular currency to which that unit belongs.

2. The invested capital is called the PRINCIPAL. The consideration for the use of capital usually becomes due at stated intervals, and, being itself of the same nature as capital, may be employed, when received, as capital. In the Theory of Compound Interest, it is assumed that the consideration will not be allowed to remain idle, but will immediately be productively invested.

3. The total interest earned on a given principal in a given time will obviously depend on (1) the given principal, (2) the interest contracted to be paid for each stated interval in respect of each unit of principal, (3) the given time. The second of these quantities is, in the strictest sense, the RATE OF INTEREST, and in some investigations it will be found convenient to take this quantity—the interest contracted to be paid in respect of each unit of principal for each stated interval—and the number of such intervals in the given time as data. The expression "the rate of interest" is, however, more generally used with reference to a *year*, the accepted unit of time in the Theory of Finance, and it is so used to denote:—

(1) the rate per unit *per annum* at which interest is calculated for each stated interval for which interest is contracted to be paid, or, in other words, the interest that would be earned on each unit of principal in a year if the interest received at the end of each stated interval were not itself productively invested;

(2) the total interest earned on each unit of principal in a year on the assumption that the actual interest as received at the end of each stated interval is invested on the same terms as the original principal.

4. It is obvious that, except in the case when the stated interval for which interest is to be paid is a year, these two senses in which the expression "the rate of interest" is employed represent two different things. To take a simple example, let it be supposed that a principal of 100 is invested in consideration of the payment of $2\frac{1}{2}$ at the end of each half-year. In this case the rate per unit *per annum* at which interest is calculated, or the interest that would be earned in a year on each unit of principal if the interest received at the end of the first half-year were not productively invested, is ·05, whereas the total interest earned on each unit of principal in a year on the assumption that the $2\frac{1}{2}$ received at the end of the first half-year is invested on the same terms as the original principal (*i.e.*, in consideration of the payment of $2\frac{1}{2}$ per-cent on the $2\frac{1}{2}$, or ·0625, at the end of each half-year) is ·050625. It is convenient, therefore, to distinguish between the two senses in which the expression "rate of interest" is employed by the use of distinct expressions and distinct symbols.

5. The rate per unit per annum at which the actual interest for each stated interval is calculated when that interval differs from a year, or, in other words, the interest that would be earned on each unit of principal in a year if the interest as received were not productively invested, is called the NOMINAL RATE OF INTEREST, and will be distinguished by the symbol j. The frequency with which interest is actually payable, or the stated interval of payment, is defined by the expressions "payable half-yearly, quarterly, or m times a year" (as the case may be), "convertible half-yearly, quarterly, monthly, &c.", or "with half-yearly, quarterly, monthly, &c., rests." Thus, when interest is said to be at the nominal rate of 5 per-cent per annum payable (or convertible) half-yearly, or at the nominal rate of 5 per-cent per annum with half-yearly rests, it is meant that $2\frac{1}{2}$ is to be paid at the end of each half year for each 100 owing at the beginning of the half year. The frequency of conversion of a given nominal rate may be denoted by means of a suffix placed in brackets at the lower right-hand corner of the symbol representing the rate. Thus $j_{(m)}$ denotes a nominal rate j convertible m times a year.

6. The total interest earned on 1 in a year, on the assumption that the actual interest (if receivable otherwise than yearly) is immediately invested as it becomes due, on the same terms as the original principal, is called the EFFECTIVE RATE OF INTEREST, and will be distinguished by the symbol i.

7. To every nominal rate of interest, convertible with a given frequency, there is a *corresponding* effective rate, for the total interest earned on each unit of principal in a year—in other words, the effective rate of interest—may be found by accumulating a unit, on the assumption of compound interest, at the given nominal rate. Thus, if the nominal rate be j, convertible m times a year, an original unit of principal, together with the interest upon it at the end of the first $\frac{1}{m}$th of a year, will amount to $1+\frac{j}{m}$. By assumption the $\frac{j}{m}$ is immediately invested on the same terms as the original unit of principal, so that the interest due at the end of the second $\frac{1}{m}$th of a year will be $\frac{j}{m}\left(1+\frac{j}{m}\right)$; hence the original unit with interest will amount to $1+\frac{j}{m}+\frac{j}{m}\left(1+\frac{j}{m}\right)$ or $\left(1+\frac{j}{m}\right)^2$. Similarly, in each $\frac{1}{m}$th of a year the amount of the original unit with interest at the beginning of the interval will be increased in the ratio of $1+\frac{j}{m}$ to 1. Consequently, at the end of a year, the unit of principal with interest will amount to $\left(1+\frac{j}{m}\right)^m$. The total interest earned on each unit of principal in the year is, therefore, $\left(1+\frac{j}{m}\right)^m-1$. In symbols,

$$i=\left(1+\frac{j}{m}\right)^m-1 \quad . \quad . \quad . \quad . \quad . \quad . \quad . \quad . \quad . \quad (1)$$

whence

$$j=m\left\{(1+i)^{\frac{1}{m}}-1\right\} \quad . \quad . \quad . \quad . \quad . \quad . \quad . \quad . \quad (2)$$

and

$$m \log\left(1+\frac{j}{m}\right)=\log(1+i) \quad . \quad . \quad . \quad . \quad (3)$$

8. From these equations the effective rate of interest corresponding to a given nominal rate convertible with a given frequency, or, conversely, the nominal rate convertible with any required frequency corresponding to a given effective rate, may be calculated.

9. It will be observed that if *two* of the three quantities j, m and i are given, the equation gives a single value for the third quantity; that is to say, to a given nominal rate convertible with a given frequency there is one, and only one, corresponding effective rate; to a given effective rate, there is one, and only one, corresponding nominal rate convertible with a given frequency; and, finally, there is one, and only one, frequency for which a given nominal rate and a given effective rate will correspond.

10. But if only *one* of the three quantities is given, any number of corresponding values may be found for either of the remaining two by assigning successive values to the other.

Thus, if j be given, any number of corresponding values of i may be found by giving successive values to m. As m increases from 1 to ∞, the value of $\left(1+\frac{j}{m}\right)^m-1$ increases from j to e^j-1. Hence the effective rate corresponding to a given nominal rate increases as the frequency of conversion of the latter is increased. For example, a nominal rate of 5 per-cent per annum convertible quarterly gives a higher effective rate than the same nominal rate convertible half-yearly. Again, if i be given, any number of corresponding values of j may be found by giving successive values to m. As m increases from 1 to ∞, the value of $m\left\{(1+i)^{\frac{1}{m}}-1\right\}$ decreases from i to $\log_e(1+i)$. Hence the nominal rate corresponding to a given effective rate *decreases* as the frequency of conversion is increased. For example, the nominal rate convertible *half-yearly* corresponding to an effective rate of 5 per-cent exceeds the nominal rate convertible *quarterly* corresponding to the same effective rate. It will be noticed, however, that the nominal rate corresponding to the effective rate i does not decrease indefinitely as m is increased, but gradually approaches the value $\log_e(1+i)$, this being the limiting value of $m\left\{(1+i)^{\frac{1}{m}}-1\right\}$, when m is made infinitely large. This limiting value is called the FORCE OF INTEREST corresponding to the effective rate i, and is distinguished by the special symbol δ.

11. The force of interest corresponding to a given effective rate i may therefore be defined as the nominal rate convertible at infinitely short intervals corresponding to that effective rate.

12. From the foregoing it will be seen that the basis upon which interest is to be calculated in any given case may be defined by means of an *effective rate of interest*, i; *a nominal rate of interest*, j, *convertible with a given frequency*, m; or, finally, a *force of interest*, δ; and that when any one of these three quantities is given the *corresponding values* of the other two may be determined by the equations

$$1+i=\left(1+\frac{j}{m}\right)^m=e^\delta \quad . \quad . \quad . \quad . \quad . \quad . \quad (4)$$

13. To proceed to the general theory of the accumulation of principal under the operation of compound interest.

Let P be a given principal, S the sum to which it will amount if accumulated at compound interest for n years, and I the total interest earned on P in the given period. Let i be the effective rate of interest at which the given principal is to be accumulated, j the corresponding nominal rate of interest convertible m times a year, and δ the corresponding force of interest. Then by reasoning precisely similar to that by which it was shown that a unit accumulated for a year at compound interest at the nominal rate j convertible m times a year will amount to $\left(1+\frac{j}{m}\right)^m$, it follows that

$$S=P(1+i)^n=P\left(1+\frac{j}{m}\right)^{mn}=Pe^{n\delta} \quad . \quad . \quad . \quad . \quad (5)$$

This system of equations affords the means of calculating the amount, in a given number of years, of a given principal at any given rate of interest—effective or nominal—provided only that rate continues uniformly in operation throughout the entire period. The appropriate formula to employ in any given case will be

$$S=P(1+i)^n$$

or

$$S=P\left(1+\frac{j}{m}\right)^{mn}$$

or

$$S=Pe^{n\delta}$$

according as the given rate is an effective rate, a nominal rate, or a force of interest. It would, of course, be practicable to obtain the amount of a given principal at a given nominal rate or force of interest, by first finding the effective rate corresponding to the given rate, and then employing the formula $S=P(1+i)^n$, but in general it will be found more convenient to use the directly appropriate formula.

14. It should be noted that tables giving the amount of 1 in any number of years (within the limits of the tables), at various effective rates of interest, may often be employed for the purpose of calculating the amount of a given principal at a given nominal rate. For example, let it be required to find the amount of 100 in 20 years at 6 per-cent convertible half-yearly. By the appropriate formula the amount $=100(1{\cdot}03)^{40}$, which also represents the amount of 100 in *40* years at 3 per-cent *effective*. Hence the required result will be obtained by taking 100 times the tabulated value of the amount of 1 in *40* years at 3 per-cent per annum. In fact, a table of amounts may be regarded more generally as a table of $(1+x)^n$, and used for any purpose for which the value of this function is required.

15. In the derivation of formula (5), it has been implicitly assumed that n is integral. In order to extend the formula to cases in which n is not an integer, it is necessary to adopt some convention as to the interest to be assumed for a fractional part of a year. When the given rate is an effective rate, or when it is a nominal rate and the fractional part of a year does not contain an integral number of the intervals of conversion, it is permissible to adopt any convention that may appear suitable, for the stated conditions do not prescribe any rule. When, however, the given rate is a nominal rate—say, j convertible m times a year—and the given period of accumulation contains an exact number of the intervals of conversion, being, say, $n+\frac{t}{m}$ years, a given principal P will amount to $P\left(1+\frac{j}{m}\right)^{nm+t}$, and this quantity, by algebraical substitution, $=P(1+i)^{n+\frac{t}{m}}$, where i is the effective rate corresponding to j. It appears, therefore, in this case, that the interest on 1 at the effective rate i for $\frac{t}{m}$ of a year is $(1+i)^{\frac{t}{m}}-1$. This result suggests the usual and convenient assumption that the interest on 1 for any fractional part, say $\frac{1}{p}$, of a year at the effective rate i, may be taken as $(1+i)^{\frac{1}{p}}-1$, and the adoption of this convention leads to the generalization that

$$S=P(1+i)^n=P\left(1+\frac{j}{m}\right)^{mn}=Pe^{n\delta}$$

for all values of n, *integral or fractional*. Similarly, the total interest earned on P will be given, in all cases, by the formula

$$I=S-P=P[(1+i)^n-1]=P\left[\left(1+\frac{j}{m}\right)^{mn}-1\right]=P[e^{n\delta}-1].$$

16. The foregoing articles deal with the *accumulation* of principal under the operation of compound interest. It is now necessary to consider the converse process of *discounting*. The general theory of compound discount may be developed on precisely the same lines as the theory of compound interest.

17. Discount may be defined as the consideration for the immediate payment of a sum due at a future date, and the total discount to be allowed for the present payment of a given sum due may be determined by reference to an *effective rate of discount* per annum, a *nominal rate of discount* per annum convertible with a given frequency, or a *force of discount*, the last-mentioned quantity being, in other words, a nominal rate of discount convertible at infinitely short intervals.

18. The sum due, less the total discount upon it, is called its Present Value.

19. As there is an effective rate of interest corresponding to any given nominal rate of interest, so also there is an effective rate of discount corresponding to a given nominal rate of discount. For, if the nominal rate of discount be f per annum convertible m times a year, the present value of 1 due $\frac{1}{m}$th of a year hence, will be $1-\frac{f}{m}$. Similarly, for each interval of conversion the sum due will be decreased in the ratio of 1 to $1-\frac{f}{m}$. The present value of 1 due a year hence will, therefore, be $\left(1-\frac{f}{m}\right)^m$. Hence the total discount on 1 for the year, or, in other words, the effective rate of discount corresponding to the nominal rate f, will be $1-\left(1-\frac{f}{m}\right)^m$. If the effective rate of discount be represented by d,

$$d=1-\left(1-\frac{f}{m}\right)^m, \text{ or } 1-d=\left(1-\frac{f}{m}\right)^m,$$

whence
$$f=m\left\{1-(1-d)^{\frac{1}{m}}\right\} \quad . \quad . \quad . \quad . \quad . \quad . \quad . \quad . \quad . \quad . \quad (6)$$

20. From these relations the effective rate of discount corresponding to a given nominal rate, or, conversely, the nominal rate convertible with any required frequency corresponding to a given effective rate, may be calculated just as in the case of the similar relations between the corresponding effective and nominal rates of interest.

As the frequency of conversion is increased, the nominal rate corresponding to a given effective rate increases. In the limiting case, when m is made infinitely large, f becomes, by definition, the force of discount corresponding to the effective rate d. Let this limiting value of f be denoted by δ'. Then

$$\delta'=\text{Limit}^{m=\infty} m\left\{1-(1-d)^{\frac{1}{m}}\right\}=-\log_e(1-d) \quad . \quad . \quad (7)$$

21. To proceed to the general problem of finding the present value of a sum due n years hence.

Let S′ be the sum due, P′ its present value, and D the total discount on S′. Let d be the effective rate at which the given sum due is to be discounted, f the corresponding nominal rate of discount convertible m times a year, and δ' the corresponding force of discount. Then, by reasoning precisely similar to that by which it was shown that the present value of 1 due a year hence at the nominal rate f is $\left(1-\frac{f}{m}\right)^m$, it follows that

$$P' = S'(1-d)^n = S'\left(1-\frac{f}{m}\right)^{mn} = S'e^{-n\delta'} \quad . \quad . \quad . \quad (8)$$

whence $D = S'[1-(1-d)^n] = S'\left[1-\left(1-\frac{f}{m}\right)^{mn}\right] = S'(1-e^{-n\delta'})$.

22. These formulas may be extended, in precisely the same way as the corresponding compound interest formulas, to cases in which n is not integral. The discount on 1 for $\frac{1}{p}$th of a year may be taken as $1-(1-d)^{\frac{1}{p}}$, and the formulas will then hold good for all values of n, integral or fractional.

23. So far, the operations of accumulating and discounting have been considered separately, and two independent systems of equations have been established. It is obvious, however, that the two processes, although admitting of independent theoretical development, will not be independent in practice, for the operation of discounting, from the point of view of the investor, differs in no essential respect from that of investing capital to accumulate at compound interest. It becomes important, therefore, to investigate the relations between the rates of interest and discount, and between the general formulas of compound interest and compound discount in the case when the rate of discount is such that the present value of a sum due n years hence is that sum which will amount in n years, under the operation of compound interest, to the given sum due. Under these conditions, if S be the amount of P in n years at the effective rate of interest i, or at the corresponding nominal rate of interest j convertible m times a year, or at the corresponding force of interest δ, then will P be the present value of S at the effective rate of discount d, or at the corresponding nominal rate of discount f convertible m times a year, or at the corresponding force of discount δ'. But by formula (5)

$$S = P(1+i)^n = P\left(1+\frac{j}{m}\right)^{mn} = Pe^{n\delta}$$

and by formula (8), if S and P be substituted for S′ and P′

$$P = S(1-d)^n = S\left(1-\frac{f}{m}\right)^{mn} = Se^{-n\delta}$$

Therefore

$$(1+i) = \left(1+\frac{j}{m}\right)^m = e^{\delta} = (1-d)^{-1} = \left(1-\frac{f}{m}\right)^{-m} = e^{\delta'} \qquad (9)$$

The assumption by which these results have been obtained—the assumption, namely, that the present value of a given sum due will, if accumulated at compound interest, amount to that sum—is implicitly made in all compound interest problems. In any given investigation, therefore, where a single uniform rate of interest is employed, formulas (9) will hold good.

24. Instead of being independently developed, the theory of compound discount may be regarded as a necessary deduction from that of compound interest. From this point of view, the present value, at a given effective rate of interest, of a given sum due, is defined to be that sum which, if accumulated at the given rate of interest, will amount to the given sum; and the effective rate of discount corresponding to a given effective rate of interest is defined to be the difference between a unit and the present value, at the given rate of interest, of a unit due a year hence. From these definitions, since 1 is the present value of $1+i$, and consequently $\frac{1}{1+i}$ is the present value of 1, it follows that $1-d=\frac{1}{1+i}$, from which formula (9) may be immediately deduced.

25. In practice it is customary to regard the operation of discounting from the point of view adopted in the last paragraph, and to speak of *discounting* a given sum, or finding its *present value*, at a given *rate of interest*—that is, at the rate of discount corresponding to that rate of interest. Financial transactions are usually based upon a given rate of interest, and the corresponding rate of discount—if required—is deduced from the given rate of interest by means of formula (9). An exception to this rule occurs in the case of bill-discounting, which is invariably based upon a rate of discount. In particular, what is termed "Bank rate" is the rate of discount charged by the Bank of England for discounting first-class bills. In employing an agreed rate of discount—f, say—to discount a bill due $\frac{1}{n}$th of a year hence the usual commercial practice is to treat the rate as a nominal rate of discount convertible n times a year, and consequently to charge discount amounting to $\frac{f}{n}$ for each unit of the amount of the bill, so that the effective rate of discount in respect of the transaction is $1-\left(1-\frac{f}{n}\right)^n$. As n is increased, the value of this expression diminishes. It appears, therefore, that, in discounting bills at the uniform rate f, the banker or bill-discounter, by following commercial usage, realizes a slightly higher effective rate on the longer bills than on the shorter ones, and that, inasmuch as practically all trade bills are drawn for periods of less than a year, he will realize all round a slightly lower effective rate than the rate f at which discount is calculated. The difference is, of course, so small as to be of no practical importance.

26. By obvious deductions from formula (9) it will be seen that, if i and d are corresponding effective rates of interest and discount, j and f the corresponding nominal rates of interest and discount convertible m times a year, and δ and δ' the corresponding forces of interest and discount, then

$$i-d=id$$

$$j-f=\frac{jf}{m}$$

and
$$\delta=\delta'.$$

The last equation establishes the important proposition that the forces of interest and discount corresponding to the same effective rate of interest are equal, and the two preceding equations suggest a verbal explanation of this fact. The difference between the effective rate of interest i and the corresponding effective rate of discount d is equal to a year's interest on d, for d is equivalent to a year's interest on the present value of 1 due a year hence, that is on $1-d$, whereas i is a year's interest on 1. Similarly, since $\frac{j}{m}$ and $\frac{f}{m}$ may be regarded as corresponding effective rates of interest and discount for the interval of $\frac{1}{m}$th of a year, $\frac{j}{m}$ exceeds $\frac{f}{m}$ by the interest for $\frac{1}{m}$th of a year on $\frac{f}{m}$, that is, $\frac{j}{m}-\frac{f}{m}=\frac{j}{m}\cdot\frac{f}{m}$, or $j-f=\frac{jf}{m}$. Now, when m is increased indefinitely, j and f become respectively, by definition, the force of interest and the force of discount, and $\frac{jf}{m}$ vanishes. Consequently, the force of interest $=$ the force of discount.

27. The question may also be considered from a slightly different point of view. If a sum P increases in $\frac{1}{m}$th of a year to S under the operation of interest, the nominal rate of interest per annum may be found by taking the ratio of S$-$P to P and multiplying by m, while the corresponding nominal rate of discount will be found by taking the ratio of S—P to S and multiplying by m—the numerator being the same in both cases, but the denominator being the *present value* in one case and the *amount* in the other. Now when the interval is indefinitely diminished the present value differs by an indefinitely small amount, so that the two operations give identical results. But in this case the nominal rates of interest and discount become the *forces* of interest and discount. Consequently, as before, the force of interest = the force of discount.

In future, the one symbol δ will be used for both the force of interest and the force of discount.

28. For convenience, the quantity $\frac{1}{1+i}$ or $(1+i)^{-1}$—the present value at the effective rate i of 1 due a year hence—is frequently denoted by the symbol v. Thus the present value, at the effective rate i, of S due n years hence, may be written either as $S(1+i)^{-n}$ or Sv^n.

29. Since $1-d=\frac{1}{1+i}$ it follows that

$$d=\frac{i}{1+i}\quad\text{or}\quad iv.$$

This relation, which will be found useful in many investigations, expresses the fact that the discount at the effective rate of interest i on 1 due a year hence is equal to the present value of a year's interest on 1, or, conversely, that the interest on 1 if paid at the beginning instead of the end of the year would be d.

30. By reference to equation (9) it will be seen that any one of the quantities i, d, j, f, δ, and v may be expressed in terms of any other.

Thus,

$$i=(1-d)^{-1}-1=d+d^2+d^3+\ldots$$

$$=\left(1+\frac{j}{m}\right)^m-1=j+\frac{m-1}{m}\cdot\frac{j^2}{2!}+\frac{\overline{m-1}\;\overline{m-2}}{m^2}\cdot\frac{j^3}{3!}+\ldots$$

$$=\left(1-\frac{f}{m}\right)^{-m}-1=f+\frac{m+1}{m}\cdot\frac{f^2}{2!}+\frac{\overline{m+1}\;\overline{m+2}}{m^2}\cdot\frac{f^3}{3!}+\ldots$$

$$=e^\delta-1=\delta+\frac{\delta^2}{2!}+\frac{\delta^3}{3!}+\ldots$$

$$=\frac{1}{v}-1$$

$$d=1-(1+i)^{-1}=i-i^2+i^3-\dots$$

$$=1-\left(1-\frac{f}{m}\right)^m=f-\frac{m-1}{m}\cdot\frac{f^2}{2!}+\frac{\overline{m-1}\,\overline{m-2}}{m^2}\cdot\frac{f^3}{3!}-\dots$$

$$=1-\left(1+\frac{j}{m}\right)^{-m}=j-\frac{m+1}{m}\cdot\frac{j^2}{2!}+\frac{\overline{m+1}\,\overline{m+2}}{m^2}\cdot\frac{j^3}{3!}-\dots$$

$$=1-e^{-\delta}=\delta-\frac{\delta^2}{2!}+\frac{\delta^3}{3!}-\dots$$

$$=1-v$$

$$j=m[(1+i)^{\frac{1}{m}}-1]=i-\frac{m-1}{m}\cdot\frac{i^2}{2!}+\frac{\overline{m-1}\,\overline{m-2}}{m^2}\cdot\frac{i^3}{3!}-\dots$$

$$=m[(1-d)^{-\frac{1}{m}}-1]=d+\frac{m+1}{m}\cdot\frac{d^2}{2!}+\frac{\overline{m+1}\,\overline{m+2}}{m^2}\cdot\frac{d^3}{3!}+\dots$$

$$=m\left[\left(1-\frac{f}{m}\right)^{-1}-1\right]=f+\frac{1}{m}f^2+\frac{1}{m^2}\cdot f^3+\dots$$

$$=m[e^{\frac{\delta}{m}}-1]=\delta+\frac{1}{m}\cdot\frac{\delta^2}{2!}+\frac{1}{m^2}\cdot\frac{\delta^3}{3!}+\dots$$

$$=m\left(\frac{1}{v^{\frac{1}{m}}}-1\right)$$

$$f=i-\frac{m+1}{m}\cdot\frac{i^2}{2!}+\frac{\overline{m+1}\,\overline{m+2}}{m^2}\cdot\frac{i^3}{3!}-\dots$$

$$=d+\frac{m-1}{m}\cdot\frac{d^2}{2!}+\frac{\overline{m-1}\,\overline{m-2}}{m^2}\cdot\frac{d^3}{3!}+\dots$$

$$=j-\frac{j^2}{m}+\frac{j^3}{m^2}-\dots$$

$$=\delta-\frac{1}{m}\cdot\frac{\delta^2}{2!}+\frac{1}{m^2}\cdot\frac{\delta^3}{3!}-\dots$$

$$=m(1-v^{\frac{1}{m}})$$

$$\delta=\log_e(1+i)=i-\frac{i^2}{2}+\frac{i^3}{3}-\dots$$

$$=-\log_e(1-d)=d+\frac{d^2}{2}+\frac{d^3}{3}-\dots$$

$$=m\log_e\left(1+\frac{j}{m}\right)=j-\frac{j^2}{2m}+\frac{j^3}{3m^2}-\dots$$

$$=-m\log_e\left(1-\frac{f}{m}\right)=f+\frac{f^2}{2m}+\frac{f^3}{3m^3}-\dots$$

$$=-\log_e v$$

$$v=(1+i)^{-1}=1-i+\frac{i^2}{2!}-\frac{i^3}{3!}-\ldots$$

$$=1-d$$

$$=\left(1+\frac{j}{m}\right)^{-m}=1-j+\frac{m+1}{m}\cdot\frac{j^2}{2!}-\frac{\overline{m+1}\,\overline{m+2}}{m^2}\cdot\frac{j^3}{3!}+\ldots$$

$$=\left(1-\frac{f}{m}\right)^{m}=1-f+\frac{m-1}{m}\cdot\frac{f^2}{2!}-\frac{\overline{m-1}\,\overline{m-2}}{m^2}\cdot\frac{f^3}{3!}-\ldots$$

$$=e^{-\delta}=1-\delta+\frac{\delta^2}{2!}-\frac{\delta^3}{3!}+\ldots$$

31. As i, d, j, f and δ are always, in practice, small quantities, the successive terms in the series given above diminish rapidly. These series afford, therefore, the means, when the numerical value of any one of the functions in question is given, of calculating the values of the others with any desired degree of accuracy. Consider, for example, the expansion of δ in terms of i:—

$$\delta=i-\frac{i^2}{2}+\frac{i^3}{3}-\ldots$$

In this series the terms are alternatively positive and negative, and each is less than the preceding one. Hence, any given term taken positively is numerically greater than the sum of all the subsequent terms. Consequently, the error resulting from the neglect of all terms after, say, the nth, is less than $\frac{i^{n+1}}{n+1}$. To take an actual example, let $i=\cdot 04$. Then, since $\frac{(\cdot 04)^5}{5}=\cdot 00000002048$, the error in taking δ as $=\cdot 04-\frac{\cdot 0016}{2}+\frac{\cdot 000064}{3}-\frac{\cdot 00000256}{4}$, or $\cdot 03922069$, will not affect the seventh place in the result.

Good approximations, either for use in algebraical analysis or for practical purposes—when an isolated value is required and great accuracy is not necessary—may also be obtained by neglecting all terms after the second. Thus

$$i=\delta+\frac{1}{2}\delta^2 \text{ approximately}$$

$$d=\delta-\frac{1}{2}\delta^2 \quad \text{,,}$$

$$\delta=i-\frac{i^2}{2} \quad \text{,,}$$

whence $$f=m\left\{1-(1-d)^{\frac{1}{m}}\right\} \quad \ldots\ldots\ldots\ldots \quad (6)$$

Also, by addition of the first and second of these approximate relations,

$$\delta = \frac{1}{2}(i+d)$$

a formula which differs from the true value of δ by only $\left(\frac{\delta^3}{3!} + \frac{\delta^5}{5!} + \ldots\right)$ in excess, and gives a result correct to at least four places of decimals for all values of i not greater than ·07. For many practical purposes, however, sufficiently accurate results may be most conveniently obtained by ordinary arithmetic or by logarithms. Thus, if i be given as ·05, the value of v will be best found by taking the reciprocal of 1·05, and that of the corresponding nominal rate of interest convertible quarterly by means of the relation $\log\left(1+\frac{j}{4}\right) = \frac{1}{4}\log 1{\cdot}05$. In the latter case it would be necessary to use a six or seven-figure logarithm table, as the first significant figure in $\log\left(1+\frac{j}{4}\right)$ will be the third.

To take another example, the value of δ corresponding to a given value of j, and the value of j corresponding to a given value of δ, would be respectively obtained by means of the relations $\delta = m\log\left(1+\frac{j}{m}\right) \div \log e$ and $\log\left(1+\frac{j}{m}\right) = \frac{\delta}{m} \times \log e$.

On page 214 will be found tables giving

(1) The values of d, δ, v, and the nominal rates of interest convertible half-yearly and quarterly, corresponding to the effective rates ·025, ·03, ·035, ·04, ·045, and ·05.

(2) The values of i corresponding to the nominal rates ·025, ·03, ·035, ·04, ·045, and ·05, convertible half-yearly and quarterly.

32. To summarize the principal results established in this chapter—

I. At *Compound Interest.* If i be an effective rate of interest, j the corresponding nominal rate payable m times a year, δ the corresponding force of interest, and S the amount of P in n years:

$$S=P(1+i)^n=\left(1+\frac{j}{m}\right)^{mn}=Pe^{n\delta}$$

$$i=\left(1+\frac{j}{m}\right)^m-1=e^\delta-1$$

$$j=m\left\{(1+i)^{\frac{1}{m}}-1\right\}=m\left\{e^{\frac{\delta}{m}}-1\right\}$$

$$\delta=\log_e(1+i)=m\log_e\left(1+\frac{j}{m}\right)$$

II. At *Compound Discount.* If d be an effective rate of discount, f the corresponding nominal rate convertible m times a year, δ' the corresponding force of discount, and P' the present value of S' due at the end of n years:

$$P'=S'(1-d)^n=S'\left(1-\frac{f}{m}\right)^{mn}=S'e^{-n\delta'}$$

$$d=1-\left(1-\frac{f}{m}\right)^m=1-e^{-\delta'}$$

$$f=m\left\{1-(1-d)^{\frac{1}{m}}\right\}=m\left\{1-e^{-\frac{\delta'}{m}}\right\}$$

$$\delta'=-\log_e(1-d)=-m\log_e\left(1-\frac{f}{m}\right)$$

III. In any given problem, when the rates of interest and discount necessarily correspond,

$$S=P\left(1+i\right)^n=P\left(1+\frac{j}{m}\right)^{mn}$$

$$=P\left(1-d\right)^{-n}=P\left(1-\frac{f}{m}\right)^{-mn}=Pe^{n\delta}$$

$$P=S\left(1+i\right)^{-n}\text{, or } Sv^n,\ =S\left(1+\frac{j}{m}\right)^{-mn}$$

$$=S\left(1-d\right)^n=S\left(1-\frac{f}{m}\right)^{mn}=Se^{-n\delta}$$

$$d=\frac{i}{1+i}=iv=1-v$$

and the Force of Interest = the Force of Discount.

and the principal of 100 on the last-mentioned date. By Art. 28, Chapter I, the present value of the first quarter's dividend will be $\cdot 875v^{\frac{1}{4}}$, that of the second $\cdot 875v^{\frac{1}{2}}$, and so on, the present value of the final dividend being $\cdot 875v^{30\frac{3}{4}}$, and the present value of the 100 receivable on 5th January, 1931, will be $100v^{30\frac{3}{4}}$. Consequently, the required price $= \cdot 875(v^{\frac{1}{4}}+v^{\frac{1}{2}}+\ .\ .\ .+v^{30\frac{3}{4}})+100v^{30\frac{3}{4}}$, which reduces, by summation of the geometrical progression, to $\cdot 875\ \dfrac{v^{\frac{1}{4}}-v^{31}}{1-v^{\frac{1}{4}}}+100v^{30\frac{3}{4}}$. By logarithms it may be easily found that the value of this expression, when $i =$ say $\cdot 025$ and v consequently $= \cdot 97561$, is $121\cdot 977$. Thus it appears that the price of India $3\frac{1}{2}$ per-cent Stock, at 5th April, 1900, to pay an effective $2\frac{1}{2}$ per-cent without allowance for income-tax, should be 122 per-cent approximately. The calculation in this case might be simplified, as will be shown subsequently, by the use of special tables, but it will be seen that the solution of the problem does not raise any new question of principle.

3. In many cases it is necessary, or convenient, in order to obtain the solution of a given problem, to write down an EQUATION OF VALUE. In an equation of this nature it is essential that all the quantities involved should be discounted or accumulated to the same moment of time—either the present moment or some future moment as may be more convenient. Let it be required, for example, to find what two sums of equal amount due six months and a year hence respectively will together be equivalent at the effective rate i to a single payment of P due nine months hence, and let each of the required sums be X. Then the equation of value may be written down either as at the present moment, or, more conveniently, as at the date when the payment of £P falls due. In the former case the equation will be

$$Xv^{\frac{1}{2}}+Xv=Pv^{\frac{3}{4}}$$

and in the latter $$X(1+i)^{\frac{1}{4}}+X(1+i)^{-\frac{1}{4}}=P.$$

In this case the two equations are equally easy to write down, and the first reduces immediately to the more symmetrical form of the second, but in some cases much trouble will be saved by selecting the most appropriate moment at which to write down the equation of value.

4. Another point to which attention may be directed is that in determining the effective rate of interest yielded by a transaction extending over a period less than a year, or by a number of transactions extending over different periods, it is not necessary to make any assumption as to the terms upon which the capital employed in any one of these transactions is or could be invested after the close of that particular transaction. Thus the effective rate realized by the purchase of a bill for 100 due 3 months hence at the price of 98 is $(1\frac{1}{49})^4-1$; it is immaterial, so far as the rate realized upon this particular transaction is concerned, whether or upon what terms the proceeds of the bill are invested for the remaining nine months of the year. So, if two sums of S_1 and S_2 due at the end of n_1 and n_2 years respectively are acquired for a present payment of P, the effective rate realized will be i, as determined from the equation $P=S_1v^{n_1}+S_2v^{n_2}$. The result means that the entire purchase-money is invested at rate i until part of it is realized on the first sum becoming due, and that thereafter the remainder is invested at the same rate until realization, and the transaction as a whole is said to yield that rate; it is immaterial how any part of the invested capital is re-invested after realization.

5. A third point, and one of considerable practical importance in the solution of problems in compound interest, is that a corresponding effective rate may always be substituted for, or employed in working in the place of, a nominal rate, and *vice versa*. Thus, if it be required to find the value of any series of payments, or to determine the conditions of some financial transaction, on the basis of interest at a given nominal rate j, the problem may be worked out on the basis of an effective rate i, and the result in terms of the given nominal rate will be obtained by substituting for i its value in terms of j. In many cases it will be found very much simpler to proceed in this way than to work throughout in terms of j. Occasionally, on the other hand, it may be found convenient to employ a nominal rate in working, and to substitute for that rate, at the final stage, its value in terms of a given effective rate. Similarly, if it be required to find the rate of interest yielded by a given transaction, it is immaterial to the result whether the effective rate or a nominal rate be determined. The object in all cases should be to determine the yield in that form—whether as an effective rate or a nominal rate—to which the conditions of the question most easily lend themselves. The yield, when determined, can of course be readily expressed as an effective rate or a nominal rate in accordance with the requirements of the question. These principles follow at once from the fundamental equation

$$(1+i)^n=\left(1+\frac{j}{m}\right)^{mn} \text{ for all values of } n.$$

6. The following examples further illustrate the principles and formulas established in the preceding chapter :—

(i) The sum of the amount of 1 in 2 years at a certain nominal rate of *interest* convertible half-yearly, and of the present value of 1 due 2 years hence at the same nominal rate of *discount* convertible half-yearly, is 2·00480032.

Find the rate.

The amount of 1 in 2 years at the nominal rate of interest $2r$ convertible half-yearly is $(1+r)^4$. And the present value of 1 due 2 years hence at the nominal rate of *discount* $2r$ convertible half-yearly is $(1-r)^4$.

∴ If $2r$ be the rate

$$(1+r)^4+(1-r)^4=2\cdot00480032,$$

whence $$r^4+6r^2-\cdot00240016=0,$$

or $$(r^2-\cdot0004)(r^2+6\cdot0004)=0,$$

giving as a practical solution $r=\cdot02$ and $2r=\cdot04$.

(ii) A money-lender makes an advance on security of a one-month bill and deducts interest in advance at the rate of 1*s.* in the £. He allows the bill to be renewed 11 times, each time for a month on payment of 1*s.* per £, and at the end of the year the bill is duly met. What rate of interest does he realize on the transaction?

The net sum invested by the money-lender in respect of each unit of the amount of the bill is (after deduction of the first month's interest) ·95. At the end of each of the first 11 months he receives ·05, and at the end of the 12th month he receives 1, that is, ·95 (the net sum invested) + ·05. Hence on each unit invested he receives interest at the rate of $\frac{12}{19}$ per annum payable monthly. This is the nominal rate of interest convertible monthly realized on the transaction. The corresponding effective rate is $\left(\frac{20}{19}\right)^{12}-1$, which $=\cdot8506$, or 85·06 per-cent per annum.

It may be observed that if the transaction had been determined at the end of the first month by the bill being then met, the effective rate realized would have been precisely the same. The successive renewals of the bill upon the same terms as those upon which it was initially discounted do not affect the rate of interest realized; they merely provide the money-lender during the remaining 11 months of the year with an investment yielding the same effective rate as that obtained on the original transaction.

(iii) In how many years will a sum of money double itself at compound interest?

If interest be assumed at the effective rate i, the required number of years will be n, where $(1+i)^n=2$. In any given case, the value of n will be most accurately obtained by ordinary logarithms. Thus, if $i=\cdot 05$,

$$n=\frac{\log 2}{\log 1\cdot 05}=\frac{\cdot 30103}{\cdot 0211893}$$

$$=14\cdot 207 \text{ nearly.}$$

But a general approximate solution, and a convenient rule for practical purposes, may be obtained by taking Napierian instead of ordinary logarithms. Proceeding in this way,

$$n=\frac{\log_e 2}{\log_e(1+i)}=\frac{\cdot 30103\times 2\cdot 3026}{i-\frac{i^2}{2}+\frac{i^3}{3}-\ldots}$$

$$=\frac{\cdot 69315}{i}\left[1+\frac{i}{2}-\frac{i^2}{12}\right]=\frac{\cdot 693}{i}+\cdot 35 \text{ approximately.}$$

The number of years in which a sum of money will double itself at a given effective rate of interest may therefore be found, with approximate accuracy, by dividing 69·3 by the rate of interest per-cent and adding ·35 to the result. Compare the common rule:—To find the number of years in which money will double itself, divide 69 by the rate of interest per-cent.

If interest be at a nominal rate j, convertible m times a year, the method of the preceding paragraph will obviously apply, for $\frac{j}{m}$ may be regarded as an effective rate for $\frac{1}{m}$th of a year. The general approximation will give $\left(\frac{\frac{\cdot693}{j}}{\frac{j}{m}}+\cdot35\right)\frac{1}{m}$ths of a year—*i.e.*, $\left(\frac{\cdot693}{j}+\frac{\cdot35}{m}\right)$ years.

(iv) By how much will the amount of a sum of money in n years, at a given rate of interest, convertible m times a year, exceed its amount at the same rate convertible annually?

Let the given sum be P, the given rate r, and the required result X. Then

$$X=P\left(1+\frac{r}{m}\right)^{mn}-P(1+r)^n=P(1+r)^n\left[\frac{\left(1+\frac{r}{m}\right)^{mn}}{(1+r)^n}-1\right]$$

For practical values of m,

$$\frac{\left(1+\frac{r}{m}\right)^m}{1+r}=1+\frac{m-1}{2m}\cdot\frac{r^2}{1+r}\text{ nearly,}$$

and, since $\frac{m-1}{2m}\cdot\frac{r^2}{1+r}$ will usually be small relatively to $\frac{1}{n}$,

$$\left(1+\frac{m-1}{2m}\cdot\frac{r^2}{1+r}\right)^n=1+\frac{n(m-1)}{2m}\cdot\frac{r^2}{1+r}\text{ approximately.}$$

Hence, as a rough approximation for cases in which n is not large,

$$X=P(1+r)^n\cdot\frac{n(m-1)}{2m}\cdot\frac{r^2}{1+r}.$$

To test the accuracy of the result, take $P=1$, $r=\cdot04$, $m=2$, and $n=50$. In this case, $P(1+r)^n=7\cdot1067$, and $X=7\cdot1067\times\frac{50}{4}\times\frac{\cdot0016}{1\cdot04}=\cdot1367$ nearly. The amount of 1 in 100 years at 2 per-cent per annum is 7·2446, and the true value of X would, therefore, be ·1379.

(v) A sum of money is to be invested and accumulated in Consols for n years from 5 April 1900. Obtain an expression for the effective rate of interest realized, on the assumptions that the investments of the original sum and of the dividends are all made at the same price, that the accumulated stock is sold at that price at the end of the n years, and that the rate of income tax remains unchanged throughout.

The dividends on Consols are payable quarterly at the rate of $2\frac{3}{4}$ per-cent per annum, on every 5 January, April, July and October up to and including 5 April 1903, and at the rate of $2\frac{1}{2}$ per-cent per annum on the same days thereafter. If, therefore, $1+k$ be the uniform price per unit of Consols at which all the dividends are invested, r per unit be the uniform rate of income tax, and i be the effective rate realized, then, since the stock is bought and sold at the same price,

$$(1+i)^n = \left[1+\frac{\cdot006875(1-r)}{1+k}\right]^{12} \cdot \left[1+\frac{\cdot00625(1-r)}{1+k}\right]^{4n-12}$$

from which i may be found by taking the nth root of the right-hand side and deducting unity. As an example, take the special case in which $n=6$, and assume that $k=\cdot05$, and $r=8d.$ in the £.

Then $$(1+i)^6 = \left[1+\frac{\cdot006646}{1\cdot05}\right]^{12}\left[1+\frac{\cdot006042}{1\cdot05}\right]^{12}$$

whence $1+i=(1\cdot00633\times1\cdot00575)^2=1\cdot02438$

As the problem is one of some practical interest to small investors, on account of the facilities that are given for the investment of Post Office Savings Bank deposits in Consols, it may be pointed out that the assumptions upon which the foregoing result is based are necessarily hypothetical. It may be anticipated that the price of Consols will be affected both by the reduction in the rate of interest and by the approach of the time at which they may be converted or redeemed. Moreover, under the arrangements for the investment of dividends on accumulating Consols accounts, the quarterly dividends are not invested until about a month after the dates on which they become due, with the result of an average loss of a month's interest on each dividend.

7. The problem of finding the *equated time* for a number of sums due at different times, or, in other words, the average date at which, on the basis of an agreed rate of interest, all the sums might be paid without theoretical advantage or disadvantage to either party, is one of some practical importance.

Let the various sums be S_1, S_2, S_3 . . . S_r, due at the end of

$n_1, n_2, n_3 \ldots n_r$ years respectively, and let n be the equated time on the basis of interest at the effective rate i. Then

$$(S_1+S_2+\ldots+S_r)v^n=S_1v^{n_1}+S_2v^{n_2}+\ldots+S_rv^{n_r} \quad . \quad . \quad . \quad . \quad (1)$$

whence $$n=\frac{\log(S_1+S_2+\ldots+S_r)-\log(S_1v^{n_1}+S_2v^{n_2}+\ldots+S_rv^{n_r})}{\log(1+i)}$$

The accurate calculation of n by this formula would not, in general, present any difficulty, but for practical purposes the following rule is frequently adopted: To find the equated time of payment of a number of different amounts due at different times, multiply each amount by the number of years to elapse before it becomes due, and divide the sum of the products by the sum of all the amounts. This rule is obtained by expanding $v^n, v^{n_1} \ldots v^{n_r}$ in formula (1) and neglecting powers of i above the first. Thus

$$(S_1+S_2+\ldots+S_r)(1-ni)=S_1(1-n_1i)+S_2(1-n_2i)+\ldots + S_r(1-n_ri) \text{ approximately}$$

whence $$n=\frac{n_1S_1+n_2S_2+\ldots+n_rS_r}{S_1+S_2+\ldots+S_r} \text{ approximately.}$$

8. An interesting question arises as to whether the approximate value of n obtained in this way is greater or less than the true value, or, in other words, whether the rule favours the debtor or the person to whom the sums are due. Suppose that $n_1, n_2 \ldots n_r$ are in ascending order of magnitude, and that n—the true equated time—lies between n_k and n_{k+1}. Then it is obvious that by paying all the sums at the end of n years the debtor gains compound interest on those sums of which the dates of payment are postponed, that is, on $S_1, S_2 \ldots S_k$, and loses compound discount on those sums of which the dates of payment are accelerated, namely, $S_{k+1} \ldots S_r$; and, as n is the true equated time, his gain and loss must be equivalent. In symbols

$$\begin{aligned}S_1[(1+i)^{n-n_1}-1]+S_2[(1+i)^{n-n_2}-1]+\ldots+S_k[(1+i)^{n-n_k}-1]\\ =S_{k+1}[1-(1+i)^{-(n_{k+1}-n)}]+\ldots+S_r[1-(1+i)^{-(n_r-n)}] \qquad (2)\end{aligned}$$

an equation which might have been obtained by a simple algebraical transformation from (1). In terms of δ, the force of interest or discount corresponding to i, equation (2) becomes

$$\begin{aligned}S_1[e^{(n-n_1)\delta}-1]+S_2[e^{(n-n_2)\delta}-1]+\ldots+S_k[e^{(n-n_k)\delta}-1]\\ =S_{k+1}[1-e^{-(n_{k+1}-n)\delta}]+\ldots+S_r[1-e^{-(n_r-n)\delta}] \quad . \quad . \quad (3)\end{aligned}$$

Now, if k be any positive quantity, e^k is $>1+k$ and e^{-k} is $>1-k$.*

It follows, therefore, since $(n-n_1)$, $(n-n_2)$ . . . $(n-n_k)$, $(n_{k+1}-n)$ . . . (n_r-n) are all positive, that the left-hand side of equation (3) is

$$>S_1(n-n_1)\delta+S_2(n-n_2)\delta+\ldots+S_k(n-n_k)\delta,$$

and that the right-hand side of the equation is

$$<S_{k+1}(n_{k+1}-n)\delta+\ldots+S_r(n_r-n)\delta$$

$$\therefore\quad S_1(n-n_1)+S_2(n-n_2)+\ldots+S_k(n-n_k)$$
$$\text{is } <S_{k+1}(n_{k+1}-n)+\ldots+S_r(n_r-n).$$

$$\therefore\quad n \text{ is } < \frac{n_1S_1+n_2S_2+\ldots+n_rS_r}{S_1+S_2+\ldots+S_k}$$

It thus appears that the ordinary approximation is in favour of the debtor.

9. The following neat alternative proof of the inequality established in the last Article appeared in the *Journal of the Institute of Actuaries* for January, 1898:—

The Arithmetical Mean of S_1 quantities, each $=v^{n_1}$, S_2 quantities, each $=v^{n_2}$, . . . S_r quantities, each $=v^{n_r}$, is $\dfrac{S_1v^{n_1}+S_2v^{n_2}+\ldots+S_rv^{n_r}}{S_1+S_2+\ldots+S_r}$.

The Geometrical Mean of the same quantities is

$$v^{\frac{n_1S_1+n_2S_2+\ldots+n_rS_r}{S_1+S_2+\ldots+S_r}}.$$

Now the Arithmetical Mean of any number of quantities is > their Geometrical Mean

$$\therefore\quad \frac{S_1v^{n_1}+S_2v^{n_2}+\ldots+S_rv^{n_r}}{S_1+S_2+\ldots+S_r} \text{ is } >v^{\frac{n_1S_1+n_2S_2+\ldots+n_rS_r}{S_1+S_2+\ldots+S_r}}$$

or

$$(S_1v^{n_1}+S_2v^{n_2}+\ldots+S_rv^{n_r}) \text{ is } >(S_1+S_2+\ldots+S_r)v^{\frac{n_1S_1+n_2S_2+\ldots+n_rS_r}{S_1+S_2+\ldots+S_r}}$$

* If k be >1 the inequality is obvious, for $1-k$ would then be a negative quantity, whereas e^{-k} is necessarily positive; if k be <1 it follows at once from the equation $e^{-k}=1-k+\frac{k^2}{2!}-\frac{k^3}{2!}+\ldots$ which may be written in the form

$$e^{-k}=1-k+\frac{k^2}{2!}\left(1-\frac{k}{3}\right)+\frac{k^4}{4!}\left(1-\frac{k}{5}\right)+\ldots$$

From this inequality it appears that the present value of S_1 due at the end of n_1 years, S_2 due at the end of n_2 years, &c., is > the present value of $(S_1+S_2+\ldots)$ due at the end of $\frac{n_1S_1+n_2S_2+\ldots}{S_1+S_2+\ldots}$ years.

The quantity $\frac{n_1S_1+n_2S_2+\ldots}{S_1+S_2+\ldots}$ is therefore > the true equated time of the sums.

10. As a practical example of the foregoing proposition, take the following:—Which would be the better investment—two bills for £5,000 each for two and four months respectively, or a three months' bill for £10,000, the same rate of discount being offered in both cases?

Since commercial discount is calculated by the formula $\frac{Sf}{m}$ where S is the amount of the bill, f the rate of discount, and $\frac{1}{m}$th of a year the time, the price of the two bills for £5,000 each will be exactly the same as that of the single bill for £10,000. But at a given rate of interest the present value of £5,000 due at the end of two months and £5,000 due at the end of four months is > that of £10,000 due at the end of three months. Therefore, at a given price, £5,000 due at the end of two months and £5,000 due at the end of four months give a better yield than £10,000 due at the end of three months; in other words, the two bills form the better investment.

Of course, in practice, other considerations would come in. The rate of discount in commercial transactions may be considered as representing partly interest and partly a premium for insurance against the risk of possible loss of principal; consequently a higher rate will generally be obtainable on bills for longer periods.

CHAPTER III.

ON THE VALUATION OF ANNUITIES-CERTAIN.

1. An ANNUITY is a series of payments made at equal intervals during the continuance of a given status.

2. When the status is a fixed term of years, the annuity is called an annuity-certain.

An ANNUITY-CERTAIN may, therefore, be defined as a series of payments made at equal intervals during a fixed term of years.

3. When the payments are of uniform amount, the annuity is measured by the total amount payable in a year, which amount is sometimes called the *annual rent*. Thus, an annuity under which a payment of $\frac{k}{m}$ is made at the end of each $\frac{1}{m}$th of a year is described as an annuity of k per annum payable m times a year, and k is said to be the annual rent of the annuity.

4. Annuities-certain may be *immediate*, in which case the first payment is made at the end of the first interval; or *due*, in which case the first payment is made at the beginning of the first interval; or *deferred*, in which case a certain number of intervals has to elapse and an immediate annuity is then entered upon.

Thus an *immediate annuity* of k per annum, payable quarterly for n years will consist of $4n$ payments of $\frac{k}{4}$ each made at quarterly intervals, the first being made at the end of three months and the last at the end of the n years. In an *annuity-due* of the same description, the first payment is made immediately and the last at the beginning of the fourth quarter of the nth year. And in a similar annuity *deferred*

m years, the first payment is to be made at the end of $(m+\frac{1}{4})$ years and the last at the end of $(m+n)$ years.

5. A *continuous* annuity is one which is assumed to be payable momently by infinitely small instalments.

6. An annuity of which the payments are to continue for ever is called a *perpetuity*. The expressions "immediate perpetuity", "perpetuity due", "deferred perpetuity", and "continuous perpetuity", are used with significations similar to those attaching to the corresponding descriptions of annuities.

7. When the successive payments of an annuity are not taken as they fall due, but are left to accumulate at compound interest, the annuity is sometimes said to be *forborne*. The sum of the amounts of the successive payments accumulated to the end of the period during which the annuity is payable is called the *amount* of the annuity. The sum of the present values of the successive payments is called the *present value* of the annuity; an annuity of which the present value is k per unit of annual rent is said to be worth *k years' purchase*.

8. The notation employed in the valuation of annuities-certain, of which the periodical payments are equal, is as follows:—

$s_{\overline{n}|}$ denotes the amount of an immediate annuity of 1 per annum payable annually for n years.

$s^{(p)}_{\overline{n}|}$ „ the amount of an immediate annuity of 1 per annum payable p times a year for n years.

$\bar{s}_{\overline{n}|}$ „ the amount of a continuous annuity of 1 per annum for n years.

$a_{\overline{n}|}$ „ the present value of an immediate annuity of 1 per annum payable annually for n years.

$a^{(p)}_{\overline{n}|}$ „ the present value of an immediate annuity of 1 per annum payable p times a year for n years.

$\bar{a}_{\overline{n}|}$ „ the present value of a continuous annuity of 1 per annum for n years.

$\mathbf{a}_{\overline{n}|}$ „ the present value of an annuity-due of 1 per annum payable annually for n years.

${}_{m|}a_{\overline{n}|}$ „ the present value of an annuity of 1 per annum, payable annually for n years, deferred m years.

The symbols $\mathbf{a}$ and $_{m|}a$ may be qualified by the affix (p) in the same way as the symbol a. In the case of a perpetuity, the suffix $\overline{n}|$ is replaced by ∞. Thus $\bar{a}_\infty$ denotes the present value of a continuous perpetuity of 1 per annum.

9. The following relations obviously hold:—

$$\mathbf{a}_{\overline{n}|}=1+a_{\overline{n-1}|} \quad \ldots \ldots \ldots \quad (1)$$

$$\mathbf{a}^{(p)}_{\overline{n}|}=\frac{1}{p}+a^{(p)}_{\overline{n-\frac{1}{p}}|} \quad \ldots \ldots \ldots \quad (2)$$

$$_{m|}a_{\overline{n}|}=a_{\overline{n+m}|}-a_{\overline{m}|} \quad \ldots \ldots \ldots \quad (3)$$

$$a_\infty=a_{\overline{n}|}+{}_{n|}a_\infty \quad \ldots \ldots \ldots \quad (4)$$

10. From the definitions given in Article 8, it will be seen that the amount or present value of an annuity at a given rate of interest may be found by summing the amounts or present values at that rate of the successive payments. Now the amount or present value of any series of payments at a given nominal rate of interest may be found by working with the corresponding effective rate and substituting for the effective rate, in the result, its value in terms of the nominal rate. Hence the general problem of finding the amount or present value of an annuity, payable p times a year, at a nominal rate of interest convertible m times a year, resolves itself into that of finding the amount or present value at an effective rate of interest.

11. To find the amount, at the effective rate of interest i, of an immediate annuity of 1 per annum payable p times a year for n years. The amount of the first payment of the annuity will be $\frac{1}{p}(1+i)^{n-\frac{1}{p}}$, that of the next $\frac{1}{p}(1+i)^{n-\frac{2}{p}}$, and so on, the amount of the last payment being $\frac{1}{p}$.

Hence
$$s^{(p)}_{\overline{n}|}=\frac{1}{p}\left[(1+i)^{n-\frac{1}{p}}+(1+i)^{n-\frac{2}{p}}+\ldots+1\right]$$

$$=\frac{1}{p}\,\frac{(1+i)^n-1}{(1+i)^{\frac{1}{p}}-1} \quad \ldots \ldots \ldots \quad (5)$$

12. This result may be readily obtained by general reasoning. A unit of capital, invested at the effective rate of interest i will yield interest amounting to $(1+i)^{\frac{1}{p}}-1$ at the end of each $\frac{1}{p}$th of a year, or, in other words, an immediate annuity of $p[(1+i)^{\frac{1}{p}}-1]$ per annum, payable p times a year, for n years, and it will remain intact at the end of the period. In the alternative, if the interest be allowed to accumulate, the original unit will amount to $(1+i)^n$ at the end of n years. These two things must be equivalent; that is to say, if the equation of value be written down as at the end of n years,

$$s_{\overline{n}|}^{(p)} \cdot p[(1+i)^{\frac{1}{p}}-1]+1=(1+i)^n$$

or, as before,

$$s_{\overline{n}|}^{(p)} = \frac{(1+i)^n-1}{p[(1+i)^{\frac{1}{p}}-1]}$$

13. To find the present value, at the effective rate of interest i, of an immediate annuity of 1 per annum payable p times a year for n years.

The present value of the first payment is $\frac{1}{p}v^{\frac{1}{p}}$, that of the second $\frac{1}{p}v^{\frac{2}{p}}$, and so on, the present value of the final payment being $\frac{1}{p}v^n$.

Hence

$$a_{\overline{n}|}^{(p)} = \frac{1}{p}[v^{\frac{1}{p}}+v^{\frac{2}{p}}+ \ldots +v^n]$$

$$= \frac{1-v^n}{p[(1+i)^{\frac{1}{p}}-1]} \quad \ldots \ldots \ldots \quad (6)$$

14. This result may be established by reasoning very similar to that of Article 12. A unit of capital invested at the effective rate of interest i will yield an immediate annuity of $p[(1+i)^{\frac{1}{p}}-1]$ per annum, payable p times a year for n years, and will remain intact at the end of the period. It must, therefore, be equal to the present value of such an annuity together with the present value of a unit due at the end of n years; that is to say:—

$$1=a_{\overline{n}|}^{(p)} \cdot p[(1+i)^{\frac{1}{p}}-1]+v^n$$

or

$$a_{\overline{n}|}^{(p)} = \frac{1-v^n}{p[(1+i)^{\frac{1}{p}}-1]}.$$

15. The argument may also be put in the following slightly different form :—An immediate annuity of 1 per annum payable p times a year for n years is obviously equivalent to a perpetuity of 1 per annum payable p times a year less a similar perpetuity deferred n years. Now a unit will produce interest of $p[(1+i)^{\frac{1}{p}}-1]$ per annum payable p times a year, in perpetuity; therefore the present value of a perpetuity of $p[(1+i)^{\frac{1}{p}}-1]$ per annum payable p times a year is 1, and by simple proportion the present value of a similar perpetuity of 1 per annum is $\dfrac{1}{p[(1+i)^{\frac{1}{p}}-1]}$. Hence

$$\begin{aligned} a_{\overline{n}|}^{(p)} &= a_{\infty}^{(p)} - v^n \,.\, a_{\infty}^{(p)} \\ &= \frac{1}{p[(1+i)^{\frac{1}{p}}-1]} - v^n \,.\, \frac{1}{p[(1+i)^{\frac{1}{p}}-1]} \\ &= \frac{1-v^n}{p[(1+i)^{\frac{1}{p}}-1]}. \end{aligned}$$

13. In establishing the formulas for $s_{\overline{n}|}^{(p)}$ and $a_{\overline{n}|}^{(p)}$ it has been implicitly assumed that np is an integer, or in other words, that the term of the annuity comprises an exact integral number of intervals. In order to extend the formulas to cases in which np is not an integer, it is necessary to adopt some convention as to the proportion of the periodical payment which should be paid in respect of a fractional part of an interval, say for $\frac{1}{m}$th part of an interval, or $\frac{1}{mp}$th of a year. For purposes of theory it is convenient to make the proportion such that the formula $a_{\overline{n}|}^{(p)} = \dfrac{1-v^n}{p[(1+i)^{\frac{1}{p}}-1]}$ may hold for all values of n. This convention gives

$$\begin{aligned} a_{\overline{n+\frac{1}{mp}}|}^{(p)} &= \frac{1-v^{n+\frac{1}{mp}}}{p[(1+i)^{\frac{1}{p}}-1]} \\ &= \frac{1-v^n}{p[(1+i)^{\frac{1}{p}}-1]} + \frac{v^n - v^{n+\frac{1}{mp}}}{p[(1+i)^{\frac{1}{p}}-1]} \\ &= a_{\overline{n}|}^{(p)} + v^{n+\frac{1}{mp}} \,.\, \frac{(1+i)^{\frac{1}{mp}}-1}{p[(1+i)^{\frac{1}{p}}-1]} \quad . \; . \; . \qquad (7) \end{aligned}$$

from which it appears that the proportionate payment for the final $\frac{1}{mp}$th of a year would be $\frac{(1+i)^{\frac{1}{mp}}-1}{(1+i)^{\frac{1}{p}}-1}\cdot\frac{1}{p}$, or the same proportion of the periodical payment as the interest on 1 for $\frac{1}{mp}$th of a year is of the interest on 1 for $\frac{1}{p}$th of a year. Subject, therefore, to the understanding that the proportion for the odd fraction of an interval is to be calculated in this way, the formula

$$a_{\overline{n}|}^{(p)}=\frac{1-v^n}{p[(1+i)^{\frac{1}{p}}-1]}$$

and, by an obvious deduction, the formula

$$s_{\overline{n}|}^{(p)}=\frac{(1+i)^n-1}{p[(1+i)^{\frac{1}{p}}-1]}$$

will hold for all positive values of n whether integral or fractional.

In practice the proportionate payment would be taken as $\frac{1}{mp}$, and the present value of an annuity of 1 per annum payable p times a year for $\left(n+\frac{1}{mp}\right)$ years would consequently be $a_{\overline{n}|}^{(p)}+\frac{1}{mp}\cdot v^{n+\frac{1}{mp}}$.

17. It will be observed that the numerators of the expressions for $s_{\overline{n}|}^{(p)}$ and $a_{\overline{n}|}^{(p)}$ are respectively the total *interest* on 1 in n years, and the total *discount* on 1 due n years hence, and that the denominator of each expression is the nominal rate of interest convertible p times a year corresponding to the given rate. It appears, therefore, that

(i) the amount of an immediate annuity of 1 per annum at a given rate of interest is the total interest on 1 in n years divided by the corresponding nominal rate of interest convertible with the same frequency as that with which the annuity is payable, and

(ii) the present value of an immediate annuity of 1 per annum at a given rate of interest is the total discount on 1 due n years hence divided by the corresponding nominal rate of interest convertible with the same frequency as that with which the annuity is payable.

These results are perfectly general, for the annuity of which the amount and present value are represented by $s_{\overline{n}|}^{(p)}$ and $a_{\overline{n}|}^{(p)}$ is the most general type of an immediate annuity payable by equal periodical instalments.

18. From formulas (5) and (6), or from the verbal expressions just given, the amount and present value, at the effective rate of interest i, of an immediate annuity of 1 per annum payable with any given frequency, may be at once written down by assigning the appropriate value to p; from the resulting formulas the amount and present value at any given nominal rate of interest may be deduced, as already explained, by substituting for i its value in terms of the given nominal rate. For convenience of reference the general formulas and the deduced expressions for certain values of p are exhibited in the following summary:—

Amounts and Present Values of an Immediate Annuity of 1 per annum for n years:

(a) In terms of the effective rate of interest i.

Annuity Payable	Amount	Present Value
p times a year	$s_{\overline{n}\vert}^{(p)}=\dfrac{(1+i)^n-1}{p[(1+i)^{\frac{1}{p}}-1]}$ $=\dfrac{\text{Total interest on 1}}{\text{Nominal rate of interest convertible } p \text{ times a year corresponding to } i}$	$a_{\overline{n}\vert}^{(p)}=\dfrac{1-v^n}{p[(1+i)^{\frac{1}{p}}-1]}$ $=\dfrac{\text{Total discount on 1}}{\text{Nominal rate of interest convertible } p \text{ times a year corresponding to } i}$
Yearly ($p=1$)	$s_{\overline{n}\vert}=\dfrac{(1+i)^n-1}{i}$ . . (8)	$a_{\overline{n}\vert}=\dfrac{1-v^n}{i}$ . . . . (9)
Continuously ($p=\infty$)	$\bar{s}_{\overline{n}\vert}=\dfrac{(1+i)^n-1}{\log_e(1+i)}$ . . (10)	$\bar{a}_{\overline{n}\vert}=\dfrac{1-v^n}{\log_e(1+i)}$ . . (11)

(b) In terms of a nominal rate of interest j convertible m times a year.

For $(1+i)$ substitute $\left(1+\frac{j}{m}\right)^m$

Annuity Payable	Amount	Present Value
p times a year	$s_{\overline{n}\mid}^{(p)} = \dfrac{\left(1+\frac{j}{m}\right)^{mn}-1}{p\left[\left(1+\frac{j}{m}\right)^{\frac{m}{p}}-1\right]}$. (12)	$a_{\overline{n}\mid}^{(p)} = \dfrac{1-\left(1+\frac{j}{m}\right)^{-mn}}{p\left[\left(1+\frac{j}{m}\right)^{\frac{m}{p}}-1\right]}$. (13)
Yearly ($p=1$)	$s_{\overline{n}\mid} = \dfrac{\left(1+\frac{j}{m}\right)^{mn}-1}{\left(1+\frac{j}{m}\right)^{m}-1}$. (14)	$a_{\overline{n}\mid} = \dfrac{1-\left(1+\frac{j}{m}\right)^{-mn}}{\left(1+\frac{j}{m}\right)^{m}-1}$. (15)
m times a year ($p=m$)	$s_{\overline{n}\mid}^{(m)} = \dfrac{\left(1+\frac{j}{m}\right)^{mn}-1}{j}$. (16)	$a_{\overline{n}\mid}^{(m)} = \dfrac{1-\left(1+\frac{j}{m}\right)^{-mn}}{j}$. (17)
Continuously ($p=\infty$)	$\bar{s}_{\overline{n}\mid} = \dfrac{\left(1+\frac{j}{m}\right)^{mn}-1}{m\log_e\left(1+\frac{j}{m}\right)}$. (18)	$\bar{a}_{\overline{n}\mid} = \dfrac{1-\left(1+\frac{j}{m}\right)^{-mn}}{m\log_e\left(1+\frac{j}{m}\right)}$. (19)

(c) In terms of a force of interest δ.

For $(1+i)$ substitute e^{δ}

Annuity Payable	Amount	Present Value
p times a year	$s_{\overline{n}\mid}^{(p)} = \dfrac{e^{n\delta}-1}{p[e^{\frac{\delta}{p}}-1]}$ . . . (20)	$a_{\overline{n}\mid}^{(p)} = \dfrac{1-e^{-n\delta}}{p[e^{\frac{\delta}{p}}-1]}$ . . . (21)
Yearly ($p=1$)	$s_{\overline{n}\mid} = \dfrac{e^{n\delta}-1}{e^{\delta}-1}$ . . . . (22)	$a_{\overline{n}\mid} = \dfrac{1-e^{-n\delta}}{e^{\delta}-1}$ . . . (23)
Continuously ($p=\infty$)	$\bar{s}_{\overline{n}\mid} = \dfrac{e^{n\delta}-1}{\delta}$ . . . . (24)	$\bar{a}_{\overline{n}\mid} = \dfrac{1-e^{-n\delta}}{\delta}$ . . . . (25)

19. If n be made infinitely great, the numerators of all the expressions on the right-hand side of the summary given in the last article become 1, and the resulting formulas give the present values of the corresponding *perpetuities* of 1 per annum. Thus the present value at the effective rate i, of an immediate perpetuity of 1 per annum payable annually is $\frac{1}{i}$; the present value, at a nominal rate j convertible m times a year, of an immediate perpetuity of 1 per annum payable m times a year is $\frac{1}{j}$; and the present value, at a force of interest δ, of an immediate continuous perpetuity is $\frac{1}{\delta}$.

20. Although the formulas exhibited under (b) and (c) in Article 18 have been deduced from the general formulas expressed in terms of the effective rate, they may of course be used without any direct reference to an effective rate. The object of expressing the amounts and present values of the annuity in the alternative forms given under (a), (b), and (c) is to have a collection of formulas which will cover all the cases that may arise, and in any given case the proper formula to employ will be that one in which the rate of interest—whether effective or nominal—to be employed in the calculation can be directly inserted. For example, if it be required to find the present value of an immediate annuity, payable quarterly for 20 years, at four per-cent convertible half-yearly, the proper formula to use will be (13), and the result will be $\frac{1-(1{\cdot}02)^{-40}}{4[(1{\cdot}02)^{\frac{1}{2}}-1]}$. Or, if it be required to find the amount of a similar continuous annuity at four per-cent effective, the proper formula to use will be (10), and the result will be $\frac{(1{\cdot}04)^{20}-1}{\log_e(1{\cdot}04)}$. If in the latter case the rate of interest were four per-cent convertible momently—that is, a force of four per-cent—the result, by formula (24) would be $\frac{e^{\cdot 8}-1}{\cdot 04}$, which may be evaluated by taking the anti-logarithm of $\frac{4}{5}$ths of the common logarithm of e, deducting 1, and dividing the result by ·04. In either the first or third of these examples precisely the same result would, of course, be obtained by first calculating the effective rate corresponding to the rate at which the calculation is to be made, and then employing the formula expressed in terms of an effective rate. Thus, in the third case, $\bar{s}_{\overline{20}|}$ at a force of interest of four per-cent $= \bar{s}_{\overline{20}|}$ at the effective rate

$(e^{\cdot 04}-1) =$ by formula (10) $\dfrac{[1+(e^{\cdot 04}-1)]^{20}-1}{\log_e[1+(e^{\cdot 04}-1)]} = \dfrac{e^{\cdot 8}-1}{\cdot 04}$ as before.
It is obviously a much shorter process to use the appropriate formula—No. (24)—without any direct reference to the effective rate corresponding to the given force.

21. A case of some special interest and practical importance is that in which interest is convertible with the same frequency as that with which the annuity is payable. In this case formula (13) gives

$$a_{\overline{n}|}^{(p)} = \frac{1-\left(1+\dfrac{j}{p}\right)^{-np}}{j} = \frac{1}{p}\cdot\frac{1-\left(1+\dfrac{j}{p}\right)^{-np}}{\dfrac{j}{p}} = \frac{1}{p}a_{\overline{np}|}$$

where $a_{\overline{np}|}$ is calculated at the *effective* rate of interest $\dfrac{j}{p}$. That is, the present value, at the nominal rate j convertible p times a year, of an immediate annuity of 1 per annum payable p times a year for n years is equal to the present value, at the *effective* rate $\dfrac{j}{p}$, of an immediate annuity of $\dfrac{1}{p}$ per annum payable annually for np years. The equality of the two is at once obvious if "year" be replaced by "interval", for each then becomes the present value of a series of np payments of $\dfrac{1}{p}$ discounted on the assumption of compound interest at the rate of $\dfrac{j}{p}$ per interval.

22. It appears, therefore, that a table giving, at various effective rates of interest, the present values of annuities of 1 per annum payable annually for various terms of years may be used (within such limits as its range allows) for finding the present value, at a nominal rate of interest convertible p times a year, of an annuity payable p times a year. For example, the present value, at 4 per-cent convertible half-yearly, of an annuity of 1 per annum payable half-yearly for n years may be found by taking one-half the present value, at 2 per-cent effective, of an annuity of 1 per annum for $2n$ years. In symbols:—
$a_{\overline{n}|}^{(2)}$ at 4 per-cent convertible half-yearly $= \frac{1}{2}a_{\overline{2n}|}$ at 2 per-cent effective.

In general, a table of the present values of immediate annuities at various effective rates of interest may be looked upon as a table of the values of $\frac{1-(1+x)^{-n}}{x}$, and may be used for any purpose for which the value of this function may be required. A similar extension may obviously be given to the application of a table of amounts.

23. Tables giving the present values and amounts, at various effective rates of interest, of an annuity of 1 per annum payable annually may also be conveniently used for calculating the present values and amounts, at the same effective rates, of a similar annuity payable p times a year. For an immediate annuity of 1 per annum payable p times a year is obviously equivalent to an annuity of $s_{\overline{1}|}^{(p)}$ per annum, payable annually, that is:—

$$a_{\overline{n}|}^{(p)} = s_{\overline{1}|}^{(p)} \cdot a_{\overline{n}|} \quad . \quad . \quad . \quad . \quad . \quad . \quad . \quad (26)$$

and

$$s_{\overline{n}|}^{(p)} = s_{\overline{1}|}^{(p)} \cdot s_{\overline{n}|} \quad . \quad . \quad . \quad . \quad . \quad . \quad . \quad (27)$$

or, since $s_{\overline{1}|}^{(p)} = \frac{(1+i)-1}{p[(1+i)^{\frac{1}{p}}-1]} = \frac{i}{p[(1+i)^{\frac{1}{p}}-1]}$,

$$a_{\overline{n}|}^{(p)} = \frac{i}{p[(1+i)^{\frac{1}{p}}-1]} \cdot a_{\overline{n}|} \quad . \quad . \quad . \quad . \quad (28)$$

and

$$s_{\overline{n}|}^{(p)} = \frac{i}{p[(1+i)^{\frac{1}{p}}-1]} \cdot s_{\overline{n}|} \quad . \quad . \quad . \quad . \quad (29)$$

These results follow at once, algebraically, from a comparison of formulas (5) and (6) with formulas (8) and (9). The factor $\frac{i}{p[(1+i)^{\frac{1}{p}}-1]}$ is independent of n, and the values of $a_{\overline{n}|}^{(p)}$ and $s_{\overline{n}|}^{(p)}$ at a given effective rate may, therefore, be found, *for any value of n*, by multiplying the tabulated values of $a_{\overline{n}|}$ and $s_{\overline{n}|}$, at that rate, by a factor which is constant for a given value of p. For example, $a_{\overline{n}|}^{(2)}$ at 4 per-cent effective $= \frac{\cdot 04}{2[\sqrt{1\cdot 04}-1]} \cdot a_{\overline{n}|}$ for all values of n. A table of the values of $\frac{i}{p[(1+i)^{\frac{1}{p}}-1]}$ for those values of i and p which occur most frequently in practice is given on p. 214.

24. By assigning to p, in formulas (5) and (6), a fractional value, say $\frac{1}{r}$, expressions may be obtained for the amount and present value of an annuity of 1 per annum payable every r years, that is, of an annuity under which a payment of r is made at the end of every rth year. Thus

$$s_{\overline{n}|}^{\left(\frac{1}{r}\right)}=\frac{r[(1+i)^n-1]}{(1+i)^r-1}=rs_{\overline{n}|}\cdot\frac{i}{(1+i)^r-1}=\frac{rs_{\overline{n}|}}{s_{\overline{r}|}} \quad . \; . \quad (30)$$

and
$$a_{\overline{n}|}^{\left(\frac{1}{r}\right)}=\frac{r[1-v^n]}{(1+i)^r-1}=ra_{\overline{n}|}\frac{i}{(1+i)^r-1}=\frac{ra_{\overline{n}|}}{s_{\overline{r}|}} \quad . \; . \; . \; . \quad (31)$$

from which it follows that the amount and present value of an annuity of 1, payable every r years throughout a period of n years are $\frac{s_{\overline{n}|}}{s_{\overline{r}|}}$ and $\frac{a_{\overline{n}|}}{s_{\overline{r}|}}$ respectively. If n be an exact multiple of r, these results may be verified by obvious general reasoning or by actual summation of the sums of the amounts and present values of the successive payments. If n bė not an exact multiple of r, they involve the same assumption as that made in Article 16, namely, that the payment to be made at the end of the nth year in respect of the final period of, say, t years (where t is $< r$), bears the same ratio to 1 as the total interest on 1 for t years bears to the total interest on 1 for r years.

25. A practical application of the formulas of the preceding article occurs in connection with leases subject to periodical renewal on payment of a fine. In the general case of a lease renewable at the end of $(t+r)$ years, and at the end of every subsequent r years during a total period of n years (where n may be assumed to be an exact multiple of r), on payment, on the occasion of each renewal, of a fine F, the series of fines will constitute an annuity of F payable every r years for a period of n years deferred t years, and their present value will, therefore, be

$$\mathrm{F}\,.\,v^t\frac{a_{\overline{n}|}}{s_{\overline{r}|}},$$

or

$$\mathrm{F}\frac{a_{\overline{n+t}|}-a_{\overline{t}|}}{s_{\overline{r}|}}.$$

The only case of much practical importance is that in which the lease is renewable every r years *in perpetuity*. In this case the expression for the present value of the future fines reduces to $\mathrm{F}\frac{v^t}{is_{\overline{r}|}}$. This formula is based on the assumption that the first fine falls due at the end of $(t+r)$ years. If the first fine is payable at the end of t years, so that the series of fines constitutes a deferred perpetuity-due instead of an ordinary deferred perpetuity, the formula for the present value will, of course, be

$$Fv^t\left(1+\frac{1}{is_{\overline{r}|}}\right)$$

or

$$F\cdot\frac{v^t}{1-v^r} \quad . \quad . \quad . \quad . \quad . \quad . \quad . \quad . \quad . \quad . \qquad (32)$$

26. The foregoing investigations relate exclusively to annuities of a uniform annual rent. It remains to consider the problem of valuing VARYING ANNUITIES, that is, annuities of which the periodical payments are not all equal. It is, of course, necessary that either the actual amounts of all the payments, or the law by which they may be calculated, should be given. An obvious method of procedure is to calculate separately the present values of the successive payments and to take the sum of the results, and in some cases, where the payments are few in number and do not follow any simple law, this will be the simplest course to adopt. But this method would obviously entail great labour if the number of payments were large, and it is therefore convenient to investigate general formulas applicable to the more important classes of cases that may occur in practice. For purposes of investigation, annuities payable *annually* need alone be considered, as the resulting formulas may be applied to annuities payable with any other frequency by appropriately changing the unit of time and the rate of interest.

27. Many simple varying annuities may be valued by elementary algebraical methods.

28. Take, for example, the case of an annuity of which the successive payments increase or decrease in arithmetic progression. Let p be the first payment, q the common difference of the series of payments, and a the present value of the annuity for n years. Then

$$a=vp+v^2(p+q)+v^3(p+2q)+\ldots+v^n(p+\overline{n-1}q)$$

and $$av=v^2p+v^3(p+q)+\ldots+v^n(p+\overline{n-2}q)+v^{n+1}(p+\overline{n-1}q)$$

$\therefore$ by subtraction, $iva=vp+v^2q+v^3q+\ldots+v^nq-v^{n+1}(p+\overline{n-1}q)$

$$=p\,.\,v(1-v^n)+qv\,.\,a_{\overline{n}|}-nqv^{n+1}$$

whence

$$a=pa_{\overline{n}|}+q\frac{a_{\overline{n}|}-nv^n}{i} \quad . \quad . \quad . \quad . \quad . \quad . \quad . \qquad (33)$$

If n be made infinite, $a_{\overline{n}|}$ becomes a_{∞}, the value of which is $\frac{1}{i}$; and nv^n, being $=\frac{n}{(1+i)^n}$, or $\frac{1}{\frac{1}{n}+i+\frac{n-1}{2!}i^2+\frac{(n-1)(n-2)}{3!}i^3+\ldots}$, vanishes. Hence the present value of a perpetuity of which the first payment is p, and the subsequent payments increase in Arithmetical Progression with a common difference q, is

$$\frac{p}{i}+\frac{q}{i^2} \quad . \quad . \quad . \quad . \quad . \quad . \quad . \quad . \quad . \quad (34)$$

This result might have been obtained by dividing the perpetuity into one of the uniform rent p, and another of which the successive payments are 0, q, $2q$, &c. The present value of the former is $\frac{p}{i}$, and that of the latter is $qv^2+2qv^3+\ldots$ *ad inf.* Now the infinite series $(1+2v+3v^2+\ldots)$ is the expansion of $(1-v)^{-2}$. Therefore

$$qv^2+2qv^3+\ \ldots\ ad\ inf.=\frac{qv^2}{(1-v)^2}=\frac{q}{i^2},$$

and the present value of the entire perpetuity is, as before, $\frac{p}{i}+\frac{q}{i^2}$

In this connection it may be pointed out that whenever the successive payments of an annuity or perpetuity can be identified with the coefficients of the successive terms of a binomial expansion, the present value of the annuity or perpetuity may be at once obtained. Thus, the present value of an annuity-due for $(n+1)$ years, whose successive payments are the coefficients of the powers of n in $(1+x)^n$ would be $(1+v)^n$, and the present value of a perpetuity whose successive payments are r, $\frac{r(r+1)}{2!}$, &c., would be $(1-v)^{-r}-1$ or $\frac{1}{i^r v^r}-1$.

29. The annuity whose successive payments are 1, 2, 3, &c., is sometimes called an INCREASING ANNUITY without definition of the nature of the increase, and its present value is denoted by the symbol $(\mathrm{I}a)$. From the foregoing it will be seen that

$$(\mathrm{I}a)_{\overline{n}|}=a_{\overline{n}|}+\frac{a_{\overline{n}|}-nv^n}{i} \quad . \quad . \quad . \quad . \quad . \quad . \quad (35)$$

and

$$(\mathrm{I}a)_{\infty}=\frac{1}{i}+\frac{1}{i^2} \quad . \quad . \quad . \quad . \quad . \quad . \quad . \quad . \quad . \quad (36)$$

30. Next consider the case of an annuity of which the payments increase in Geometric Progression, and let k be the first payment, and r the common ratio of the series of payments. Then the present value of the annuity for n years

$$=kv+krv^2+kr^2v^3+\ .\ .\ .\ +kr^{n-1}v^n$$

$$=kv\frac{1-r^nv^n}{1-rv} \text{ or } k\frac{1-r^nv^n}{1+i-r}$$

The present value of the corresponding perpetuity will be $\frac{k}{1+i-r}$, if r is $<1+i$, and an infinitely large quantity if r be$=$or $>1+i$. If rv be put$=v'$, so that $i'=\frac{1+i}{r}-1$, the expression $kv\frac{1-r^nv^n}{1-rv}$ takes the form $\frac{k}{r}v'\frac{1-v'^n}{1-v'}$ or $\frac{k}{r}a'_{\overline{n}|}$. Hence it appears that the present value at rate i of an annuity of which the first payment is k, and the subsequent payments increase in Geometric Progression with the common ratio r is equal to the present value at rate i' of an ordinary annuity of $\frac{k}{r}$ per annum, where $i'=\frac{1+i}{r}-1$.

When the value of r is such that the resulting value of i' comes within the range of rates of interest for which the present values of annuities are tabulated, the relation just established affords a convenient means of obtaining approximately, without the labour of actual calculation, the present value of an increasing annuity.

31. As an example of the subject discussed in the foregoing article, suppose that a company applies its surplus profits, after declaring a certain fixed rate of dividend on its ordinary shares, to the allotment to its ordinary shareholders of further shares, and that it is required to find the present value, at say 5 per-cent, of the dividends for the next ten years in respect of a present holding on which a dividend of k has just been paid, on the assumption that the annual allotment of new shares will be at the rate of two per-cent on the total number of shares existing at the date of each allotment. Here the dividends will form an annuity of which the payments increase in Geometric Progression with a common ratio of 1·02, and i' will$=\frac{1\cdot05}{1\cdot02}-1$ or ·03 approximately. The present value of the dividends will, therefore, be roughly $k\times a_{\overline{10}|}$ at three per-cent $=k\times 8{\cdot}53$. The true value obtained by the formula $k(1{\cdot}02)\cdot\dfrac{1-(1{\cdot}02)^{10}v^{10}}{1{\cdot}05-1{\cdot}02}$, would be $k\times 8{\cdot}56$.

32. The practical utility of replacing an increasing (or decreasing) annuity by an ordinary annuity at a changed rate of interest will be limited to those cases in which the rate of increase lies between $(1+i)$ and 1, or in which the rate of decrease is only a small fraction less than 1. If $r=1+i$, the rate of increase exactly counteracts the rate of discount, and the present value of the increasing annuity becomes that of an ordinary annuity of $\dfrac{k}{r}$ calculated on the assumption that money yields no interest, that is to say, in the case of an annuity to continue for n years, $\dfrac{nk}{r}$. If r is $>1+i$, i' becomes negative. This, of course, means that the rate of increase more than counteracts the rate of discount, so that the present values of the successive payments of the increasing annuity form a series of increasing quantities. In each of the last two cases the present value of the increasing perpetuity will obviously be infinitely great.

33. A class of varying annuities of a more general type than either of those discussed in the preceding articles—and one which, in fact, includes most of the varying annuities that arise in practice—is that in which the successive payments form a series of which the rth term is a rational integral function of r. If the function be assumed to be of the mth order, the present value of an n-year annuity of this type may be written in the form

$$\Sigma_{r=1}^{r=n}(a_0+a_1r+a_2r^2+\ .\ .\ .\ +a_mr^m)v^r.$$

34. The summation of this series in any given case may be effected by repeated multiplications by $1-v$ or iv, for it is obvious that each multiplication by this factor will reduce the order of the function by unity. Take, for example, the case of an annuity whose successive payments are the 2nd powers of the natural numbers. Here

$$a=1^2v.+2^2v^2+3^2v^3+\ .\ .\ .\ +n^2.v^n$$

$$a(1-v)=1v+3v^2+5v^3+\ .\ .\ .\ +(2n-1)v^n-n^2v^{n+1}$$

$$a(1-v)^2=v+2v^2+2v^3+\ .\ .\ .\ +2v^n-(n^2+2n-1)v^{n+1}+n^2v^{n+2}$$

and
$$a=\frac{2a_{\overline{n}|}-v-(n^2+2n-1)v^{n+1}+n^2v^{n+2}}{i^2v^2}$$

If n be made infinitely great, this expression reduces to

$$\frac{\frac{2}{i}-v}{i^2v^2} \text{ or } \frac{v(1+v)}{(1-v)^3}.$$

The infinite series $1^2+2^2v+3^2v^2+4^2v^3+\ldots$ is, in fact, the expansion of $(1+v)(1-v)^{-3}$ in powers of v.

35. When, as in the example just given, the function is of a low order—say the 2nd or 3rd—the process of reduction by successive multiplications by $1-v$ does not entail much labour. For functions of higher orders, and for the development of the general theory, a different method of procedure must be adopted. This method, which involves the use of the calculus of finite differences, is discussed in Chapter X, but it will be convenient to consider, in this place, a special class of varying annuities which are required in its application. These are the annuities whose successive payments are the successive terms of the various orders of *figurate numbers*. Information upon the subject of figurate numbers will be found in any standard work on algebra, but it will be convenient to recapitulate briefly their method of formation and principal properties.

36. The FIGURATE NUMBERS are the terms of certain series of numbers constructed in accordance with a certain law. The series are called *Orders*, and their laws of formation are as follows:—

(i) Each term of the first order is unity.

(ii) If $t_{\overline{m}|\,\overline{r}|}$ is the mth term of the rth order $t_{\overline{m}|\,\overline{r}|}=\Sigma_1^{m-1}t_{\overline{m}|\,\overline{r-1}|}$.

By means of these laws the successive series may be formed. Thus:

Term No.	Order No.						
	1	2	3	4	5	6	7
1	1	0	0	0	0	0	0
2	1	1	0	0	0	0	0
3	1	2	1	0	0	0	0
4	1	3	3	1	0	0	0
5	1	4	6	4	1	0	0
6	1	5	10	10	5	1	0
7	1	6	15	20	15	6	1

37. To find the value of $t_{\overline{m}|\,\overline{r}|}$, the mth term of the rth order.

By the first law of formation $t_{\overline{m}|\,\overline{1}|}=1$.

By the second law $t_{\overline{m}|\,\overline{2}|}=(t_{\overline{1}|\,\overline{1}|}+t_{\overline{2}|\,\overline{1}|}+\ldots+t_{\overline{m-1}|\,\overline{1}|})$

$$=1+1+1+\ldots \text{ to } (m-1) \text{ terms}=m-1.$$

$$t_{\overline{m}|\,\overline{3}|}=t_{\overline{1}|\,\overline{2}|}+t_{\overline{2}|\,\overline{2}|}+\ldots+t_{\overline{m-1}|\,\overline{2}|}$$

$$=0+1+2+\ldots+\overline{m-2}=\frac{\overline{m-1}\;\overline{m-2}}{2!}$$

$$t_{\overline{m}|\,\overline{4}|}=t_{\overline{1}|\,\overline{3}|}+t_{\overline{2}|\,\overline{3}|}+\ldots+t_{\overline{m-1}|\,\overline{3}|}$$

$$=0+0+1+3+\ldots+\frac{\overline{m-2}\;\overline{m-3}}{2!}=\frac{\overline{m-1}\;\overline{m-2}\;\overline{m-3}}{3!}$$

Assume that $t_{\overline{m}|\,\overline{r}|}=\dfrac{\overline{m-1}\ldots\overline{m-r+1}}{\overline{r-1}!}$

Then $t_{\overline{m}|\,\overline{r+1}|}=t_{1\,\overline{r}|}+t_{\overline{2}|\,\overline{r}|}+\ldots+t_{\overline{m-1}|\,\overline{r}|}$

$$=0+0+\ldots+1+r+\ldots+\frac{\overline{m-2}\ldots\overline{m-r}}{\overline{r-1}!}$$

$$=\frac{\overline{m-1}\ldots\overline{m-r}}{r!}$$

This expression is of precisely the same form as that assumed for $t_{\overline{m}|\,\overline{r}|}$. Therefore, by induction,

$$t_{\overline{m}|\,\overline{r}|}=\frac{\overline{m-1}\;\overline{m-2}\ldots\overline{m-r+1}}{\overline{r-1}!}=\frac{\overline{m-1}!}{\overline{m-r}!\,\overline{r-1}!}\quad\ldots\quad(35)$$

The following relations are evident:—

$$t_{\overline{m}|\,\overline{r}|},\text{ where } m \text{ is } <r,=0\quad\ldots\ldots\ldots\quad(36)$$

$$t_{\overline{r}|\,\overline{r}|}=1\quad\ldots\ldots\ldots\quad(37)$$

$$t_{\overline{m}|\,\overline{r}|}=t_{\overline{m-1}|\,\overline{r}|}+t_{\overline{m-1}|\,\overline{r-1}|}\quad\ldots\quad(38)$$

38. Since

$$(1-x)^{-r}=1+rx+\frac{r\,\overline{r+1}}{2!}x^2+\ldots+\frac{\overline{m-1}!}{\overline{m-r}!\,\overline{r-1}!}x^{m-r}+\ldots$$

$$=t_{\overline{r}|\,\overline{r}|}+t_{\overline{r+1}|\,\overline{r}|}\cdot x+t_{\overline{r+2}|\,\overline{r}|}\cdot x^2+\ldots+t_{\overline{m}|\,\overline{r}|}\cdot x^{m-r}+\ldots$$

it appears that the terms of the rth order of figurate numbers consist of $(r-1)$ 0's followed by the successive coefficients in the expansion of

$(1-x)^{-r}$, and that $t_{\overline{m|}\,\overline{r|}}$ is the coefficient of x^m in the expansion of $x^r(1-x)^{-r}$.

39. An annuity of which the successive payments are the successive terms of the rth order of figurate numbers is called an *annuity of the rth order*. The amount and present value of an n-year annuity of the rth order are represented by the symbols $s_{\overline{n|}\,\overline{r|}}$ and $a_{\overline{n|}\,\overline{r|}}$.

$$\text{Obviously} \qquad a_{\overline{n|}\,\overline{r|}} = v^n s_{\overline{n|}\,\overline{r|}} \quad . \quad . \quad . \quad . \quad . \quad . \quad . \quad . \quad . \qquad (39)$$

40. To find the relation between $s_{\overline{n|}\,\overline{r|}}$ and $s_{\overline{n|}\,\overline{r-1|}}$.

$$s_{\overline{n|}\,\overline{r|}} = t_{\overline{n|}\,\overline{r|}} + (1+i)t_{\overline{n-1|}\,\overline{r|}} + \ldots + (1+i)^{n-1}t_{\overline{1|}\,\overline{r|}}$$

$$(1+i)s_{\overline{n|}\,\overline{r|}} = \qquad (1+i)t_{\overline{n|}\,\overline{r|}} \quad + \ldots + (1+i)^{n-1}t_{\overline{2|}\,\overline{r|}} + (1+i)^n t_{\overline{1|}\,\overline{r|}}$$

by subtraction with the aid of formula (38)

$$i s_{\overline{n|}\,\overline{r|}} = (1+i)t_{\overline{n-1|}\,\overline{r-1|}} + (1+i)^2 t_{\overline{n-2|}\,\overline{r-1|}} + \ldots$$

$$+ (1+i)^{n-1}t_{\overline{1|}\,\overline{r-1|}} + (1+i)^n t_{\overline{1|}\,\overline{r|}} - t_{\overline{n|}\,\overline{r|}}$$

$$= s_{\overline{n|}\,\overline{r-1|}} + (1+i)^n t_{\overline{1|}\,\overline{r|}} - t_{\overline{n|}\,\overline{r|}} - t_{\overline{n|}\,\overline{r-1|}}$$

$$= s_{\overline{n|}\,\overline{r-1|}} + (1+i)^n t_{\overline{1|}\,\overline{r|}} - t_{\overline{n+1|}\,\overline{r|}}$$

$$\text{or} \qquad s_{\overline{n|}\,\overline{r|}} = \frac{s_{\overline{n|}\,\overline{r-1|}} + (1+i)^n t_{\overline{1|}\,\overline{r|}} - t_{\overline{n+1|}\,\overline{r|}}}{i} \quad . \quad . \quad . \quad . \quad . \quad . \quad . \qquad (40)$$

41. To find the relation between $a_{\overline{n|}\,\overline{r|}}$ and $a_{\overline{n|}\,\overline{r-1|}}$

$$a_{\overline{n|}\,\overline{r|}} = \qquad v t_{\overline{1|}\,\overline{r|}} + v^2 t_{\overline{2|}\,\overline{r|}} + \ldots + v^{n-1} t_{\overline{n-1|}\,\overline{r|}} + v^n t_{\overline{n|}\,\overline{r|}}$$

$$(1+i)a_{\overline{n|}\,\overline{r|}} = t_{\overline{1|}\,\overline{r|}} + v t_{\overline{2|}\,\overline{r|}} + v^2 t_{\overline{3|}\,\overline{r|}} + \ldots + v^{n-1} t_{\overline{n|}\,\overline{r|}}$$

by subtraction with the aid of formula (38)

$$i a_{\overline{n|}\,\overline{r|}} = v t_{\overline{1|}\,\overline{r-1|}} + v^2 t_{\overline{2|}\,\overline{r-1|}} + \ldots + v^{n-1} t_{\overline{n-1|}\,\overline{r-1|}} + t_{\overline{1|}\,\overline{r|}} - v^n t_{\overline{n|}\,\overline{r|}}$$

$$= a_{\overline{n|}\,\overline{r-1|}} - v^n t_{\overline{n|}\,\overline{r-1|}} + t_{\overline{1|}\,\overline{r|}} - v^n t_{\overline{n|}\,\overline{r|}}$$

$$= a_{\overline{n|}\,\overline{r-1|}} + t_{\overline{1|}\,\overline{r|}} - v^n t_{\overline{n+1|}\,\overline{r|}}$$

$$\text{or} \quad a_{\overline{n|}\,\overline{r|}} = \frac{a_{\overline{n|}\,\overline{r-1|}} + t_{\overline{1|}\,\overline{r|}} - v^n t_{\overline{n+1|}\,\overline{r|}}}{i} \quad . \quad . \quad . \quad . \quad . \quad . \quad . \quad . \quad . \quad . \quad . \qquad (41)$$

42. From formulas (40) and (41) the amounts and present values of the annuities of the various orders can be successively calculated. Thus:—

Order of Annuity	Amount	Present Value
1	$s_{\overline{n}\|} = \dfrac{(1+i)^n-1}{i}$	$a_{\overline{n}\|} = \dfrac{1-v^n}{i}$
2	$s_{\overline{n}\|\,\overline{2}\|} = \dfrac{s_{\overline{n}\|}-n}{i}$	$a_{\overline{n}\|\,\overline{2}\|} = \dfrac{a_{\overline{n}\|}-nv^n}{i}$
3	$s_{\overline{n}\|\,\overline{3}\|} = \dfrac{s_{\overline{n}\|\,\overline{2}\|} - \dfrac{n(n-1)}{2}}{i}$	$a_{\overline{n}\|\,\overline{3}\|} = \dfrac{a_{\overline{n}\|\,\overline{2}\|} - \dfrac{n(n-1)}{2}v^n}{i}$
&c.	&c.	&c.

It will be observed that, in the derivation of $s_{\overline{n}|}$ and $a_{\overline{n}|}$ from the general formulas, $s_{\overline{n}|\,\overline{0}|}$ and $a_{\overline{n}|\,\overline{0}|}$ are taken as 0, and that in the derivation of the amounts and present values of the annuities of orders higher than the first, the terms $(1+i)^n t_{\overline{1}|\,\overline{r}|}$ and $t_{\overline{1}|\,\overline{r}|}$ vanish.

43. Since the numbers of the rth order, beginning with the first significant number, namely, $t_{\overline{r}|\,\overline{r}|}$, are the coefficients of the successive powers of x in the expansion of $x^r(1-x)^{-r}$, it follows that the present value of an n-year annuity of the rth order=the sum of the first $(n-r+1)$ terms of $v^r(1-v)^{-r}$. Hence the present value of a *perpetuity* of the rth order is

$$\frac{v^r}{(1-v)^r}, \text{ that is } \frac{1}{i^r} \quad . \quad . \quad . \quad . \quad . \quad . \quad . \quad . \qquad (42)$$

44. The relations between the amounts and present values of annuities of the successive orders may be established by general reasoning. The successive payments of an annuity of the $(r-1)$th order, if invested at rate i, will yield, by way of interest, $it_{\overline{r-1}|\,\overline{r-1}|}$, which is equal to $it_{\overline{r}|\,\overline{r}|}$, at the end of the rth year, $i(t_{\overline{r-1}|\,\overline{r-1}|}+t_{\overline{r}|\,\overline{r-1}|})$, which again is equal to $it_{\overline{r+1}|\,\overline{r}|}$, at the end of the $(r+1)$th year, and, generally, $i(t_{\overline{r-1}|\,\overline{r-1}|}+t_{\overline{r}|\,\overline{r-1}|}+ \ldots +t_{\overline{m-1}|\,\overline{r-1}|})$, or $it_{\overline{m}|\,\overline{r}|}$, at the end of the mth year, that is, an annuity of the rth order $\times i$; and, at the end of n years, the total payments, amounting in all to $(t_{\overline{r-1}|\,\overline{r-1}|}+t_{\overline{r}|\,\overline{r-1}|}+\ldots +t_{\overline{n}|\,\overline{r-1}|})$, or $t_{\overline{n+1}|\,\overline{r}|}$, will remain intact. Therefore, an n-year annuity of the $(r-1)$th order is equivalent to an n-year annuity of the rth order $\times i$ together with $t_{\overline{n+1}|\overline{r}|}$ in hand at the end of the term. If these equivalents be equated at the present time and at the end of n years respectively, it follows that—

$$a_{\overline{n}|\overline{r-1}|}=ia_{\overline{n}|\overline{r}|}+v^n t_{\overline{n+1}|\overline{r}|}$$

and

$$s_{\overline{n}|\overline{r-1}|}=is_{\overline{n}|\overline{r}|}+t_{\overline{n+1}|\overline{r}|}$$

These results agree with those obtained by the algebraical method for values of r greater than unity.

By a similar argument, it follows that a perpetuity of the $(r-1)$th order is equivalent to a perpetuity of the rth order $\times i$, so that

$$a_{\overline{\infty}|\overline{r-1}|}=ia_{\overline{\infty}|\overline{r}|}$$

and, as before,

$$a_{\overline{\infty}|\overline{r}|}=\frac{1}{i^r}.$$

45. It will be observed that the first significant payment of an annuity of the rth order does not become due until the end of the rth year, so that the annuities of all orders higher than the first are practically, although not in theory, deferred annuities. Thus, an annuity of the second order is an ordinary increasing annuity deferred one year. In Article 29 it was shown that $(Ia)_{\overline{n}|}=a_{\overline{n}|}+\dfrac{a_{\overline{n}|}-nv^n}{i}$, and it may be easily verified that this expression is equal to $(1+i)a_{\overline{n+1}|\overline{2}|}$.

CHAPTER IV.

Analysis of the Annuity.

1. In the preceding chapter the annuity has been considered as a given series of payments, of which it is required to find the present value or amount at a specified rate of interest. Conversely it may be regarded as the *equivalent*, in the form of a series of future payments, of a given present value or principal. Thus, an annuity of 1 per annum payable p times a year for n years is the equivalent, at the effective rate of interest i, of a given principal of $\dfrac{1-v^n}{p\{(1+i)^{\frac{1}{p}}-1\}}$. Hence, an investor proposing to purchase an n-year annuity payable p times a year, and intending to realize interest on the transaction at the effective rate i, would expect to receive $\dfrac{1}{a_{\overline{n}|}^{(p)}}$ per annum for each unit invested. Similarly, the vendor of such an annuity, if willing to sell at a net price calculated at the effective rate i, would be prepared to give an annuity of $\dfrac{1}{a_{\overline{n}|}^{(p)}}$ per annum for each unit of the purchase-money. Investment transactions involving the payment of an annuity frequently occur in practice, and it becomes important, therefore, to analyze the successive payments of the annuity in order to determine how they should be dealt with, on an investment basis, by the respective parties to the transaction.

2. In the first place, the present value of an annuity may be regarded as a fund which, if accumulated at the assumed rate of interest, will exactly provide the successive payments of the annuity as

they fall due. In the case of an ordinary annuity-certain payable annually

$$(1+i)a_{\overline{n}|}=1+v+v^2+\ldots+v^{n-1}=1+a_{\overline{n-1}|} \quad \ldots \quad (1)$$

and in the case of a similar annuity payable p times a year

$$(1+i)^{\frac{1}{p}}a^{(p)}_{\overline{n}|}=\frac{1}{p}\{1+v^{\frac{1}{p}}+v^{\frac{2}{p}}+\ldots+v^{n-\frac{1}{p}}\}=\frac{1}{p}+a^{(p)}_{\overline{n-\frac{1}{p}}|} \quad \ldots \quad (2)$$

These relations are merely the algebraical expression of what must obviously be the case, namely, that the accumulated amount of the purchase-money at the end of the first interval will provide the payment then due and leave in hand a fund equal to the present value of the annuity for the remainder of the term. Similar relations will clearly obtain for the second and subsequent intervals, until just after the last payment but one the fund will be reduced to $a_{\overline{1}|}$ or $a^{(p)}_{\overline{\frac{1}{p}}|}$, as the case may be, which will exactly provide the final payment. It appears, therefore, that by investing the purchase-money at the effective rate i, and by keeping the residue of the fund, as diminished from time to time by the periodical payments, strictly invested at that rate, the vendor or grantor of the annuity will be enabled to meet the successive payments, while from the point of view of the purchaser or grantee the transaction is essentially the same as if he placed his principal on deposit, on the basis of interest at the effective rate i being allowed from time to time on the balance standing at his credit, and withdrew at the end of every year or $\frac{1}{p}$th of a year, as the case may be, an amount equal to the periodical payment of the annuity.

3. In the next place, an annuity may be regarded as a means of liquidating a debt carrying interest at the assumed rate, the original sum owing being the present value of the annuity. From this point of view each payment may be considered as consisting partly of interest on so much of the debt as was outstanding after the last preceding payment and partly of a repayment of principal.

In the general case of a debt of $a^{(p)}_{\overline{n}|}$ which is to be repaid, with interest at the effective rate i, by an annuity of 1 per annum payable p times a year, the interest for the first $\frac{1}{p}$th of a year will be

$\{(1+i)^{\frac{1}{p}}-1\}a_{\overline{n}|}^{(p)}$, which $=\dfrac{1-v^n}{p}$. Hence the principal contained in the first payment of the annuity will be $\dfrac{1}{p}-\dfrac{1-v^n}{p}$, or $\dfrac{v^n}{p}$. And the principal outstanding after this payment will be $a_{\overline{n}|}^{(p)}-\dfrac{v^n}{p}$, which $=a_{\overline{n-\frac{1}{p}}|}^{(p)}$. Similarly, the interest for the second $\dfrac{1}{p}$th of a year will be $\{(1+i)^{\frac{1}{p}}-1\}a_{\overline{n-\frac{1}{p}}|}^{(p)}$, which $=\dfrac{1-v^{n-\frac{1}{p}}}{p}$; the principal contained in the second payment will be $\dfrac{1}{p}-\dfrac{1-v^{n-\frac{1}{p}}}{p}$, or $\dfrac{v^{n-\frac{1}{p}}}{p}$, and the principal outstanding after this payment will be $a_{\overline{n-\frac{1}{p}}|}^{(p)}-\dfrac{v^{n-\frac{1}{p}}}{p}$, which $=a_{\overline{n-\frac{2}{p}}|}^{(p)}$. By proceeding in this way, the successive payments of the annuity may be divided into their component elements of interest and principal-repayments in the manner shown in the following schedule:

No. of interval	Principal owing at beginning of interval	Interest for interval	Principal repaid at end of interval
1	$a_{\overline{n}|}^{(p)}$	$\dfrac{1}{p}(1-v^n)$	$\dfrac{v^n}{p}$
2	$a_{\overline{n-\frac{1}{p}}|}^{(p)}$	$\dfrac{1}{p}(1-v^{n-\frac{1}{p}})$	$\dfrac{v^{n-\frac{1}{p}}}{p}$
⋮	⋮	⋮	⋮
np	$a_{\overline{\frac{1}{p}}|}^{(p)}$	$\dfrac{1}{p}(1-v^{\frac{1}{p}})$	$\dfrac{v^{\frac{1}{p}}}{p}$

The final repayment of $\dfrac{v^{\frac{1}{p}}}{p}$ pays off the balance of $a_{\overline{\frac{1}{p}}|}^{(p)}$ owing at the beginning of the npth interval, and the successive principal-repayments in the final column add up, as they ought to do, to the original amount of the debt, namely, $a_{\overline{n}|}^{(p)}$.

In the special case in which $p=1$, the schedule will stand as follows:

Year	Principal owing at beginning of year	Interest for year	Principal repaid at end of year
1	$a_{\overline{n}\vert}$	$1-v^n$	v^n
2	$a_{\overline{n-1}\vert}$	$1-v^{n-1}$	v^{n-1}
⋮	⋮	⋮	⋮
n	$a_{\overline{1}\vert}$	$1-v$	v
Total principal repaid	...	...	$a_{\overline{n}\vert}$

4. On reference to the schedules given in the last article it will be seen that the successive repayments of principal are in Geometrical Progression with a common ratio of $(1+i)^{\frac{1}{p}}$ in the one case (where the annuity is payable p times a year), and of $(1+i)$ in the other (where the annuity is payable annually). It may be readily shown that when a debt is being repaid by an annuity of equal periodical payments, the successive repayments of principal must necessarily increase in Geometrical Progression. For let $C_{\frac{m}{p}}$ denote the principal included in the mth payment of an annuity of 1 per annum payable p times a year. Then the repayment of this amount will reduce by $C_{\frac{m}{p}}$, the outstanding principal upon which interest has to be charged. Consequently the interest included in the $(m+1)$th payment will be less by $\{(1+i)^{\frac{1}{p}}-1\}C_{\frac{m}{p}}$ than that included in the mth payment. Therefore, the principal included in the $(m+1)$th payment—being the balance thereof after deduction of interest for the interval—will be greater by $\{(1+i)^{\frac{1}{p}}-1\}C_{\frac{m}{p}}$ than that included in the mth payment. That is to say,

$$C_{\frac{m+1}{p}}=C_{\frac{m}{p}}+\{(1+i)^{\frac{1}{p}}-1\}C_{\frac{m}{p}}$$

or

$$C_{\frac{m+1}{p}}=(1+i)^{\frac{1}{p}}C_{\frac{m}{p}} \quad . \quad . \quad . \quad . \quad . \quad . \quad . \quad . \quad (3)$$

5. The relation between the principal repayments suggests an instructive method of finding the present value of an annuity-certain. For, since the successive repayments of principal form a Geometrical Progression with a common ratio of $(1+i)^{\frac{1}{p}}$ it follows that

$$C_n=(1+i)^{n-\frac{1}{p}}C_{\frac{1}{p}} \quad . \quad . \quad . \quad . \quad . \quad . \quad . \quad (4)$$

Now $C_{\frac{1}{p}}$, being the principal included in the first payment of the annuity, is $=\frac{1}{p}-\left\{(1+i)^{\frac{1}{p}}-1\right\}a_{\overline{n}|}^{(p)}$. And, since the final payment of the annuity must exactly suffice to repay the principal outstanding at the beginning of the final interval together with interest thereon, it follows that

$$\frac{1}{p}=(1+i)^{\frac{1}{p}}C_n.$$

Substituting for C_n and $C_{\frac{1}{p}}$ in (4)

$$\frac{1}{p}v^n=\frac{1}{p}-\left\{(1+i)^{\frac{1}{p}}-1\right\}a_{\overline{n}|}^{(p)}$$

whence

$$a_{\overline{n}|}^{(p)}=\frac{1-v^n}{p\{(1+i)^{\frac{1}{p}}-1\}}.$$

6. It will be observed that the schedules of Article 3 give not only *a law of relation* between the successive repayments of principal, but also their *absolute values*. Thus:—

$$C_{\frac{m}{p}}=\frac{1}{p}v^{n-\frac{m-1}{p}} \quad . \quad . \quad . \quad . \quad . \quad . \quad . \quad (5)$$

and

$$C_m=v^{n-m+1} \quad . \quad . \quad . \quad . \quad . \quad . \quad . \quad (6)$$

It follows, therefore, that any given payment of an annuity may be resolved into its component elements of principal and interest without reference to a complete schedule showing the respective amounts of principal and interest contained in each payment. Thus in the general case of a debt of $a_{\overline{n}|}^{(p)}$ repayable with interest at the effective rate i by an annuity of 1 per annum payable p times a year:—

The Principal contained in the mth payment $=\frac{1}{p}v^{n-\frac{m-1}{p}}$,

The Interest contained in the mth payment $=\frac{1}{p}\left(1-v^{n-\frac{m-1}{p}}\right)$,

And the Outstanding Principal just after the mth payment $=a_{\overline{n-\frac{m}{p}}|}$.

7. In practice loans are often made on the basis of the principal, with interest at an agreed rate, being repaid by a terminable annuity. This mode of repayment is specially authorised or prescribed by Act of Parliament in certain cases, where loans are raised by local authorities on security of the rates or by life-tenants of settled estates for improvement purposes, and it is also not infrequently adopted when money is advanced on mortgage of depreciating securities such as leasehold property.

In transactions of this nature a nominal rate of interest convertible half-yearly is usually charged, and the principal, with interest at that rate, is made repayable by an annuity payable half-yearly. If K be the amount of the loan, n the number of years over which the payments are to extend, and j convertible half-yearly, the rate of interest to be paid, then the uniform half-yearly payment to be made by the borrower will evidently be $\frac{K}{a_{\overline{2n}|}}$ where the annuity-value is to be taken at the effective rate $\frac{j}{2}$; the principal and interest included in the mth half-yearly payment will be $\frac{Kv^{2n-m+1}}{a_{\overline{2n}|}}$ and $\frac{K}{a_{\overline{2n}|}}(1-v^{2n-m+1})$ respectively, and the principal outstanding just after the mth payment will be $\frac{Ka_{\overline{2n-m}|}}{a_{\overline{2n}|}}$; where all the quantities are taken at the effective rate $\frac{j}{2}$. The transaction, in fact, takes the form of the liquidation of a debt of K by means of an annuity extending over $2n$ intervals, interest being at the effective rate of $\frac{j}{2}$ per interval.

8. The successive payments of the annuity, in such transactions as those discussed in the last article, are subject to income-tax only to the extent of the *interest* element contained in them. It is usual, therefore, to insert in the deed creating the security a schedule showing the amounts of interest and principal respectively contained in each payment. If the borrower has the right to pay off the balance of the

loan at any time during its currency—or, in other words, to redeem the remainder of the annuity on payment of a sum equal to the present value of the remaining payments calculated at the rate of interest payable on the loan—the schedule also serves the purpose of showing the amount payable on redemption at the end of each interval; if the borrower has no such right of redemption, and is entitled to re-purchase the remainder of the annuity only on terms acceptable to the lender or fixed by the deed, then the schedule must be regarded merely as showing how the amount of interest contained in each payment is arrived at, and not as fixing the amount of principal repaid. From the foregoing analysis it appears that the schedule might be constructed in any of the three following ways:—

(i) by the method of Article 3—that is, by calculating the interest for the first interval, deducting the result from the periodical annuity-payment in order to find the amount of principal contained in the first payment of the annuity, deducting this amount from the original debt and so obtaining the principal outstanding at the beginning of the second interval, calculating the interest for the second interval, and so on, from interval to interval.

(ii) by constructing the complete column of principal-repayments in the first instance, and obtaining therefrom, by subtraction, the columns of interest and outstanding principal. The principal-repayments may be readily calculated by reference to the fact that they form a series in Geometrical Progression (Art. 4). The first step in the process will be to calculate the amount of principal included in the first payment of the annuity, which may be done either by means of the formula $\frac{v^n}{p}$ or by deducting the interest for the first interval from the periodical annuity-payment, and the subsequent repayments may then be obtained by repeated multiplications by the common ratio of the series.

(iii) by constructing in the first instance the column showing the principal outstanding at the beginning of each interval, and obtaining the other two columns by subtraction. The successive amounts of principal outstanding may of course be obtained by multiplying the periodical annuity-payment by the successive values of $a^{(p)}_{\overline{n-\frac{m}{p}}|}$.

In theory it is a matter of indifference which of these methods is employed, but in practice it will be desirable to select that one which, with the least expenditure of labour, minimizes the error resulting from the necessary limitation of the number of decimal places retained in the calculations. From this point of view the third method is inadmissible—on account of the comparatively large numerical values of the factors which have to be multiplied together to obtain the successive values of the outstanding principal—while the first and second methods are equally satisfactory. Perhaps the most convenient plan to adopt is to employ the first method—checking the work at intervals, in the case of a loan extending over a long period, by independently calculating periodical values of the principal repayments—and to finally adjust the figures by inspection. The process is illustrated by the following example:—A loan of £1,000 is to be repaid in five years, with interest at 4 per-cent per annum convertible half-yearly, by equal half-yearly instalments including principal and interest. It is required to construct a schedule showing the amounts of principal and interest respectively contained in each half-yearly payment.

The half-yearly payment will be $\frac{1,000}{a_{\overline{10|}}}$, where the annuity-value is calculated at 2 per-cent, that is 111·32653 . . . As the term of repayment extends over only ten half-years, it will not be necessary to employ any intermediate checks, and the entire calculations, taken to the nearest third place, will be as shown by the original figures in the following schedule:—

Half-year No.	Outstanding Principal at beginning of Half-year	Interest for Half-year	Principal contained in Payment for Half-year
1	1000	20	91·327
2	908·673	18·1734	93·1543
3	815·519 20	16·3101	95·0176
4	720·502 4	14·4101	96·9176
5	623·585 8	12·472	98·855
6	524·730 3	10·495	100·832
7	423·898901	8·478	102·849
8	321·049 52	6·421	104·906
9	216·143 6	4·323	107·004
10	109·139 42	2·183	109·144
			1000·0052

Here there is an error of ·005 in excess, in the principal repayments, resulting from the fact that the annuity-payment upon which the calculations are based is too large by nearly ·0005. This error must be removed by diminishing five of the values in the last column by ·001, and as each such adjustment will entail a corresponding increase of the values in the interest column—which, again, must be kept in close agreement with the column of outstanding principal—it will be convenient to determine the values to be adjusted by inspection of the interest column. It will be observed that the interest for the first half-year is absolutely correct, and that in calculating the interest for each half-year from the fifth to the tenth inclusive, the final figure has been already increased. Hence it will be proper to increase by 1 the final figures of the interest for the second, third, and fourth half-years, and to diminish the corresponding principal-repayments by ·001 each. This reduces the total error to ·002, and at the same time increases the amounts of principal outstanding as shown in the schedule. On further inspection it appears that the interest for the seventh and eighth half-years, calculated on the *corrected* amounts of principal outstanding, is now in excess of the amounts scheduled in the original calculations. The requisite further adjustment will, therefore, be obtained by increasing the final figure in the interest for the seventh and eighth half-years by ·001 each, and by diminishing the corresponding principal-repayments. Hence the finally adjusted figures will stand as follows:—

Half-year No.	Outstanding Principal at beginning of Half-year	Interest for Half-year	Principal contained in Payment for Half-year
1	1000	20	91·327
2	908·673	18·174	93·153
3	815·520	16·311	95·016
4	720·504	14·411	96·916
5	623·588	12·472	98·855
6	524·733	10·495	100·832
7	423·901	8·479	102·848
8	321·053	6·422	104·905
9	216·148	4·323	107·004
10	109·144	2·183	109·144
			1000·000

If the original figures be expressed (as will usually be the case) in pounds, shillings, and pence, correct to the nearest penny, similar principles of adjustment will apply.

9. In the analysis of Article 3 it has been assumed that the balance of each annuity-payment after deduction of interest will be applied directly to reduce the amount of the debt. The purchaser of the annuity may, however, prefer to deal with the payments of the annuity in a different way. Instead of periodically writing down the principal as each payment is made, he may leave it at its original amount until the end of the term and carry to a separate capital-redemption account so much of the periodical annuity-payment as is not required for interest; the sums thus carried to a separate account, being available for investment, will of course accumulate at compound interest. Under this mode of dealing with the transaction a uniform amount out of each annuity-payment will be required for interest (since the original principal is treated, for purposes of account, as outstanding throughout), and consequently a uniform amount will remain to be carried to capital redemption account at the end of each interval and accumulated at compound interest. This uniform sum periodically transferred to the redemption account is called a *sinking-fund.*

In the case of a loan of $\overset{(p)}{a}_{\overline{n}|}$ repayable, with interest at rate i, by an annuity of 1 per annum payable p times a year for n years, each payment of the annuity will provide $\{(1+i)^{\frac{1}{p}}-1\}\overset{(p)}{a}_{\overline{n}|}$ for *interest* and $\frac{1}{p}-\{(1+i)^{\frac{1}{p}}-1\}\overset{(p)}{a}_{\overline{n}|}$ for *sinking-fund.* Now

$$\frac{1}{p}-\{(1+i)^{\frac{1}{p}}-1\}\overset{(p)}{a}_{\overline{n}|}=\frac{v^n}{p}=\frac{\overset{(p)}{a}_{\overline{n}|}}{p\overset{(p)}{s}_{\overline{n}|}},$$

Hence, the sinking fund, if accumulated at rate i, will amount at the end of n years to $\frac{\overset{(p)}{a}_{\overline{n}|}}{\overset{(p)}{s}_{\overline{n}|}}\times\overset{(p)}{s}_{\overline{n}|}$, that is, to $\overset{(p)}{a}_{\overline{n}|}$, which will exactly repay the principal of the loan. Further, the accumulations of the sinking-fund at any intermediate period, say after m years, will amount to $\frac{\overset{(p)}{a}_{\overline{n}|}}{\overset{(p)}{s}_{\overline{n}|}}\cdot\overset{(p)}{s}_{\overline{m}|}$, and the deduction of this sum from the original principal would leave $\overset{(p)}{a}_{\overline{n}|}\left(1-\frac{\overset{(p)}{s}_{\overline{m}|}}{\overset{(p)}{s}_{\overline{n}|}}\right)$, which may easily be shown to be equal to $\overset{(p)}{a}_{\overline{n-m}|}$. It appears, therefore, that, as should obviously be the case, the balance of the original principal after deduction of the sinking-fund accumulations is the same as the principal outstanding as obtained by the method of Article 3. In fact, the two methods of dealing with the annuity-payments differ only in *form*; in the one case the sinking-fund is carried to a separate account and accumulated at compound interest, while in the other it is invested in reducing the amount of principal.

10. In the foregoing article the amount of the loan has been taken as $a_{\overline{n}|}^{(p)}$ and the annuity as 1 per annum payable p times a year. If the amount of the loan be taken as unity, the annual annuity-payment required to repay the principal in n years will be $\frac{1}{a_{\overline{n}|}}$, the annual interest will be i, and the sinking-fund will be $\frac{1}{a_{\overline{n}|}} - i$, that is $\frac{v^n}{a_{\overline{n}|}}$ or $\frac{1}{s_{\overline{n}|}}$. The algebraical identity

$$\frac{1}{a_{\overline{n}|}} = i + \frac{1}{s_{\overline{n}|}} \quad . \quad . \quad . \quad . \quad . \quad . \quad . \quad . \quad (7)$$

shows, therefore, the relation between the annuity which 1 will purchase and the annual payment which will accumulate to 1 in n years, and expresses the fact that the annuity-payment must provide (a) interest on the amount invested and (b) the necessary sinking-fund to replace the invested capital on the expiration of the annuity.

In the case of a loan of K repayable in n years, with interest at rate j convertible half-yearly, by an annuity payable half-yearly the constituent elements of the half-yearly annuity-payment will be given by the formula

$$\frac{K}{a_{\overline{2n}|}} = \frac{K \cdot j}{2} + \frac{K}{s_{\overline{2n}|}}$$

where $a_{\overline{2n}|}$ and $s_{\overline{2n}|}$ are taken at the effective rate $\frac{j}{2}$.

11. It will be observed that in Article 9 it has been assumed that the sinking fund will be accumulated at rate i, that is, at the rate realized on the invested capital. In the ordinary formula for the present value of the annuity no question arises as to how that part of each payment representing a repayment of the invested principal is re-invested, because it is implicitly assumed that the principal repayments go to reduce the outstanding principal—in accordance with the analysis of Article 1—and cease forthwith to bear interest in

connection with this particular transaction; in fact, from the investment point of view the transaction is one under which the investor has a gradually diminishing amount of capital invested. In the analysis of Article 9, on the other hand, it has been assumed that the investor is to obtain interest at rate i, not merely on so much of the debt as may remain owing from time to time, but on the whole of the original principal throughout the entire term of the annuity, and this assumption involves the accumulation of the sinking fund at that rate. Obviously, if the sinking fund were not invested at so high a rate, and the investor were in the meantime to take interest at the full rate i on his original principal, the sinking fund accumulations at the end of the term of the annuity would be insufficient to replace the invested capital. The question therefore arises, what price should be paid for an n-year annuity of 1 per annum in order that the purchaser may realize interest on the whole of the purchase-money for the entire term of the annuity at rate i', and replace his invested capital by means of a sinking fund to be accumulated at some other—usually lower—rate i? Formula (7) at once suggests the answer. If the invested capital be taken as unity, a year's interest will be i' and the annual sinking fund must be $\frac{1}{s_{\overline{n}|}}$, where $s_{\overline{n}|}$ is calculated at rate i. Hence, if the present value of the annuity under the specified conditions be denoted by $a^{(i'\&i)}$,

$$\frac{1}{a_{\overline{n}|}^{(i'\&i)}}=i'+\frac{1}{s_{\overline{n}|}}=\frac{1}{a_{\overline{n}|}}+i'-i \quad . \quad . \quad . \quad . \quad . \quad . \quad . \quad (8)$$

That is to say, the annuity per annum which 1 will purchase on this special basis=the annuity per annum which 1 will purchase on the ordinary basis at rate i+the extra annual interest to be realized by the purchaser on the investment.

The corresponding relation for an annuity payable p times a year will take different forms according as the interest included in each periodical payment is assumed to be (a) interest for $\frac{1}{p}$th of a year at the effective rate i', or (b) such that the total interest received in each year would, if accumulated to the end of the year at rate i, provide a year's interest at rate i'. In the first case

$$\begin{aligned}\frac{1}{a_{\overline{n}|}^{(p)(i'\&i)}}&=p\{(1+i')^{\frac{1}{p}}-1\}+\frac{1}{s_{\overline{n}|}^{(p)}}\\&=\frac{1}{a_{\overline{n}|}^{(p)}}+p\{(1+i')^{\frac{1}{p}}-(1+i)^{\frac{1}{p}}\} \quad . \quad . \quad (9)a\end{aligned}$$

and, in the second case,

$$\frac{1}{a_{\overline{n}|}^{(p)(i'\&i)}} = \frac{i'}{s_{\overline{1}|}^{(p)}} + \frac{1}{s_{\overline{n}|}^{(p)}}$$

$$= \frac{1+i's_{\overline{n}|}}{s_{\overline{n}|}^{(p)}} \quad . \quad . \quad . \quad . \quad . \quad . \quad . \quad . \quad (9)b$$

From formulas (8), (9)a and (9)b it follows that

$$a_{\overline{n}|}^{(i'\&i)} = \frac{s_{\overline{n}|}}{1+i's_{\overline{n}|}} \quad . \quad . \quad . \quad . \quad . \quad . \quad . \quad . \quad . \quad . \quad . \quad . \quad . \quad . \quad (10)$$

and $$a_{\overline{n}|}^{(p)(i'\&i)} = \frac{s_{\overline{n}|}^{(p)}}{1+p\{(1+i')^{\frac{1}{p}}-1\}s_{\overline{n}|}^{(p)}} \text{ on assumption } (a) \quad . \quad (11)a$$

or $$\frac{s_{\overline{n}|}^{(p)}}{1+i's_{\overline{n}|}} \text{ on assumption } (b) \quad . \quad (11)b$$

When two rates of interest are employed, as in the foregoing investigation, they are usually distinguished as the *remunerative* and *reproductive* rates respectively—i' in the case considered above, being the remunerative rate and i the reproductive rate.

12. It has been shown that the periodical payment of an annuity calculated on the assumption that the reproductive rate differs from the remunerative rate is equal, for a given invested capital, to the periodical payment of an annuity calculated in the ordinary way on the basis of the former rate together with interest on the invested capital at a rate equal to the excess of the remunerative rate over the reproductive rate. Hence it follows that the analysis of the annuity based on a remunerative rate i' and a reproductive rate i is the same as that of an ordinary annuity based on the single rate i, except that the interest portion of each payment will include interest at rate $(i'-i)$ on the whole of the original principal as well as interest at rate i on the outstanding principal, or, what is the same thing, interest at rate $(i'-i)$ on the principal repaid as well as interest at rate i' on the outstanding principal.

Thus, in the practical case of a loan of K repayable by an annuity payable half-yearly for n years, the remunerative rate being j' convertible half-yearly and the reproductive rate j convertible half-yearly, the half-yearly annuity payment will be $\frac{\text{K}}{a_{\overline{2n}|}} + \frac{\text{K}}{2}(j'-j)$, the principal and interest contained in the mth half-yearly payment will be $\frac{Kv^{2m-n+1}}{a_{\overline{2n}|}}$ and $\frac{K}{a_{\overline{2n}|}}(1-v^{2n-m+1})+\frac{K}{2}(j'-j)$ respectively, the principal outstanding just after the mth payment will be $\frac{Ka_{\overline{2n-m}|}}{a_{\overline{2n}|}}$, and the principal repaid will be $\frac{K(a_{\overline{2n}|}-a_{\overline{2n-m}|})}{a_{\overline{2n}|}}$; all the present values in these expressions being calculated at the effective rate $\frac{j}{2}$. On comparison of these expressions with those given in Art. 7 it will be found that the only differences are in the amount of the annuity-payment and the periodical interest. The effect of the lender realizing the higher remunerative rate j', instead of the lower rate j at which the sinking fund can be accumulated, is that the half-yearly annuity-payment and the interest contained in each instalment are increased by $\frac{K}{2}(j'-j)$, as compared with what they would be if the annuity were calculated in the ordinary way at j convertible half-yearly.

$$\text{Since } \frac{K}{a_{\overline{2n}|}}(1-v^{2n-m+1})+\frac{K}{2}(j'-j)=\frac{j}{2}\cdot\frac{K}{a_{\overline{2n}|}}\cdot a_{\overline{2n-m+1}|}+\frac{K}{2}(j'-j)$$

$$=\frac{j'}{2}\cdot\frac{K}{a_{\overline{2n}|}}\cdot a_{\overline{2n-m+1}|}+\tfrac{1}{2}(j'-j)\frac{K(a_{\overline{2n}|}-a_{\overline{2n-m+1}|})}{a_{\overline{2n}|}}$$

it will be seen that, as has already been stated, the interest for each interval is equal to the interest at the remunerative rate on the outstanding principal together with interest at a rate equal to the excess of the remunerative over the reproductive rate on the principal repaid.

13. In constructing a schedule showing the interest and principal contained in the successive payments of an annuity calculated to pay one rate of interest on a loan and to admit of the replacement of capital at another, it will merely be necessary to construct a preliminary schedule in the ordinary way at the latter rate and to increase the amounts in the interest column by the extra interest on the whole loan. Suppose, for example, that in the case considered in Art. 8 the annuity had been calculated to yield the lender 5 per-cent convertible half-yearly on the entire loan for the whole duration of the transaction and to admit of the replacement of principal at 4 per-cent convertible half-yearly. The half-yearly annuity-payment would then have been 111·32653 . . . + ·005 × 1000, which = 116·32653 . . ., and the final schedule would have stood as follows—

Half-year No.	Outstanding Principal at beginning of Half-year	Interest for Half-year	Principal contained in Payment for Half-year
1	1000	25	91·327
2	908·673	23·174	93·153
3	815·520	21·311	95·016
4	720·504	19·411	96·916
5	623·588	17·472	98·855
6	524·733	15·495	100·832
7	423·901	13·479	102·848
8	321·053	11·422	104·905
9	216·148	9·323	107·004
10	109·144	7·183	109·144

It will be observed that the interest for each half year—although most simply obtained by adding 5 to the interest given in the schedule of Art. 8—may also be considered as made up of $2\frac{1}{2}$ per-cent on the outstanding principal and $\frac{1}{2}$ per-cent on the principal repaid. Thus, for the 9th half year, 9·323 = ·025 × 216·148 + ·005 × 783·852.

14. It will be understood that the expressions "principal repaid" and "principal outstanding" are employed, in connection with an annuity based on differing remunerative and reproductive rates, in a purely technical sense, and that they do not necessarily or usually define any practical relations between the parties to the transaction. They are merely introduced for purposes of analysis to show how much of each payment is of the nature of interest and consequently subject to income-tax. Different remunerative and reproductive rates may occasionally arise in practice, as, for example, when a purchaser has bought an annuity to pay a high rate of interest and prefers to treat it for purposes of account as yielding a somewhat lower rate for the entire term on the whole invested capital and admitting of the replacement of capital at a still lower rate, but they very seldom form any part of the contract between a borrower and a lender. In the practical example discussed in the last article it is obvious that if the transaction were a loan, subject to the ordinary right of redemption, the borrower would pay off the outstanding balance long before the expiration of the term of the annuity; 4 per-cent convertible half-yearly being by hypothesis the rate at which re-investments can be made, and, therefore, the rate at which money could be borrowed on reasonable security, it would not suit the borrower to pay the high and increasing rates (as compared with the principal nominally outstanding) exhibited in the latter part of the schedule. A transaction involving different remunerative and reproductive rates must, in fact, be regarded as of the nature of a sale and purchase, rather than a loan. If, therefore, in the case of an annuity based on two rates of interest either party desires, or both desire, to terminate the contract, the terms of re-purchase—apart from any special provision in the security—will generally be a matter for negotiation. Either party is entitled to the complete fulfilment of the contract, and the amount to be paid by the original grantor of the annuity for the re-purchase of the remaining instalments will have to be settled by agreement.

Three formulas suggest themselves as affording reasonable bases for negotiation. To fix ideas, consider the case of an annuity of 1 per annum payable annually for n years and originally bought at the price of $a_{\overline{n}|}^{(i' \& i)}$, or $\dfrac{1}{\dfrac{1}{s_{\overline{n}|}}+i'}$, to pay i' on the purchase-money for the entire term of n years, and to admit of the replacement of capital by a sinking fund accumulated at rate i, and suppose that the annuity is to be redeemed just after the tth payment. Then:

(i) If the vendor desires to re-purchase, it appears reasonable that he should put the purchaser in a position to buy a similar annuity for the remaining $(n-t)$ years in the open market. The rate at which re-investments can be made being, by hypothesis, i, it may be assumed that this is the rate at which an annuity could be bought on the ordinary basis. Hence in this case the re-purchase price would be $a_{\overline{n-t}|}$ calculated in the ordinary way at rate i.

(ii) If the purchaser desires to obtain the immediate use of his invested capital it may be considered that he ought to give the vendor credit for the entire accumulations of the sinking fund—that is, for the principal technically assumed to be repaid—and to accept the balance of his invested capital in commutation of the remaining payments of the annuity. On this basis the re-purchase-price would be

$$a_{\overline{n}|}^{(i'\&i)} - (1 - i'a_{\overline{n}|}^{(i'\&i)})s_{\overline{t}|}, \text{ or } \frac{1}{\frac{1}{s_{\overline{n}|}} + i'} - \frac{s_{\overline{t}|}}{s_{\overline{n}|}} \cdot \frac{1}{\frac{1}{s_{\overline{n}|}} + i'}.$$

(iii) If both parties desire to close the transaction it may be argued that the purchaser should sell back the remainder of the annuity on the basis on which he originally bought it, that is, at a price to yield rate i' and to admit of the replacement of the principal at rate i. In these circumstances the re-purchase-price would be

$$a_{\overline{n-t}|}^{(i'\&i)} \text{ or } \frac{1}{\frac{1}{s_{\overline{n-t}|}} + i'}.$$

Let the amounts to be paid on re-purchase on these three bases be respectively denoted by R_1, R_2 and R_3.

Then $$R_2 = \frac{1}{\frac{1}{s_{\overline{n}|}} + i'} - \frac{s_{\overline{t}|}}{s_{\overline{n}|}} \cdot \frac{1}{\frac{1}{s_{\overline{n}|}} + i'}$$

$$= \frac{s_{\overline{n}|} - s_{\overline{t}|}}{1 + i's_{\overline{n}|}} = \frac{(1+i)^t s_{\overline{n-t}|}}{1 + i's_{\overline{n}|}} = \frac{(1+i)^n a_{\overline{n-t}|}}{1 + i's_{\overline{n}|}}$$

$$= \frac{(1 + is_{\overline{n}|})a_{\overline{n-t}|}}{1 + i's_{\overline{n}|}} = a_{\overline{n-t}|}\left[1 - \frac{i' - i}{\frac{1}{s_{\overline{n}|}} + i'}\right]$$

$$= R_1 - a_{\overline{n-t}|} \cdot (i' - i) a_{\overline{n}|}^{(i'\&i)}$$

And $$R_3 = \frac{1}{\frac{1}{s_{\overline{n-t}|}} + i'} = \frac{s_{\overline{n-t}|}}{1 + i's_{\overline{n-t}|}}$$

$$= \frac{(1+i)^{n-t} a_{\overline{n-t}|}}{1 + i's_{\overline{n-t}|}} = \frac{(1 + is_{\overline{n-t}|})a_{\overline{n-t}|}}{1 + i's_{\overline{n-t}|}}$$

$$= a_{\overline{n-t}|}\left[1 - \frac{i' - i}{\frac{1}{s_{\overline{n-t}|}} + i'}\right]$$

$$= R_1 - a_{\overline{n-t}|} \cdot (i' - i) a_{\overline{n-t}|}^{(i'\&i)}$$

Hence $$R_1 = R_2 + a_{\overline{n-t}|} \cdot (i' - i) a_{\overline{n}|}^{(i'\&i)}$$

$$= R_3 + a_{\overline{n-t}|} \cdot (i' - i) a_{\overline{n-t}|}^{(i'\&i)} \quad . \; . \; . \; . \; . \; . \; . \; . \quad (12)$$

These relations bring out clearly the differences between the three methods of calculating the re-purchase price. In the first case the purchaser receives the full present value of the remaining instalments of the annuity. In the second case he gives up the extra interest which he would have obtained during the remaining $(n-t)$ years on the whole of his original capital if he had retained the annuity, the present value of this extra interest being $a_{\overline{n-t}|} \times (i'-i) a_{\overline{n}|}^{(i' \& i)}$. In the third case he gives up the extra interest which he would have obtained during the remaining $(n-t)$ years on the sum actually paid to him by the vendor for the re-purchase of the remainder of the annuity, the present value of this extra interest being $a_{\overline{n-t}|} \times (i'-i) . a_{\overline{n-t}|}^{(i' \& i)}$. Obviously R_1 gives the *largest* and R_2 the *smallest* re-purchase price, the result given by R_3 being intermediate in amount. In practice the price obtainable on re-purchase of such an annuity as that under consideration may be expected to be determined almost entirely by the market rate of interest obtainable on similar security, that is—on the assumption that the reproductive rate coincides closely to the market rate—to approximate to R_1 rather than R_2 or R_3, for the purchaser, if desirous of realizing, will generally be able to find some third party who will be willing to take over the investment in the event of the original vendor not wishing to re-purchase. Hence the formulas R_2 and R_3 must be considered as chiefly of theoretical interest.

15. So far, the investigation has been confined to the case of an ordinary immediate annuity, but it is obvious that similar methods of analysis may be applied to any definite and certain series of payments. Any such series of payments may be regarded as the equivalent—at the rate of interest employed in the calculations—of its present value, and the successive payments may be divided into their component elements of principal and interest. The general principle to be observed is that so much of each payment as is not required for interest will be applicable to the reduction of the outstanding principal. The only case which it is necessary to discuss here is that of the annuity of which the successive payments form one of the orders of figurate numbers. Let the annuity be an n-year annuity of the rth order and let i be the effective rate of interest. Then the general algebraical form of schedule of interest and principal-repayments will be as follows:

Year	Principal outstanding at beginning of year	Interest contained in payment for year	Principal repaid at end of year
1	$a_{\overline{n}\|\overline{r}\|}$	$ia_{\overline{n}\|\overline{r}\|}$	$t_{\overline{1}\|\overline{r}\|}-ia_{\overline{n}\|\overline{r}\|}$
2	$(1+i)a_{\overline{n}\|\overline{r}\|}-t_{\overline{1}\|\overline{r}\|}$	$i[(1+i)a_{\overline{n}\|\overline{r}\|}-t_{\overline{1}\|\overline{r}\|}]$	$t_{\overline{2}\|\overline{r}\|}-i[(1+i)a_{\overline{n}\|\overline{r}\|}-t_{\overline{1}\|\overline{r}\|}]$
3	$(1+i)^2a_{\overline{n}\|\overline{r}\|}-(1+i)t_{\overline{1}\|\overline{r}\|}-t_{\overline{2}\|\overline{r}\|}$	&c.	&c.
⋮	⋮	⋮	⋮

The principal outstanding at the beginning of the mth year will be

$$(1+i)^{m-1}a_{\overline{n}|\overline{r}|}-(1+i)^{m-2}t_{\overline{1}|\overline{r}|}-(1+i)^{m-3}t_{\overline{2}|\overline{r}|}- \ldots\ldots -t_{\overline{m-1}|\overline{r}|}.$$

The interest for the mth year will be obtained by multiplying the principal outstanding at the beginning of the year by i, and the principal contained in the mth payment of the annuity will, therefore, be

$$t_{\overline{m}|\overline{r}|}-i[(1+i)^{m-1}a_{\overline{n}|\overline{r}|}-(1+i)^{m-2}t_{\overline{1}|\overline{r}|}- \ldots\ldots -t_{\overline{m-1}|\overline{r}|}].$$

Hence the sum of all the principal-repayments

$$=\sum_{m=1}^{m=n} t_{\overline{m}|\overline{r}|}-i[s_{\overline{n}|}.a_{\overline{n}|\overline{r}|}-s_{\overline{n-1}|}.t_{\overline{1}|\overline{r}|}- \ldots\ldots -t_{\overline{n-1}|\overline{r}|}]$$

$$=t_{\overline{n}|\overline{r}|}+(1+i)t_{\overline{n-1}|\overline{r}|}+ \ldots\ldots +(1+i)^{n-1}t_{\overline{1}|\overline{r}|}-[(1+i)^n-1]a_{\overline{n}|\overline{r}|}$$

$$=s_{\overline{n}|\overline{r}|}-[(1+i)^n-1]a_{\overline{n}|\overline{r}|}=a_{\overline{n}|\overline{r}|}.$$

That is, the total principal repaid is, as it should be, the same as the present value of the annuity.

16. Since $t_{\overline{m}|\overline{r}|}=0$ for all values of m less than r—or, what is the same thing, since the first actual payment of the annuity of the rth order does not become due until the end of the rth year—it follows that the principal-repayments for the first $(r-1)$ years will be *negative*; in other words they represent the *capitalization* of unpaid interest. Thus, at the beginning of the rth year the original $a_{\overline{n}|\overline{r}|}$ will have accumulated to $(1+i)^{r-1}a_{\overline{n}|\overline{r}|}$, and the actual payments of interest and principal will begin at the end of the rth year. It may happen that the early payments of the annuity will be insufficient to meet the interest and that there will consequently be no balance available to reduce the principal; this will be the case, in regard to the payment due at the end of the rth year, if $a_{\overline{n}|\overline{r}|}$ is $> \frac{1}{i(1+i)^{r-1}}$. This would merely mean that part of the interest would still have to be capitalized for a certain number of years after the actual payments had begun, but it would not, of course, affect the algebraical accuracy of the analysis or the eventual repayment of the principal (with accumulations of capitalized interest) by the end of the n years.

17. It has been shown in Article 4 that the successive principal-repayments in the case of an ordinary annuity—that is, an annuity of the *first* order—are in Geometrical Progression. A somewhat similar relation exists between the principal-repayments for annuities of the higher orders. For let $C_{\overline{m}|\overline{r}|}$ denote the principal contained in the mth payment of an annuity of the rth order. Then the repayment of this amount will reduce by $C_{\overline{m}|\overline{r}|}$ the outstanding principal upon which interest has to be charged. Consequently, the interest contained in the $(m+1)$th payment will be less by $iC_{\overline{m}|\overline{r}|}$ than that contained in the mth payment, and the principal contained in the $(m+1)$th payment will exceed by $iC_{\overline{m}|\overline{r}|}$ *on this account* the principal contained in the mth payment. But the $(m+1)$th payment exceeds the mth payment in actual amount by $t_{\overline{m+1}|\overline{r}|}-t_{\overline{m}|\overline{r}|}$, that is, by $t_{\overline{m}|\overline{r-1}|}$. Therefore, on the whole, the principal contained in the $(m+1)$th payment will exceed that contained in the mth payment by $iC_{\overline{m}|\overline{r}|}+t_{\overline{m}|\overline{r-1}|}$

$$\therefore \quad C_{\overline{m+1}|\overline{r}|}=(1+i)C_{\overline{m}|\overline{r}|}+t_{\overline{m}|\overline{r-1}|} \quad . \quad . \quad . \quad (13)$$

By means of this relation the present value of the annuity may be deduced by a process similar to that of Article 5. By repeated application of formula (13) it follows that

$$C_{\overline{n}|\overline{r}|}=t_{\overline{n-1}|\overline{r-1}|}+(1+i)t_{\overline{n-2}|\overline{r-1}|}+(1+i)^2t_{\overline{n-3}|\overline{r-1}|}+\ldots$$

$$\ldots+(1+i)^{n-2}t_{\overline{1}|\overline{r-1}|}+(1+i)^{n-1}C_{\overline{1}|\overline{r}|}$$

$$=s_{\overline{n-1}|\overline{r-1}|}+(1+i)^{n-1}C_{\overline{1}|\overline{r}|}$$

Now $$C_{\overline{1}|\overline{r}|}=t_{\overline{1}|\overline{r}|}-ia_{\overline{n}|\overline{r}|}$$

and since the principal contained in the final payment of the annuity must be equal to the principal outstanding at the beginning of the nth year

$$t_{\overline{n}|\overline{r}|}=iC_{\overline{n}|\overline{r}|}+C_{\overline{n}|\overline{r}|}.$$

$$\therefore \quad vt_{\overline{n}|\overline{r}|}=s_{\overline{n-1}|\overline{r-1}|}+(1+i)^{n-1}(t_{\overline{1}|\overline{r}|}-ia_{\overline{n}|\overline{r}|})$$

whence
$$a_{\overline{n}|\,\overline{r}|}=\frac{a_{\overline{n-1}|\,\overline{r-1}|}+t_{\overline{1}|\,\overline{r}|}-v^n t_{\overline{n}|\,\overline{r}|}}{i}$$

$$=\frac{a_{\overline{n}|\,\overline{r-1}|}+t_{\overline{1}|\,\overline{r}|}-v^n(t_{\overline{n}|\,\overline{r}|}+t_{\overline{n}|\,\overline{r-1}|})}{i}$$

$$=\frac{a_{\overline{n}|\,\overline{r-1}|}+t_{\overline{1}|\,\overline{r}|}-v^n t_{\overline{n+1}|\,\overline{r}|}}{i}$$

18. In order to find the present value of an annuity of the rth order to pay interest at one rate on the whole invested capital for the entire term of the annuity, and to admit of the replacement of the capital by a sinking fund accumulated at another rate, it will be necessary to proceed by a different method from that of Article 11. Let the annuity be for n years, let the remunerative and reproductive rates be i' and i respectively, and let the present value of the annuity on the special basis under consideration be denoted by $a^{(i'\&i)}_{\overline{n}|\,\overline{r}|}$.

Then the annuity must be equivalent to (a) an ordinary annuity for n years of $i'a^{(i'\&i)}_{\overline{n}|\,\overline{r}|}$, this being the annual yield which the purchaser proposes to obtain from the investment, together with (b) $a^{(i'\&i)}_{\overline{n}|\,\overline{r}|}$ due n years hence, this being the sum which must then have been accumulated to replace the purchaser's invested capital. In equating the present value of the annuity to the sum of the present values of these elements, all the quantities must be discounted at rate i, since this, by hypothesis, is the rate at which investments can be made.

$$\therefore\quad i'a^{(i'\&i)}_{\overline{n}|\,\overline{r}|}.a_{\overline{n}|}+v^n.a^{(i'\&i)}_{\overline{n}|\,\overline{r}|}=a_{\overline{n}|\,\overline{r}|}$$

whence
$$a^{(i'\&i)}_{\overline{n}|\,\overline{r}|}=\frac{a_{\overline{n}|\,\overline{r}|}}{v^n+i'a_{\overline{n}|}}\quad\text{or}\quad\frac{s_{\overline{n}|\,\overline{r}|}}{1+i's_{\overline{n}|}}\quad .\ .\ .\ (14)$$

The method of this Article will be found useful in the following chapter.

CHAPTER V.

On the Valuation of Debentures and other Securities— Miscellaneous Problems.

1. It is proposed in this chapter to consider the application of the Theory of Compound Interest to some representative examples of that class of problems in which it is required to find the present value of a given obligation or combination of obligations, or the terms of a given transaction, in order that a specified rate of interest may be realized. It does not come within the scope of this work to consider the nature of the security for the due fulfilment of the conditions of the contract in any particular case, or the legal incidents affecting any such contract, or the rate of interest which may properly be employed in valuation. It will be assumed in all cases that the payments provided for under any given contract will be certainly made at the stipulated dates, and it will be understood that the rate of interest that may be used in any example is employed merely for purposes of numerical illustration without reference to its applicability to the particular security in question.

2. The most important problems of the class under consideration are those that arise in connection with the valuation of redeemable securities—that is to say, securities under which there is an obligation or an option (exercisable by the debtor) to pay a given sum on a given date, and an obligation to pay in the meantime a fixed periodical dividend.

3. Ordinary Stocks and Shares do not lend themselves to exact valuation at a specified rate of interest owing to the liability of the dividends to fluctuate from year to year, and preference, guaranteed and perpetual debenture stocks—or, in fact, any pre-ordinary stocks carrying a fixed annual dividend without any express provision for repayment of the capital—may obviously be valued by simple proportion; for example, the present value, to pay 3 per-cent convertible half-yearly, of a 5 per-cent perpetual preference stock on which the dividends are payable half-yearly—the next being due in six months' time—would be $100 \times \frac{2\frac{1}{2}}{1\frac{1}{2}}$ or $166\cdot\dot{6}$ per-cent, and the present value of the same stock to pay 3 per-cent effective would be $100 \times \frac{2\frac{1}{2}(1+\sqrt{1\cdot 03})}{3}$ or 167·9; if the next dividend fell due in less than six months it would merely be necessary to accumulate the present value as obtained by the method just explained for the period elapsed since the due date of the last dividend.

4. The valuation of redeemable securities presents a more complex problem inasmuch as the arrangements in regard to redemption have to be taken into account. As a preliminary to the investigation of the subject the following general points may be mentioned:

(i) When the price at which a debenture or other security is redeemable differs from its nominal amount, it is the former which must be taken into account in the valuation of the security. Apart from the bearing it may have upon the rights of the holder in the event of a winding-up—a contingency which will be disregarded here—the nominal amount of a debenture, in such a case as that under consideration, is of no importance except as a factor in the determination of the amount of the periodical dividend. Thus, a debenture for 100 bearing interest at 5 per-cent payable half-yearly and redeemable at the end of 15 years at 110 represents, for present purposes, a contract to pay 110 at the end of 15 years and $2\frac{1}{2}$ half-yearly during that period; the fact that the debenture is nominally for 100 merely assists in fixing the amount of the half-yearly dividend.

(ii) The so-called "rate of interest" on a debenture has no necessary connection with the true rate of interest employed in valuation, and would be more conveniently termed a "rate of dividend." Like the nominal amount of the debenture it should be regarded merely as a factor in the determination of the periodical dividend. In the case of a debenture bearing interest at, say, 5 per-cent payable half-yearly, it would be incorrect to regard this rate as a nominal rate, and to treat it as equivalent to an effective rate of $(1{\cdot}025)^2-1$, *unless* the true rate of interest employed in valuation were also 5 per-cent convertible half-yearly. In general, the equivalent annual dividend per-cent in such a case would be $2\frac{1}{2}\times\{(1+i)^{\frac{1}{2}}+1\}$ where i is the true rate of interest employed in valuation. Thus in the example of Art. 3 the equivalent annual dividend has been taken as $2\frac{1}{2}(1+\sqrt{1{\cdot}03})$, not as $5{\cdot}0625$.

(iii) When a debenture is only redeemable *at the option* of the debtor, it will be necessary in valuing the debenture at an effective rate of interest *less than* the ratio of the equivalent annual dividend to the price at which the debenture would be redeemable to assume that the option to redeem *will* be exercised, and in valuing it at an effective rate exceeding that ratio to assume that the option will *not* be exercised. The reason for this will be best seen by consideration of an actual example. Take, for instance, the case of a debenture bearing interest at 5 per-cent payable annually and redeemable at the option of the issuing company at 125, so that the ratio of the annual dividend to the redemption price is 4 per-cent. The issuing company is, in this case, practically in the position of owing a sum of 125—repayable or not at its option—upon which it pays interest at the rate of 4 per-cent. If, now, the credit of the company or the nature of the security is such that the debenture would be valued by an investor at a lower rate than 4 per-cent, it is probable that the company could re-borrow at a rate of less than 4 per-cent, while, if the converse were the fact, it is probable that the company would have to offer a higher rate of interest than 4 per-cent if it sought to raise money to repay its existing debentures. Hence, in the first case, it may be assumed that the option would certainly be exercised; and in the second case, that it would not be exercised.

5. To proceed now to the problem of valuation. It will be convenient to begin with the case of a debenture or other security under which the principal is redeemable in one sum.

Let C_1 represent the price to be paid on redemption.

,, n_1 ,, the number of years at the expiration of which the security becomes redeemable.

,, K_1 ,, the present value of C_1 due n_1 years hence at the rate of interest employed in the valuation of the security.

,, g ,, the ratio of the dividend *per annum* to C_1.

,, A_1 ,, the present value of the security, including brokerage or commission and any other costs incidental to purchase.

Then, if the security be definitely redeemable at the expiration of n_1 years, and the dividend be payable p times a year—the next dividend being due $\frac{1}{p}$th of a year hence—the purchaser will be entitled to a sum of C_1 payable at the end of n_1 years, and a periodical dividend of $\frac{gC_1}{p}$ payable at the end of every $\frac{1}{p}$th of a year throughout the period of n_1 years, or, in other words, an annuity of gC_1 payable p times a year for n_1 years. Hence the value of the security to pay the effective rate i will be given by the formula

$$A_1 = C_1 v^{n_1} + gC_1 . a^{(p)}_{\overline{n_1}|} \quad . \quad . \quad . \quad . \quad . \quad . \quad . \quad . \quad (1)$$

or, since

$$a^{(p)}_{\overline{n_1}|} = \frac{1-v^{n_1}}{p[(1+i)^{\frac{1}{p}}-1]} = s^{(p)}_{\overline{1}|} . \frac{1-v^{n_1}}{i},$$

$$A_1 = C_1 v^{n_1} + gC_1 . s^{(p)}_{\overline{1}|} . \frac{1-v^{n_1}}{i}$$

$$= C_1 v^{n_1} + \frac{gs^{(p)}_{\overline{1}|}}{i} . (C_1 - C_1 v^{n_1})$$

$$= K_1 + \frac{gs^{(p)}_{\overline{1}|}}{i} (C_1 - K_1) \quad . \quad . \quad . \quad . \quad . \quad . \quad (2)$$

where K_1 represents the present value of the capital repayable.

By substitution of $\left(1+\frac{j}{m}\right)^m - 1$ for i, it follows that the value of the security to pay the nominal rate j convertible m times a year will be given by the formulas

$$A_1 = C_1\left(1+\frac{j}{m}\right)^{-mn_1} + gC_1 \frac{1-\left(1+\frac{j}{m}\right)^{-mn_1}}{p\left[\left(1+\frac{j}{m}\right)^{\frac{m}{p}}-1\right]} \quad . \quad . \quad (3)$$

or

$$A_1 = K_1 + \frac{g s_{\overline{1}|}^{(p)}}{\left(1+\frac{j}{m}\right)^m - 1} \cdot (C_1 - K_1) \quad . \quad . \quad . \quad . \quad (4)$$

where in the latter formula $s_{\overline{1}|}^{(p)}$ and K_1 are both to be calculated at the nominal rate j convertible m times a year.

6. If m be put$=p$, formulas (3) and (4) take the form

$$A_1 = C_1 v^{pn_1} + g\frac{C_1}{p} a_{\overline{pn_1}|} \quad . \quad . \quad . \quad . \quad . \quad . \quad (5)$$

or

$$A_1 = K_1 + \frac{g}{j}(C_1 - K_1) \quad . \quad . \quad . \quad . \quad . \quad . \quad (6)$$

where v^{pn_1} and $a_{\overline{pn_1}|}$ are to be calculated at the effective rate $\frac{j}{p}$, and K_1 represents the present value, at the nominal rate j convertible p times a year, of C_1 due n_1 years hence.

It appears, therefore, that the present value of a security such as that under consideration, at a nominal rate of interest *convertible with the same frequency as that with which the dividend is payable*, may in all cases be written in the simple form

$$K_1 + \frac{g}{j}(C_1 - K_1)$$

where j is the given nominal rate of interest and K_1 is the present value, at that rate, of the capital repayable. This result admits of a simple verbal proof. For if the dividend were at the rate of j per unit per annum, payable p times a year, calculated on C_1, it is obvious that the present value of the entire security to pay the *rate of interest* j convertible p times a year would be C_1, and since the present value of C_1 due n_1 years hence is, by definition, K_1, it follows that the present value of a dividend of jC_1 per annum payable p times a year, for the term of n_1 years, would be $C_1 - K_1$. By simple proportion, the present value of a dividend of 1 per annum payable p times a year for the term of n_1 years would be $\frac{C_1 - K_1}{jC_1}$, and the present value of a dividend of gC_1 per annum payable p times a year for n_1 years would be $gC_1 \times \frac{C_1 - K_1}{jC_1}$ or $\frac{g}{j}(C_1 - K_1)$. But the present value of the entire security is the sum of the present value of C_1 due n_1 years hence, and the present value of a dividend of gC_1 payable p times a year throughout the term of n_1 years. Hence

$$A_1 = K_1 + \frac{g}{j}(C_1 - K_1)$$

Formula (2) may be established by precisely similar reasoning, if the effective rate i be written for j and the equivalent annual dividend $gs^{(p)}_{\overline{1|}}$ for the dividend of g payable p times a year.

7. In the special case in which $p = m = 1$, when the problem becomes that of finding the present value, to pay the effective rate i, of a security yielding an annual dividend of gC_1 and redeemable in n_1 years at the price of C_1, the alternative formulas take the form

$$A_1 = C_1 v^{n_1} + gC_1 a_{\overline{n_1|}} \quad . \quad . \quad . \quad . \quad . \quad . \quad (7)$$

and

$$A_1 = K_1 + \frac{g}{i}(C_1 - K_1) \quad . \quad . \quad . \quad . \quad . \quad . \quad (8)$$

8. In practice the periodical dividend (commonly called "interest") is almost invariably paid half-yearly or quarterly.

If it be paid *half-yearly* the value of the security to pay the effective rate i will be

$$C_1 v^{n_1} + gC_1 a^{(2)}_{\overline{n_1|}} \quad . \quad . \quad . \quad . \quad . \quad . \quad . \quad (9)$$

or

$$K_1 + \frac{g(1 + \sqrt{1+i})}{2i}(C_1 - K_1) \quad . \quad . \quad . \quad . \quad (10)$$

while the value to pay the nominal rate j convertible *half-yearly*, may be written in the form

$$C_1 v^{2n_1} + g\frac{C_1}{2} a_{\overline{2n_1|}} \quad . \quad . \quad . \quad . \quad . \quad . \quad . \quad (11)$$

or

$$K_1 + \frac{g}{j}(C_1 - K_1) \quad . \quad . \quad . \quad . \quad . \quad . \quad . \quad (12)$$

where v^{2n_1} and $a_{\overline{2n_1|}}$ are calculated at the *effective* rate $\frac{j}{2}$ and K_1 is written for $C_1 v^{2n_1}$.

Similarly, if the dividend be paid quarterly, the value of the security to pay the effective rate i will be

$$C_1 v^{n_1} + g C_1 a^{(4)}_{\overline{n_1}|} \quad . \quad . \quad . \quad . \quad . \quad . \quad . \quad . \quad (13)$$

or

$$K_1 + \frac{g[1+(1+i)^{\frac{1}{4}}+(1+i)^{\frac{1}{2}}+(1+i)^{\frac{3}{4}}]}{4i}(C_1-K_1) \quad . \quad (14)$$

and the value to pay the nominal rate j convertible quarterly may be written in the form

$$C_1 v^{4n_1} + g\frac{C_1}{4} \cdot a_{\overline{4n_1}|} \quad . \quad . \quad . \quad . \quad . \quad . \quad . \quad (15)$$

or

$$K_1 + \frac{g}{j}(C_1 - K_1) \quad . \quad . \quad . \quad . \quad . \quad . \quad . \quad . \quad (16)$$

where v^{4n_1} and $a_{\overline{4n_1}|}$ are both to be calculated at the *effective* rate $\frac{j}{4}$, and K_1 is written for $C_1 v^{4n_1}$.

9. On comparison of the alternative formulas given in the foregoing articles, it will be observed that in each case the first formula entails the calculation of two quantities, namely, the present value of 1 due n_1 years hence and the present value of an n_1-year annuity; while the second formula involves the calculation of only the single quantity K_1. Consequently, in any case where the rate of interest employed, or the value of n_1, is such as to necessitate the actual calculation of v^{n_1}, it will clearly save labour to use the second formula. But when all the required quantities are tabulated, it will generally be found more convenient to employ the first formula, or, what is the same thing, to dispense with a formula and to write down the value by reference to the general principle that the present value of the entire security is the sum of the present values of the capital repayable, due at the end of the term, and of an annuity of the dividend. For example, if it be required to find the present value, at 4 per-cent convertible half-yearly, of a debenture for 100 bearing interest at 5 per-cent payable half-yearly and redeemable in 20 years at 105, it is simpler to write down the value as $105v^{40} + 2{\cdot}5a_{\overline{40}|}$ at 2 per-cent, and to turn up v^{40} and $a_{\overline{40}|}$ in the 2 per-cent tables, than to go through the process of putting $g = \frac{5}{105}$ and using the general formula $K_1 + \frac{g}{j}(C_1 - K_1)$.

10. When a redeemable security is bought to pay a rate of interest *lower* than the ratio of the dividend to the redemption price—that is, if j be $< g$ where interest is convertible with the same frequency as that with which the dividend is payable, or if i be $< gs_{\overline{1}|}^{(p)}$ where interest is convertible yearly and the dividend is payable p times a year—it is clear that the price paid for the security will *exceed* the redemption-price; in these circumstances, the security is said to be bought *at a premium*. In the notation of Art. 5, the premium will be $A_1 - C_1$. Now, if the rate of interest employed in valuation be j convertible p times a year, and the dividend be payable with the same frequency,

$$A_1 - C_1 = C_1 v^{pn_1} - C_1 + \frac{gC_1}{p} a_{\overline{pn_1}|}$$

where v^{pn_1} and $a_{\overline{pn_1}|}$ are to be calculated at the effective rate $\frac{j}{p}$,

$$= \frac{(g-j)\,C_1}{p} \cdot a_{\overline{pn_1}|} .$$

Or, if k be the premium per unit on the redemption-price,

$$k = \frac{g-j}{p} a_{\overline{pn_1}|} \quad . \quad . \quad . \quad . \quad . \quad . \quad . \quad . \quad (17)$$

This equation expresses the fact that the premium per unit is equivalent to an annuity, at the rate employed in valuation, of the excess of the dividend per annum over the valuation rate of interest. It is obvious that this must be the case, for the present value, to pay j per annum convertible p times a year, of each unit of capital repayable, together with a dividend of j per annum payable p times a year, will clearly be unity, and the extra value—or premium—due to the dividend being at the rate of g, instead of j, per annum must be the present value of an annuity of the excess of g over j for the term during which the dividend is payable. In general, if a debenture redeemable in n_1 years, and bearing interest at the rate of g per unit per annum on the redemption-price payable p times a year, be bought to pay the effective rate i, the premium, per unit of the redemption-price, paid by the purchaser, will be given by the formula

$$k = (gs_{\overline{1}|}^{(p)} - i) a_{\overline{n_1}|} \quad . \quad . \quad . \quad . \quad . \quad . \quad . \quad (18)$$

11. In the investigations of Arts. 5 to 10, the security has been assumed to be *certainly* redeemable on the expiration of the specified term of years. On this assumption, the resulting formulas hold equally whether the rate of interest employed in valuation is less or greater than the rate of dividend—except that in the latter case the k of Art. 10 becomes *negative*, and the security may be said to be bought at a *discount* on its redemption-price. If, however, the security be only redeemable at the option of the debtor, the distinction explained in Art. 4 (iii) must be borne in mind; for valuation at a rate lower than the ratio of the dividend to the redemption-price, all the formulas (1) to (18) will hold good, but in valuing the security at a rate *exceeding* that ratio it must be assumed that the option to redeem will not be exercised, in which case the value of the security will be merely that of a perpetuity of the dividend, namely, $\frac{gC_1 s_{\overline{1}|}^{(p)}}{i}$ or $\frac{gC_1}{j}$ according as an effective rate or a nominal rate convertible p times a year is employed.

12. It will be convenient, at this point, to consider some actual examples of the valuation of securities of the class under consideration, which includes the various British, Indian, and Colonial Government Securities, many British, Colonial, and Foreign Municipal Stocks, the majority of American Railway Mortgage Bonds, and numerous Brewery, Commercial and other Debentures.

13. Take, first, the case of Consols. In this case, dividends are payable quarterly, at the rate of $2\frac{3}{4}$ per-cent per annum, on every 5 January, April, July, and October, up to and including 5 April 1903, and at the rate of $2\frac{1}{2}$ per-cent per annum on the same days thereafter, and the Stock is redeemable at par on or after 5 April 1923 at the option of the Government. The security is, therefore, equivalent to a stock bearing interest at the rate of $2\frac{1}{2}$ per-cent per annum payable quarterly and redeemable at the option of the Government on 5 April 1923, together with an annuity of $\frac{1}{4}$ per-cent per annum payable quarterly up to 5 April 1903. Hence the value to pay any rate of interest exceeding $2\frac{1}{2}$ per-cent convertible quarterly will be that of a perpetuity of $2\frac{1}{2}$ per-cent per annum payable quarterly, together with an annuity of $\frac{1}{4}$ per-cent payable quarterly ceasing in April 1903. For example, the value per-cent as at 5 April 1900 to pay 3 per-cent convertible quarterly would be

$$\frac{2\frac{1}{2}}{3} \times 100 + \tfrac{1}{16} a_{\overline{12}|}^{\frac{3}{4}\%}.$$

If it be required to find the value to pay $2\frac{1}{2}$ per-cent convertible quarterly —that is to say, the same rate as the ultimate rate of dividend—it is immaterial whether the option to redeem be taken into account or not. If it be assumed that the stock will be redeemed on 5 April 1923, formula (16), with the addition of the value of the extra dividend for the first 3 years, will give for each 100 Consols

$$A_1 = K_1 + \frac{\cdot 025}{\cdot 025}(C_1 - K_1) + \tfrac{1}{16} a_{\overline{12}|}^{\frac{5}{8}\%}$$

$$= 100 + \tfrac{1}{16} a_{\overline{12}|}^{\frac{5}{8}\%},$$

which is the same thing as the value to pay $2\frac{1}{2}$ per-cent convertible quarterly of a perpetuity of $2\frac{1}{2}$ per annum payable quarterly, together with an annuity of $\frac{1}{4}$ per annum payable quarterly for three years

If, however, the rate of interest to be employed were *less than* $2\frac{1}{2}$ per-cent convertible quarterly, it would be necessary to assume that the option to redeem will certainly be exercised. Thus, to pay $2\frac{1}{2}$ per-cent *effective*, the value, per-cent, at 5 April 1900 by formula (14), with the addition of the value of the extra dividend would be

$$K_1 + \frac{\cdot 025\, s_{\overline{1}|}^{(4)}}{\cdot 025}(C_1 - K_1) + \tfrac{1}{4} a_{\overline{3}|}^{(4)} = K_1 + s_{\overline{1}|}^{(4)}(C_1 - K_1) + \tfrac{1}{4} s_{\overline{1}|}^{(4)} \cdot a_{\overline{3}|}$$

where $K_1 = 100v^{23}$; $C_1 = 100$; and all the quantities involved are to be calculated at $2\frac{1}{2}$ per-cent effective. Again, to pay 2 per-cent convertible quarterly, the value at the same date would be

$$100 + \tfrac{1}{8} a_{\overline{92}|} + \tfrac{1}{16} a_{\overline{12}|}$$

where both annuity-values are to be calculated at $\frac{1}{2}$ per-cent effective. It may be useful to compare the numerical results obtained by valuing at the different rates of interest assumed above.

By Spitzer's Interest Tables:—

$a_{\overline{12}|}$	at	$\frac{3}{4}$	per-cent	= 11·4349
v^{23}	,,	$2\frac{1}{2}$	,,	= ·566697
$a_{\overline{3}|}$	,,	$2\frac{1}{2}$	,,	= 2·8560
$a_{\overline{92}|}$	,,	$\frac{1}{2}$	,,	= 73·5985
$a_{\overline{12}|}$	,,	$\frac{1}{2}$	,,	= 11·6189
$a_{\overline{12}|}$	,,	$\frac{5}{8}$	,,	= 11·5264

and by Table VIII on page 214 of this work:—

$s_{\overline{1}|}^{(4)}$ at $2\frac{1}{2}$ per-cent = 1·00933

On insertion of these values in the formulas, the results given in the following Table are obtained:

Value of 100 *Consols at* 5 *April* 1900 *to pay the undermentioned rates.*

3 per-cent Convertible Quarterly	$2\frac{1}{2}$ per-cent Convertible Quarterly	$2\frac{1}{2}$ per-cent Effective	2 per-cent Convertible Quarterly
84·048	100·720	101·125	109·926

14. Consider, next the following group of British and Indian Government Securities—the dividends in all cases being payable quarterly on 5 January, April, July, and October:

$2\frac{3}{4}$ per-cents redeemable at par	5 January	1905
$2\frac{1}{2}$ „ „ „	5 January	1905
Local Loans 3 per-cent Stock redeemable at par	1 April	1912
India $3\frac{1}{2}$ per-cents „ „	5 January	1931
India 3 „ „ „	5 October	1948

By formula (17) the values of these stocks per-cent as at 5 April 1900, to pay $2\frac{1}{2}$ per-cent convertible quarterly, will be as follows:

$2\frac{3}{4}$ per-cents	$100+\frac{1}{16}a_{\overline{19}|}$
$2\frac{1}{2}$ „	100
Local Loans	$100+\frac{1}{8}a_{\overline{48}|}$
India $3\frac{1}{2}$ per-cents . .	$100+\frac{1}{4}a_{\overline{123}|}$
India 3 „ . .	$100+\frac{1}{8}a_{\overline{194}|}$

where the annuity-value in each case is to be calculated at the effective rate of $\frac{5}{8}$ths per-cent.

The requisite annuity-values may be obtained from Spitzer's Tables—$a_{\overline{19}|}$ and $a_{\overline{48}|}$ directly, and $a_{\overline{123}|}$ and $a_{\overline{194}|}$ by means of the formulas $a_{\overline{100}|}+v^{100}a_{\overline{23}|}$ and $a_{\overline{100}|}+v^{100}a_{\overline{94}|}$; or they may all be taken direct from Werker's Tables.

The values of the stocks in question as at 5 April 1900, to pay

$2\frac{1}{2}$ per-cent convertible quarterly, will then be found to be as shown in the following table:

Stock	Value per-cent
$2\frac{3}{4}$ per-cents . . .	101·116
$2\frac{1}{2}$ per-cents . . .	100·000
Local Loans . . .	105·170
India $3\frac{1}{2}$ per-cents .	121·412
India 3 per-cents . .	114·028

15. British Municipal Stocks are usually definitely redeemable at par at fixed dates, in which case the method of valuation will be precisely similar to that already exemplified. There are, however, numerous exceptions to this rule. The Stocks of some Corporations are redeemable only by purchase in the open market. Such Stocks will, of course, be properly valued as perpetuities of the annual dividend. Others are redeemable at par not later than certain fixed dates, but may be redeemed at par on or after certain earlier dates at the option of the borrowers. In any such case it should be assumed that the option to redeem will be exercised at the earlier or later date according as the rate of interest employed in valuation is less than or greater than the rate of dividend. The Sheffield Water Progressive Annuities present an example of a somewhat unusual type. On the acquisition of the water undertaking by the Corporation the ordinary shareholders were offered for each £100 Stock (*a*) £82 in cash, or (*b*) an annuity of £3 per annum payable half-yearly, or (*c*) an annuity of £2 for the first two years, £2. 5*s*. for the second two years, £2. 10*s*. for the third two years, &c., up to £4 for every year after the first 16, both the (*b*) and (*c*) annuities being redeemable on or after the expiration of 60 years at 25 years' purchase.

What were the present values, at the outset, of the (*b*) and (*c*) annuities, interest being assumed at 4 per-cent convertible half-yearly?

Since a perpetuity of 1 per annum payable half-yearly is worth, at

4 per-cent convertible half-yearly, 25 years' purchase, it follows that for the purposes of a valuation at 4 per-cent convertible half-yearly the option of redemption may be disregarded. Hence the present value of the (*b*) annuity would have been $1\frac{1}{2}a_{\infty}^{2\%}=\frac{1\frac{1}{2}}{\cdot 02}=75$.

Similarly, the present value of the (*c*) annuity would have been

$$2a_{\infty}-\cdot 125(a_{\overline{32}|}+a_{\overline{28}|}+\ldots+a_{\overline{4}|})$$

where all the annuity-values are to be calculated at 2 per-cent.

Now $a_{\infty}=\frac{1}{\cdot 02}=50$, and

$$a_{\overline{32}|}+a_{\overline{28}|}+\ldots+a_{\overline{4}|}=\frac{1-v^{32}}{i}+\frac{1-v^{28}}{i}+\ldots+\frac{1-v^{4}}{i}$$

$$=\frac{1}{i}\left(8-\frac{a_{\overline{32}|}}{s_{\overline{4}|}}\right)=115\cdot 3.$$

Therefore, the present value of the (*c*) annuity at the assumed rate of interest would have been $100-14\cdot 4=85\cdot 6$.

It need hardly be said that the assumption of a different rate of interest would materially alter the values of the two annuities both absolutely and relatively.

16. The "B" Annuities of the East Indian and other Indian Railways present a problem of a slightly different nature from those already discussed. The railways in question were originally constructed and worked by private companies under concessions from the Indian Government, and were subsequently acquired by the Government under powers reserved in the contracts by which the concessions were granted. On taking over these railways the Government exercised an option of paying out the stockholders by means of *terminable annuities*, and to meet the convenience of those stockholders who desired to keep their capital intact, it was arranged that a certain sum should be deducted from each payment of the terminable annuity and invested as a sinking fund to replace the capital on the expiration of the term of the annuity The reduced annuities thus created, with provision for a sinking fund, were called "B" annuities.

In the case of the East Indian Railway the annuity is payable half-yearly for approximately 73 years from 1880, and is subject to a half-yearly deduction of $\frac{1}{2}d.$ for management and $8d.$ for sinking fund. The sinking fund was originally estimated to accumulate by 1953 (when the annuity ceases) to $22\frac{1}{4}$, "as near as may be", per each 1 of the full annuity, but it is obvious that the actual amount then available to replace capital will depend upon the rate of interest realized on the sinking fund investments. Hence, the first step, in valuing the "B" Annuity, would be to estimate the amount receivable on the cessation of the annuity. To do this as accurately as possible, it would be desirable to ascertain the amount of the sinking fund investments at the date of valuation and to assume the most probable rate of accumulation for the remainder of the period. But for present purposes let it be assumed that the sinking fund will accumulate throughout the entire term at the rate of $2\frac{1}{2}$ per-cent with half-yearly rests. Then the capital repayable in 1953 per each 1 of annuity may be estimated at $\cdot 0\dot{3} \times s_{\overline{146}|}^{1\frac{1}{4}\%}$. Hence the value per unit of the "B" Annuity in 1900, to pay 3 per-cent convertible half-yearly, would be

$$\cdot 46458\dot{3}a_{\overline{106}|}^{1\frac{1}{2}\%} + \cdot 0\dot{3}s_{\overline{146}|}^{1\frac{1}{4}\%} \,.\, v^{106^{1\frac{1}{2}\%}},$$

which will be found to be 24·6.

17. American Railway Bonds and Brewery and Commercial Debentures present no special features—apart from the question of exchange in the former case and the liability in the latter case to redemption at par—in the absence of any special provision to the contrary—in the event of a winding-up. As a representative example of the latter type the following may be taken:

Required the value per-cent at 1 January 1900, to yield 4 per-cent effective, of debentures bearing interest at $4\frac{1}{2}$ per-cent payable half-yearly on 1 January and 1 July, and redeemable on 1 January 1960 at par or on or after 1 January 1910, at the option of the issuing Company (or in the event of voluntary liquidation) at 10 per-cent premium.

A dividend of $4\frac{1}{2}$ payable half-yearly represents $4\cdot\dot{0}\dot{9}$ per-cent on 110. This exceeds an effective rate of 4 per-cent. It must be assumed, therefore, that the option to redeem will be exercised. Hence, by formula (10), the required present value will be

$$110v^{10} + \frac{\cdot 04\dot{0}\dot{9}(1+\sqrt{1\cdot 04})}{\cdot 08}(110-110v^{10})$$

where v^{10} is to be calculated at 4 per-cent. The numerical result will be found to be 111·172.

18. In all the foregoing examples the date of valuation has been taken as one of the days on which the dividend is payable, so that the dividend begins to accrue from the date of purchase. In practice it will, of course, more often happen that it is required to find the value of a security at a date intermediate between the dates on which the dividend is payable. In such cases the security will include a certain amount of accrued dividend (unless the date of purchase precedes the dividend due-date by a few days only, in which case the security may be sold *ex dividend*), and it will be necessary to allow for this in calculating the price. The simplest course to pursue in all such cases is to value the security just after payment of the *last* dividend or just before payment of the *next* dividend, and to accumulate the former or discount the latter to the actual date of purchase. Take, as an example, a redeemable debenture carrying a half-yearly dividend, and let it be required to find its value with accrued dividend $\frac{1}{m}$th of a half-year before the next dividend due-date, to pay j per annum convertible half-yearly. The value just before the next dividend is paid may be written symbolically as $A_1+\frac{gC_1}{2}$, and the discounted value $\frac{1}{m}$th of a half-year previously will, therefore, be $\left(1+\frac{j}{2}\right)^{-\frac{1}{m}}\left(A_1+\frac{gC_1}{2}\right)$. At the end of the half-year the interest to date on the purchaser's outlay will amount to

$$\left[\left(1+\frac{j}{2}\right)^{\frac{1}{m}}-1\right]\left(1+\frac{j}{2}\right)^{-\frac{1}{m}}\left(A_1+\frac{gC_1}{2}\right)$$

which is identically equal to

$$\frac{gC_1}{2}-\left[\left(1+\frac{j}{2}\right)^{-\frac{1}{m}}\left(A_1+\frac{gC_1}{2}\right)-A_1\right]$$

Hence it appears that the dividend payable at the end of the half year will suffice, as it ought, to pay interest for $\frac{1}{2m}$th of a year and to write down the invested capital to A_1. In practice, interest for $\frac{1}{m}$th of a half year would be taken as $\frac{j}{2m}$, and the value of the security would accordingly be taken as

$$\frac{A_1+\frac{gC_1}{2}}{1+\frac{j}{2m}} \quad . \quad . \quad . \quad . \quad . \quad . \quad . \quad . \quad (19)$$

19 Marketable securities are usually dealt in on the basis of the purchaser taking the whole of the accruing dividend, without apportionment, and are quoted accordingly at an inclusive price. To this rule, however, there is one important exception. In the case of the enfaced promissory notes of the Indian Government—commonly called "enfaced rupee paper," or simply "rupee paper"—it is the custom for the purchaser to give the vendor, in addition to the market price, the interest accrued from the last dividend-date to the date of purchase, and the price is accordingly quoted exclusive of accrued dividend.

20. When a redeemable security is bought to pay a rate of interest differing from the ratio of the dividend to the redemption price—that is, when it is bought at a premium or discount on the redemption price—a question arises as to how it should be dealt with on an investment basis, in order that the required rate of interest may be realized and that the invested capital may be gradually written down, or up, to the redemption value of the security. In the case of securities dealt in on the Stock Exchange the plan very frequently adopted is to debit the account for a given security with the market-value of the security at the beginning of the year or half-year, to credit it with dividends received and with the market-value of the security at the end of the period, and to determine the interest for the period by balancing the account; this method may be expected to approximate roughly to the theoretical method of procedure, and it has the advantage of obviating any risk of a security being valued, as an asset, at a price exceeding its market-value.

21. It may, however, be considered desirable to deal with securities of this nature independently of the more or less accidental fluctuations of Stock Exchange quotations, and there are, besides, many such securities which are not publicly dealt in. A different method of procedure must then be adopted. It has been shown in Art. 10 that when a redeemable security is bought to pay a rate of interest differing from the rate of dividend, the premium paid for the security over and above its redemption value, or the discount at which it is obtained, is the present value of an annuity of the excess of the rate of interest over the rate of dividend, or *vice versâ*. It follows, therefore, that a possible method of procedure would be to construct a schedule for this annuity in the manner explained in Chapter IV; the principal-repayments would represent the amounts to be written off, or added to, the invested capital at the end of each interval, and the periodical dividend decreased or increased by these amounts would give the interest for each interval.

Thus, in the case of a debenture for 100 redeemable at par in 10 years, bearing interest at 5 per-cent payable half-yearly, and bought to yield 4 per-cent convertible half-yearly, the premium of 8·176 paid by the purchaser would represent the value of $\frac{1}{2}a_{\overline{20}|}$ at the effective rate ·02. The successive principal-repayments in the case of this annuity will be $\frac{1}{2}v^{20}$, $\frac{1}{2}v^{19}$, &c.—all at 2 per-cent—that is, ·3365, ·3432, &c. These are the amounts which must be written off half-yearly from the purchase-money of 108·176, and the balance of the dividend available for interest will be 2·1635 for the first half-year, 2·1568 for the second half-year, &c., which will be found to represent, as they ought, 2 per-cent on the amount of capital outstanding at the beginning of the first, second, &c., half-years.

If the debenture had borne interest at the rate of 3 per-cent and had been bought to yield 4 per-cent, the purchaser would have obtained it at a *discount* of 8·176, which again represents the value of $\frac{1}{2}a_{\overline{20}|}$ at ·02 effective. The principal-repayments contained in the successive payments of the annuity, must in this case be *written on* half-yearly to the purchase-money, and the interest for each half-year will be found by *adding* to the dividend the amount written on to capital at the end of the half-year.

22. It appears, therefore, that the amounts by which the capital invested in a redeemable security should be periodically written up or written down, as the case may be, could be ascertained by constructing a schedule showing the principal and interest contained in the successive payments of an annuity of the difference between the dividend and the rate of interest required to be realized. But the same result may be more directly attained on a book-keeping basis by debiting the security from interval to interval with interest at the requisite rate on the capital outstanding at the beginning of the interval, crediting it with the dividend, and writing the difference on to or off the capital according as the interest is $>$ or $<$ the dividend. If a schedule be required to check the accuracy of the entries, it may be constructed at the outset by a similar method. For example, the schedule in the case of a debenture for 100 redeemable in $5\frac{1}{4}$ years at par, bearing interest at 6 per-cent payable half-yearly (the next payment being due three months hence), and bought to yield 4 per-cent convertible half-yearly, will be as follows:

$$\text{Invested Capital} = \frac{108{\cdot}983 + 3{\cdot}000}{1{\cdot}01} = 110{\cdot}874.$$

Half-Year No.	Capital outstanding	Interest	Dividend *less* Interest (to be written off Capital)
0	110·874	1·109	1·891
1	108·983	2·180	·820
2	108·163	2·163	·837
3	107·326	2·147	·853
4	106·473	2·129	·871
5	105·602	2·112	·888
6	104·714	2·094	·906
7	103·808	2·076	·924
8	102·884	2·058	·942
9	101·942	2·039	·961
10	100·981	2·019	·981

23. An interesting question arises as to the incidence of income-tax in relation to the class of securities under consideration. It has been stated in Chapter IV that when a loan or debt is repayable by an annuity income-tax is chargeable on that part only of each annuity-payment which represents interest. But in the case of redeemable securities bought at a premium or at a discount, income-tax is invariably charged on the dividend without any reference to the fact that in the one case part of each dividend consists of capital applicable to the gradual reduction of the premium, or that in the other the dividend does not represent the whole of the interest realized by the investor. The question may therefore be asked, What would be the present value, to pay a given rate of interest subject to a fixed rate of income-tax, of a redeemable security bought at a premium—income-tax being chargeable on the full dividend?

It will be convenient to determine, as a preliminary, the present value to yield the effective rate i, subject to income-tax at rate t per unit, of an annuity of 1 per annum payable annually for n years, the whole of each annuity payment being chargeable with income-tax at rate t per unit. The net amount of each annuity-payment, after deduction of tax, will be $1-t$, and the net rate of interest to be realized on the annuity is $i(1-t)$. Hence it follows that the present value of the annuity under the conditions specified is $(1-t)a'_{\overline{n}|}$, where the dash denotes that the annuity-value is to be calculated at the effective rate $i(1-t)$ instead of i.

Consider, now, the case of an n-year debenture of 1 redeemable at par, bearing interest at g per unit, payable half-yearly and bought at a premium of k per unit to yield rate j convertible half-yearly, subject to income-tax at the rate of t per unit. Each half-yearly dividend may be divided into two parts—both subject to tax—namely, $\frac{j}{2}$, which represents interest on 1 at rate j convertible half-yearly, and $\frac{1}{2}(g-j)$, which represents the half-yearly payment to liquidate the premium of k with interest. Now the former, after deduction of tax, represents interest less tax on 1, and the value of the latter, after deduction of tax, to yield j convertible half-yearly subject to tax, is the same as the present value to yield the effective rate $\frac{j}{2}$ subject to tax, of a $2n$-year annuity of $\frac{1}{2}(g-j)$, the whole of each payment being chargeable with tax. Hence the present value of the debenture under the specified conditions will be

$$1+\tfrac{1}{2}(1-t)(g-j)a'_{\overline{2n}|}. \quad . \quad . \quad . \quad . \quad . \quad (20)$$

where the dash denotes that the annuity-value is to be calculated at the effective rate $(1-t)\frac{j}{2}$.

As an example, let it be required to find the value at 4 per-cent convertible half-yearly, subject to tax at 1*s*. in the £, of a debenture for 100 redeemable in 10 years at par, and bearing interest at 6 per-cent payable half-yearly. Here $t=\cdot05$; $g=\cdot06$; $j=\cdot04$; and $a'_{\overline{2n}|}=\dfrac{1-(1\cdot019)^{-20}}{\cdot019}$ which$=16\cdot510$. Hence the required present value$=115\cdot684$. If the fact of income-tax being chargeable on the entire dividend be left out of account, the present value would be $[1+\cdot01\times \overset{2\%}{a_{\overline{20}|}}]\times 100$ which$=116\cdot351$ It will be seen, therefore, that the adjustment is of some practical importance.

24. The investigations of Arts. 5 to 23 have been limited to securities redeemable in one sum, but they may be extended, by a simple generalization, to securities redeemable by any fixed instalments and bearing interest at a fixed rate on the outstanding instalments. This follows at once from the fact that any such security may be considered as consisting of a number of separate securities each of which is redeemable in one sum. As an example of the method of generalization it will be sufficient to consider the fundamental problem of valuation.

Let $C_1, C_2, \ldots C_r$ represent the successive instalments by which the principal is to be redeemed.

" $n_1, n_2, \ldots n_r$ " the respective numbers of years at the expiration of which the successive instalments become payable.

" $K_1, K_2, \ldots K_r$ " the present values, at the valuation-rate of interest, of C_1 due n_1 years hence, &c.

" g " the fixed rate of dividend to be paid on the outstanding instalments.

" $A_1, A_2, \ldots A_r$ " the present values, at the valuation-rate, of the separate instalments with the relative dividends.

Assume the dividend to be payable p times a year—the next dividend being due $\frac{1}{p}$th of a year hence—and let it be required to find the value of the entire security at the effective rate i.

Then, by formula (2),

$$A_1 = K_1 + \frac{g s_{\overline{1}|}^{(p)}}{i}(C_1 - K_1)$$

$$A_2 = K_2 + \frac{g s_{\overline{1}|}^{(p)}}{i}(C_2 - K_2)$$

$$\vdots \qquad \vdots$$

$$A_r = K_r + \frac{g s_{\overline{1}|}^{(p)}}{i}(C_r - K_r)$$

Hence, by addition, if A, K, and C, respectively, be written for $(A_1 + A_2 + \ldots + A_r)$, $(K_1 + K_2 + \ldots + K_r)$, and $(C_1 + C_2 + \ldots + C_r)$,

$$A = K + \frac{g s_{\overline{1}|}^{(p)}}{i}(C - K) \quad . \quad . \quad . \quad . \quad . \quad . \quad (21)$$

where C represents the total capital repayable, K the sum of the present values, at the valuation-rate, of the successive instalments of C, each being discounted for the period to elapse before it becomes payable, and A the present value, at the valuation-rate, of the total security.

25. The advantage of the algebraical transformation by which formula (2) is obtained from formula (1)—or, by which, in other words, the present value of the dividend is expressed in terms of the present value of the capital repayable—becomes very apparent in connection with securities under which the principal is repayable by instalments instead of in one sum. In such cases, if it be necessary to value the several instalments with the dividends thereon by individual calculation, a considerable saving of labour will obviously be effected by expressing the value of the dividends in terms of the value of the capital repayable, while, if it be possible to find algebraical formulas for the sum of the present values of the successive instalments and the sum of the present values of the dividends, the expression for the latter sum will generally be found to be much more complex than that for the former. For example, let it be required to find the present value, at the effective rate i, of a debenture for 1 redeemable at par by equal annual instalments spread over t years and bearing interest, payable annually, at rate g on the amount from time to time outstanding. The value might obviously be written in the form

$$\frac{1}{t}(v+v^2+\ldots+v^t)+\frac{g}{t}(t.v+\overline{t-1}.v^2+\ldots+v^t)$$

$$=\frac{1}{t}\cdot a_{\overline{t}|}+\frac{g}{t}(ta_{\overline{t}|}-a_{\overline{t}|\overline{2}|})$$

which would involve the evaluation of an annuity of the second order.

By means of formula (21), in which K will $=\frac{1}{t}a_{\overline{t}|}$ and C will $=1$, the result is at once obtained in the simple form

$$\frac{1}{t}\cdot a_{\overline{t}|}+\frac{g}{i}\left(1-\frac{1}{t}a_{\overline{t}|}\right).$$

26. Formula (21) may be established by general reasoning precisely similar to that of Art. 6. If the dividend were payable annually at rate i, the present value of the whole security, to yield the effective rate i, would obviously be C, and the present value of the dividends alone would consequently be C−K. But the dividends are actually at rate g payable p times a year, which is equivalent, at the effective rate i, to an annual rate of $gs_{\overline{1}|}^{(p)}$, and their value by simple proportion will, therefore, be $\frac{gs_{\overline{1}|}^{(p)}}{i}(C-K)$. Hence, the value of the entire security is $K+\frac{gs_{\overline{1}|}^{(p)}}{i}(C-K)$.

27. The method of repayment by fixed instalments has been extensively adopted by foreign governments in connection with their loan-issues. In such cases interest is usually payable half-yearly, and the general valuation formula will take the form

$$K+\frac{g(1+\sqrt{1+i})}{2i}(C-K).$$

As an example, the Chinese 6 per-cent Gold Loan of April 1895 may be taken. In this case interest is payable half-yearly on 1 January and 1 July, and the principal is repayable at par by annual drawings in 15 approximately equal annual instalments, of which the first is to be paid on 1 July 1901. Let it be required to find the price per-cent at which a syndicate could have taken up the entire loan as at 1 July 1895 in order to realize interest at the effective rate of $5\frac{1}{2}$ per-cent.

Here $K=\frac{100}{15}(v^6+v^7+\ldots+v^{20})$ at $5\frac{1}{2}$ per-cent

$$=\frac{100}{15}(a_{\overline{20}|}-a_{\overline{5}|})=51{\cdot}201$$

$$C=100$$

$$g(1+\sqrt{1+i})={\cdot}06(1+\sqrt{1{\cdot}055})={\cdot}12163$$

Hence the required price per-cent $=51{\cdot}201+1{\cdot}1057\times48{\cdot}799=105{\cdot}158$.

Another example, of a rather more complex character, is afforded by the French 3 per-cent Redeemable Rentes. This loan originally consisted of 175 series, redeemable by annual drawings at par, as follows:

1	series in	each of the	years	1879	to	1907
2	„	„	„	1908	„	1925
3	„	„	„	1926	„	1938
4	„	„	„	1939	„	1945
5	„	„	„	1946	„	1950
6	„	„	„	1951	„	1953

Interest is payable quarterly on 16 January, April, July, and October.

On the assumption that the series drawn for redemption are paid off annually on 16 April, let it be required to find, on the basis of an effective rate of $3\frac{1}{8}$ per-cent, the capitalized value per-cent of the entire outstanding balance of the loan as on 16 April 1900.

Twenty-two series having been paid off in 1879–1900, there remain

153 series outstanding, to be repaid as shown above. Hence if C be taken as 100,

$$K = \frac{100}{153}[(v + v^2 + \ldots + v^7) + 2(v^8 + v^9 + \ldots v^{25})$$

$$+ 3(v^{26} + v^{27} + \ldots + v^{38}) + 4(v^{39} + v^{40} + \ldots v^{45})$$

$$+ 5(v^{46} + v^{47} + \ldots + v^{50}) + 6(v^{51} + v^{52} + v^{53})]$$

$$= \frac{100}{153}[6a_{\overline{53}|} - (a_{\overline{7}|} + a_{\overline{25}|} + a_{\overline{38}|} + a_{\overline{45}|} + a_{\overline{50}|})]$$

the numerical value of which must be calculated at $3\frac{1}{8}$ per-cent.

By Oakes's Interest Tables $6a_{\overline{53}|}$ at $3\frac{1}{8}$ per-cent=		154·415
,, ,, ,, $a_{\overline{7}|}$,, ,,	= 6·201	
,, ,, ,, $a_{\overline{25}|}$,, ,,	=17·173	
,, ,, ,, $a_{\overline{38}|}$,, ,,	=22·062	
,, ,, ,, $a_{\overline{45}|}$,, ,,	=23·987	
,, ,, ,, $a_{\overline{50}|}$,, ,,	=25·130	
		94·553

whence $K = \frac{100}{153} \times 59·862$

Also the equivalent annual dividend

$$= ·03 \times s_{\overline{1}|}^{(4)} \text{ at } 3\tfrac{1}{8} \text{ per-cent} = ·03035$$

Hence the required value per-cent

$$= 39·125 + \frac{·03035}{·03125} \times 60·875 = 98·247$$

28. It should be carefully noted that the values found in the examples given in the last article are in both cases values of the *entire* loan per-cent, not those of individual bonds for 100. It is not possible to value a loan redeemable by drawings, otherwise than as a *whole*—except as a matter of average—because the value of any given bond will depend upon when that particular bond may happen to be drawn for repayment. For instance, in the case of the Chinese loan discussed above, it has been shown that the value of the whole loan, as at 1 July 1895, to pay $5\frac{1}{2}$ per-cent, would have been 105·158 per-cent, but the value of any one of the bonds which may happen to be drawn for repayment in 1901 would be only $100v^6 + 6·0815a_{\overline{6}|}$ at $5\frac{1}{2}$ per-cent, or

102·905; whereas the value of a bond which remains outstanding until 1915 would be $100v^{20}+6\cdot0815a_{\overline{20}|}$, or 106·949.

Inasmuch, however, as bonds forming part of a loan redeemable by drawings are frequently bought—as an investment with an element of speculation—at a price proportionate to the value of the entire loan, it becomes a matter of some interest to determine when any given bond should become repayable in order that it may yield the same rate of interest as the entire loan. Let the symbols K, C, and g refer, with the usual significations, to the whole loan, let C_1 be the capital repayable under the particular bond, and let n be the number of years that should elapse before this bond is drawn for repayment in order that it may yield the same rate of interest—i say—as the whole loan. Then the value of the particular bond will be $C_1v^n+\frac{g}{i}(C_1-C_1v^n)$; and the value of the entire loan is $K+\frac{g}{i}(C-K)$. Then, since the price given for the particular bond is, by hypothesis, proportionate to the value of the entire loan, it follows that

$$Cv^n+\frac{g}{i}(C-Cv^n)=K+\frac{g}{i}(C-K)$$

whence

$$Cv^n=K.$$

It appears, therefore, that n=the *equated time*, at the rate of interest required to be realized, for the several instalments by which the loan is redeemable. Thus, in the case of a loan standing at a premium, any particular bond will yield a lower or higher rate than that yielded by the loan as a whole, according as it is drawn for repayment before or after the equated time for the outstanding instalments, while in the case of a loan standing at a discount the converse will hold.

29. Another method of repayment frequently adopted by foreign governments—and also by some commercial companies—is that of the *cumulative* or *accumulative sinking-fund*. A loan is said to be redeemable by a cumulative sinking-fund when a fixed sum is periodically applied to the service of the loan—that is, to payment of interest and to repayment of principal by drawings, purchase or otherwise—so that the sum available for repayment of principal is increased from time to time by the interest that would have been payable on the repaid portion of the principal if it had been still outstanding. The only case that it is necessary to consider is that in which the sinking-fund is applied to redeem the loan by drawings made at regular intervals. In this case, if the periodical drawings take place with the same frequency as that with which interest is payable, the transaction simply takes the form of the repayment of principal and interest by an annuity. Let C be the capital repayable, g the rate of dividend per annum, payable half-yearly, reckoned on the capital repayable, z the rate of sinking-fund per annum, payable half-yearly, also reckoned on the capital repayable, and j convertible half-yearly, the rate of interest on which the transaction is based. Then the sum to be applied half-yearly to the service of the loan will be $\frac{1}{2}(g+z)$C, and since the principal of C, with interest at rate g payable half-yearly, is to be liquidated by an annuity of $(g+z)$C payable half-yearly, it follows that, if n be the number of years which will elapse before the whole loan is repaid,

$$C=\tfrac{1}{2}(g+z)C\,.\,a_{\overline{2n}|}\text{ at rate }\tfrac{1}{2}g\,.$$

whence
$$1=\tfrac{1}{2}(g+z)\frac{1-\left(1+\dfrac{g}{2}\right)^{-2n}}{\tfrac{1}{2}g}$$

or
$$z=(g+z)\left(1+\frac{g}{2}\right)^{-2n}$$

and
$$n=\frac{\log(g+z)-\log z}{2\log\left(1+\dfrac{g}{2}\right)}$$

Now from the point of view of the lender the security consists of an annuity of $(g+z)$C per annum payable half-yearly for this term of n years. Hence its value, to pay j convertible half-yearly, is given by the formula

$$A=\tfrac{1}{2}(g+z)C\,.\,a_{\overline{2n}|}\text{ at rate }\frac{j}{2}\,.\quad .\quad .\quad .\quad .\quad (22)$$

where n has the value obtained above.

30. In practice, the drawings usually take place *annually*, whereas interest is payable *half-yearly*. Let the rate of dividend be, as before, g payable half-yearly, let the cumulative sinking-fund be z per unit payable annually, and let it be required to find the value of the whole loan to yield the effective rate i. Then, in these circumstances, the fixed annual sum set aside for the service of the loan will be $(g+z)$C, but the portion applicable in any year to the payment of interest will be paid in two equal parts, namely, one-half at the end of the first half of the year, and the other one-half at the end of the year; hence the sum applied to the service of the loan for, say, the rth year would be equivalent, for the purposes of a valuation at the effective rate i, to a sum of $(g+z)C+\frac{g}{2}(\sqrt{1+i}-1)X$ paid at the *end* of the year, where X is used to denote the amount of the loan outstanding at the beginning of the rth year. Now the fact of the dividend being payable half-yearly does not affect the rate of accumulation of the sinking-fund, for, by hypothesis, the portion of the fixed annual sum of $(g+z)C$, available in any year for repayment of principal is found by deducting from $(g+z)C$ the sum actually applied to payment of interest irrespective of the actual dates of payment. Hence, if n be the number of years within which the loan will be entirely redeemed,

$$C=(g+z)C\,.\,a_{\overline{n}|} \text{ at rate } g$$

whence
$$n=\frac{\log(g+z)-\log z}{\log(1+g)}$$

and the amounts of principal drawn for repayment at the end of the 1st, 2nd, 3rd, years, &c., will be zC, $zC(1+g)$, $zC(1+g)^2$, &c. It follows, therefore, that the total amount repaid in the first $(r-1)$ years will be $zC\,.\,s_{\overline{r-1}|}$ calculated at rate g, and that the amount outstanding at the beginning of the rth year will be $C(1-zs_{\overline{r-1}|})$.

Consequently, from the point of view of the investor, the security consists of an annuity, payable annually for n years, of which the rth payment is

$$(g+z)C+\frac{gC}{2}(\sqrt{1+i}-1)(1-zs_{\overline{r-1}|}),$$

or, in other words, an ordinary annuity of $(g+z)C$ per annum and a relatively small decreasing annuity of which the rth payment is $\frac{gC}{2}(\sqrt{1+i}-1)(1-zs_{\overline{r-1}|})$, where $s_{\overline{r-1}|}$ is calculated at rate g.
In theory, both annuities should be valued at rate i, but it will make very little difference for practical purposes if the latter be valued at rate g. Hence, approximately, the required value of the total loan

$$=(g+z)Ca_{\overline{n}|}^{(i)}+\frac{gC}{2}(\sqrt{1+i}-1)\left(a_{\overline{n}|}-z\sum_{r=1}^{r=n-1}v^r\,.\,s_{\overline{r-1}|}\right)^{(g)}$$

$$=(g+z)Ca_{\overline{n}|}^{(i)}+\frac{gC}{2}(\sqrt{1+i}-1)\left(a_{\overline{n}|}-z\,.\,\frac{nv-a_{\overline{n}|}}{g}\right)^{(g)} \qquad (23)$$

The Chinese Gold Loan of 1896 bears interest at 5 per-cent payable half-yearly, and is redeemable by annual drawings spread over 36 years.

In this case $z = \frac{1}{s_{\overline{36}|}}$ at 5 per-cent $= \cdot 0104345$

$$a_{\overline{36}|} - z \cdot \frac{36v - a_{\overline{36}|}}{\cdot 05} \quad \text{,,} \quad \text{,,} \quad = 12 \cdot 845$$

Hence the value of the loan per-cent at date of issue, to pay $5\frac{1}{2}$ per-cent effective, would have been 93·891 + ·871, or 94·762.

It will be observed that in the above example the value of the loan has been found as at the date of issue, but precisely the same method will be applicable to a valuation at any annual date during the currency of the loan, except that the cumulative sinking fund must be taken as the ratio of the sum applicable to repayment of principal at the next annual drawing to the amount of principal outstanding at date of valuation.

31. It may here be mentioned that in the case of a loan repayable by drawings by means of a cumulative sinking fund, the schedule showing the operation of the sinking fund would differ slightly from the ordinary repayment schedule for a loan repayable by a terminable annuity, owing to the fact that only an *integral* number of bonds could be repaid at each drawing. The necessary adjustment may be easily made by carrying forward the unapplied balance from each drawing to the next following drawing. Thus, in the case of a 5 per-cent loan of 1,000,000 in 10,000 bonds of 100 each, repayable at par in 30 years by annual drawings by the operation of a cumulative sinking fund, the total amount to be applied annually to the service of the loan would be $\frac{1,000,000}{a_{\overline{30}|}}$ at 5 per-cent, or 65,051·44, and the schedule showing the number of bonds to be drawn for repayment each year would be as follows:

n	$\frac{1,000,000}{s_{\overline{30}|}}(1+i)^{n-1}$	Amount available for nth Drawing	Number of Bonds Repaid at nth Drawing	Balance Forward
1	15,051·44	15,051·44	150	51·44
2	15,804·01	15,855·45	158	55·45
3	16,594·21	16,649·66	166	49·66
4	17,423·92	17,473·58	174	73·58
&c.	&c.	&c.	&c.	&c.

Or, a full schedule, showing the interest and drawings for each year, might be constructed in the following way:

n	Amount of Bonds outstanding at beginning of nth year	Interest for nth year	65,051·44 *less* interest for nth year	Amount available for nth drawing	No. of Bonds repaid at nth drawing	Balance after nth drawing	Interest at 5 per-cent on Balance
1	1,000,000	50,000	15,051·44	15,051·44	150	51·44	2·57
2	985,000	49,250	15,801·44	15,855·45	158	55·45	2·77
3	969,200	48,460	16,591·44	16,649·66	166	49·66	2·48
4	952,600	47,630	17,421·44	17,473·58	174	73·58	3·68
5	935,200	46,760	18,291·44	18,368·70	183	68·70	3·44
&c.	&c.	&c.	&c.	&c.	&c.	&c.	&c.

As a result of the practical adjustment of the periodical drawings, the series of payments made by the borrower takes the form of a slightly varying annuity, instead of an annuity of uniform amount. Thus, in the example discussed above, the successive annual payments made on foot of principal and interest are 65,000, 65,050, 65,060, 65,030, 65,060, &c., instead of 65,051·44 each year. This, however, would not make any appreciable difference in the value of the loan.

32. In the foregoing discussion of the subject of loans repayable by instalments, it has been assumed throughout that the principal is to be repaid in some definite way. It may, however, often happen—apart from any question of default (a contingency which does not enter into the theory of the subject)—that the borrower has power to suspend or increase the sinking fund, or other provision for redemption, at his option. In such cases theoretical methods of valuation would have to be employed with caution. In fact, in every case the precise terms of the contract must be studied, and due consideration must be given to all their bearings on the problem of valuation.

33. The method of gradually writing down or writing up a redeemable security to its redemption price has been discussed in Art. 20–22 for the case of a security redeemable in one sum, and an identically similar process will obviously apply to a loan redeemable by instalments, or, in fact, as stated in Art. 15 of Chapter IV, to any series of payments. As an alternative method, in all cases, the security may be kept at its purchase-price until redemption, or during any other period, and the sinking fund for writing the capital value up or down may be carried to a separate account. But if that course be adopted, the sinking fund must be accumulated at the rate of interest realized on the purchase price of the security; otherwise there will be a discrepancy between the accumulations of the sinking fund and the sum required to write down, or write up, the capital value of the security. It may happen, however, that an investor desires to realize a certain rate of interest on his original invested capital for a certain period, and to accumulate his sinking fund at some other—usually lower—rate. This suggests the general question, What price should be paid for a security to yield the investor a given effective rate, i' say, on his original invested capital for a term of n years, on the assumption that the effective rate of interest realizable on investments is i? It will be observed that i' and i correspond to the *remunerative* and *reproductive* rates of Arts. 11–14 and 18 in Chapter IV. Let A be the present value of the security at the effective rate i, and let X be the required price. Then, since the investor desires to realize interest on X at the effective rate i' for n years, or, in other words, to obtain an annuity of $i'X$ per annum payable annually for n years, and to have his original capital of X intact at the end of the period, it is obvious that the present value of these benefits at the investment rate i must be equal to the present value of the security at that rate. Hence

$$i'X.a_{\overline{n}|}+X.v^n=A$$

whence
$$X=\frac{A}{i'a_{\overline{n}|}+v^n}=\frac{A(1+i)^n}{1+i's_{\overline{n}|}} \quad . \quad . \quad . \quad . \quad . \qquad (21)$$

That is to say, the required price = (*a*) the present value of the security at rate i divided by $i'a_{\overline{n}|}+v^n$ or $1+(i'-i)a_{\overline{n}|}$, or (*b*) the accumulated *amount* of the security in n years at rate i divided by $1+i's_{\overline{n}|}$. It will be seen that the problem resolves itself simply into that of converting the given security into an equivalent n-year debenture redeemable at par and bearing interest at rate i'. Formulas (10), (11)*b* and (14) of Chapter IV may be at once deduced from the formula given above. Similarly, the value per unit to pay the effective rate i' on the invested capital, and to admit of the accumulation of the necessary sinking fund at rate i, of a debenture redeemable at par in n years and bearing interest at rate g payable annually will be $\dfrac{1+gs_{\overline{n}|}}{1+i's_{\overline{n}|}}$.

34. Many problems arise in practice in connection with the conversion of securities and the consolidation of loans. The fundamental principle to be observed in transactions of this nature is that the converted or consolidated security should be equivalent to the old security. Hence, apart from any special circumstances which might render it proper to value the new and old securities at different rates of interest, the procedure in all cases will be in the first place to fix the rate of interest upon which the conversion or consolidation is to be based, and then to so adjust the terms of the transaction that the new security shall be equivalent, at that rate of interest, to the security which it replaces. In the case of the conversion of a marketable security, the rate of interest to be employed should be such as to leave the market value unaltered, and it would, therefore, be determined by ascertaining the rate of interest yielded by the old security on its market price; in other cases the rate to be employed would have to be determined by reference to the rate obtainable, at the time of conversion, on similar securities.

The following examples will sufficiently illustrate the subject—

(*a*) A company proposes to convert its existing debentures, bearing interest at 6 per-cent payable half-yearly, and redeemable at par in 5 years, into an equal amount of debentures bearing interest at $4\frac{1}{2}$ per-cent payable half-yearly. On the assumption that the existing debentures are quoted at a price to pay 4 per-cent convertible half-yearly, when should the new debentures be redeemable?

Let n be the number of years at the expiration of which the converted debentures should be redeemed.

Then $1+(\cdot 03-\cdot 02)a_{\overline{10}|}=1+(\cdot 0225-\cdot 02)a_{\overline{2n}|}$ where the annuity-values are to be calculated at 2 per-cent.

$$\therefore \quad a_{\overline{2n}|}=\frac{\cdot 01}{\cdot 0025}a_{\overline{10}|}=35\cdot 93.$$

On reference to a 2 per-cent annuity table it will be found that $a_{\overline{64}|}=35\cdot 92$.

Hence the new debentures should be redeemable at par in 32 years.

(*b*) A borrower has obtained at different times three loans of £5,000, £2,000, and £4,000, repayable with interest at the respective rates of 5, $4\frac{1}{2}$, and 4 per-cent, convertible half-yearly, by annuities payable half-yearly on 1 June and 1 December, each annuity having been originally for a term of 30 years. He proposes to consolidate the loans as on 1 June 1900, when 20 instalments remain to be paid in respect of the £5,000 loan, 25 in respect of the £2,000 loan, and 35 in respect of the £4,000 loan, into a single loan repayable with interest by a single terminable annuity payable half-yearly from the following 1 December, and he desires to know (i) what annuity he would have to pay in order to redeem the consolidated loan in 15 years; (ii) what would be the term of the annuity if he were to pay a half-yearly instalment equal to the sum of the annuities at present payable in respect of the existing loans.

It must be assumed that the borrower is not entitled to pay off the loans otherwise than by the stipulated annuities, otherwise he would have exercised his right to pay off the balance of the 5 per-cent loan when obtaining the $4\frac{1}{2}$ loan, and similarly to pay off the balance of the $4\frac{1}{2}$ per-cent loan when obtaining the loan at 4 per-cent.

The first point to be decided will be the rate of interest at which the consolidation is to be effected. Let it be assumed that $3\frac{1}{2}$ per-cent convertible half-yearly is now obtainable on similar security, and that this rate is to be employed in the calculation.

The half-yearly payments in respect of the three loans will be as follows—

For the £5,000 loan, $\dfrac{5{,}000}{a_{\overline{60}|}}$ at $2\frac{1}{2}$ per-cent, or 161·767

" " £2,000 " $\dfrac{2{,}000}{a_{\overline{60}|}}$ " $2\frac{1}{4}$ " " 61·071

" " £4,000 " $\dfrac{4{,}000}{a_{\overline{60}|}}$ " 2 " " 115·072

Hence (i), if X be the half-yearly amount of the consolidated annuity for 15 years,

$$X \,.\, a_{\overline{30}|} = 161{\cdot}767 a_{\overline{20}|} + 61{\cdot}071 a_{\overline{25}|} + 115{\cdot}072 a_{\overline{35}|}$$

where all the annuities are to be taken at $1\frac{3}{4}$ per-cent, whence it will be found that X=298·9 approximately. And (ii), if n be the number of years in which the consolidated loan would be redeemed by a half-yearly payment of 161·767+61·071+115·072, or 337·910,

$$337{\cdot}910 \times a_{\overline{2n}|} = 161{\cdot}767 a_{\overline{20}|} + 61{\cdot}071 a_{\overline{25}|} + 115{\cdot}072 a_{\overline{35}|}$$

where again all the annuities are to be taken at $1\frac{3}{4}$ per-cent, from which it will be found that $n=12\cdot815$ nearly. This means, of course, that 25 half-yearly payments of $337\cdot910$ would be payable and that a final fractional payment would have to be made at the end of 13 years.

The result obtained in answer to the second part of the question may be defined as the *equated term* of the three annuities. It will be found to be slightly *less* than the result obtained by multiplying the several annuities by their outstanding terms and dividing the sum of the products by the consolidated annuity. It may be shown generally that this must always be the case. For let there be any number of annuities of K_1, K_2, K_3, &c., for n_1, n_2, n_3, &c., years, and let n be their equated term.

Then $$a_{\overline{n}|} \times \Sigma K = K_1 a_{\overline{n_1}|} + K_2 a_{\overline{n_2}|} + \&c.$$

$$\therefore \qquad \frac{1-v^n}{i} \cdot \Sigma K = K_1 \cdot \frac{1-v^{n_1}}{i} + K_2 \frac{1-v^{n_2}}{i} + \ldots .$$

$$\therefore \qquad v^n . \Sigma K = v^{n_1} K_1 + v^{n_2} K_2 + \ldots .$$

whence it appears that n is the *equated time* for sums of K_1, K_2, &c., due n_1, n_2, &c., years hence.

Now it has been shown in Art. 8 of Chap. II, that the true equated time is $<$ the result obtained by dividing the sum of the products of the amounts due and their respective times by the sum of the amounts. Hence it follows that the *equated term* of any number of annuities is $<$ the result obtained by dividing the sum of the products of their periodical payments and their respective terms by the sum of the payments. The latter will, however, be a rough approximation to the true result.

CHAPTER VI.

On the Determination of the Rate of Interest involved in a given Transaction.

1. In the preceding chapters, methods have been investigated for determining the present value or amount of a given series of payments, or the terms of a given transaction, on the basis of a specified rate of interest. In the present chapter, it is proposed to consider the converse problem of determining at what rate of interest a given series of payments would have a given present value or amount, or, more generally, the rate involved in carrying out any given financial transaction on specified terms. This problem will obviously reduce in all cases to the solution of an equation for i, or j, or δ, as the case may be. For since the successive payments of the given series, or the terms of the given transaction, are assumed to be given, it follows that an equation may be obtained by finding an algebraical expression, on the basis of an assumed rate of interest i, j, or δ, for the present value or amount of the given series, or for some one of the quantities involved in the given transaction, and equating the result to the given present value or amount, or to the known value of the quantity in question. In this equation the assumed rate of interest will be the only unknown quantity, and the problem of determining its value consequently resolves itself into that of solving an equation for a single unknown. The equation will, however, generally be found to be of such a nature that it will be impracticable to obtain an exact solution, and it becomes, therefore, a matter of importance to consider the special problems that most frequently arise in financial transactions, and to investigate convenient methods of obtaining approximate solutions.

2. At the outset, one consideration of a general nature presents itself. Since an effective rate may be converted into a nominal rate convertible with a given frequency, or *vice versa*, it follows that it is immaterial whether the rate involved in a given transaction be determined, in the first instance, in the form of an effective rate or in that of a nominal rate. Hence, in any given case it will be most convenient to assume as the rate to be determined a rate convertible with such a frequency as will lead to an equation of the simplest possible form.

For example, suppose it to be required to find at what effective rate an ordinary annuity payable half-yearly for a given number of years will have a given present value. The algebraical expression for the present value of an annuity payable half-yearly assumes its simplest form in terms of a nominal rate of interest convertible half-yearly. The best course to adopt, therefore, would be to determine, as accurately as may be necessary, the nominal rate payable half-yearly which would produce the given present value, and then to convert that nominal rate into the corresponding effective rate. Similarly, if it were required to find the nominal rate of interest, convertible half-yearly, realized on the purchase of Consols at a given price, the best plan would be to determine the yield, in the first instance, in the form of a nominal rate convertible quarterly—because, the dividends on Consols being payable quarterly, the algebraical expression for the value of Consols per-cent can be most simply written down in terms of a nominal rate convertible quarterly—and then to convert the result into a nominal rate convertible half-yearly.

In general, the interval of conversion of the assumed rate may be made the same as the interval of payment in the annuity or other transaction under consideration. It will be sufficient, therefore, in most of the investigations that follow, to consider the problem of determining the *effective* rate involved in an annuity or other transaction under which the interval of payment is a *year*, for, by substitution of an *interval* for a *year*, the resulting formulas will become immediately applicable to the determination of the nominal rate convertible p times a year involved in an annuity or other transaction in which the interval of payment is $\frac{1}{p}$th of a year.

3. To proceed now to the discussion of the problem. An obvious method of procedure would be to endeavour to find the unknown rate

by successive independent trials. Thus, suppose it were required to find the effective rate of interest realized on the purchase, at the price of 135·187 per-cent, of debentures redeemable in 20 years at par and bearing interest at the rate of 5 per-cent payable annually, or, in symbols, to find the value of i satisfying the equation

$$100v^{20} + 5a_{\overline{20}|} = 135{\cdot}187.$$

Since the premium of 35·187 has to be written off out of the dividends in 20 years, it is obvious that the rate of interest realized will be very considerably below 5 per-cent. If 3 per-cent and $2\frac{1}{2}$ per-cent be successively taken as trial rates it will be found, by actual evaluation of the expression $100v^{20}+5a_{\overline{20}|}$, that the debentures would be worth 129·755 per-cent at the former rate and 138·973 at the latter. The given price lies between these two values, and it is obvious, therefore, that the required rate lies between $2\frac{1}{2}$ and 3 per-cent. If now $2\frac{3}{4}$ per-cent be tried, it will be found that at this rate the value would be 134·261, which shows that $2\frac{3}{4}$ per-cent is slightly above the required rate. By proceeding to make further trials, it might ultimately be found that the true yield is 2·7 per-cent. But this method, although an admissible process for obtaining a rough idea of the required rate, would clearly be too laborious for general use, and it becomes necessary to investigate more systematic methods of approximation. Three such methods suggest themselves, namely, (1) the method of approximation, without the aid of tables, by direct expansion of the algebraical expression involving the unknown rate of interest; (2) the method of approximation, with the aid of tables, by expansion of a modified expression obtained by substituting for the unknown rate a nearly correct rate (determined by trial) plus or minus a relatively small unknown quantity; (3) the method of approximation, with the aid of tables, by interpolation between two or more trial rates giving nearly correct results. It will be convenient to consider the application of these methods, in the order in which they have been stated, to the two representative problems of determining the rate of interest at which a given annuity has a given present value or amount, and of finding the yield on the purchase of a redeemable security at a given price.

4. The first method to be discussed is the method of approximation, without the aid of tables, by direct expansion.

5. Consider, first, the case of an annuity of 1 per annum payable annually for n years. Let a be the given present value of the annuity, s its amount in n years, and i the unknown rate of interest.

Then $$a=\frac{1-v^n}{i}=\frac{1-(1+i)^{-n}}{i}$$

$$=n-\frac{n(n+1)}{2}i+\frac{n(n+1)(n+2)}{6}i^2-\ldots$$

This series ultimately becomes convergent, and it would, therefore, appear that an approximate solution might be obtained by neglecting the terms involving the higher powers of i. For example, for a first approximation,

$$a=n-\frac{n(n+1)}{2}i$$

whence $$i=\frac{2(n-a)}{n(n+1)} \quad \ldots\ldots\ldots \quad (1)$$

and for a second approximation, by substitution of the first approximation in the term involving i^2,

$$a=n-\frac{n(n+1)}{2}i+\frac{(n-a)(n+2)}{3}i$$

whence $$i=\frac{6(n-a)}{n^2-n+2an+4a} \quad \ldots\ldots\ldots \quad (2)$$

Similarly, it may be shown that, as a first approximation,

$$i=\frac{2(s-n)}{n(n-1)} \quad \ldots\ldots\ldots \quad (3)$$

and, as a second approximation,

$$i=\frac{6(s-n)}{n^2+n+2sn-4s} \quad \ldots\ldots\ldots \quad (4)$$

To test the accuracy of the results given by this method, let $n=30$, and $a=20$.

Formula (1) gives $i=\cdot021505$ . .

" (2) " $i=\cdot027906$ . . .

The *true* value of i to six places is ·028446. It appears, therefore, that the approximations given by formulas (1)—(4) are too wide of the mark to be reliable. This might have been anticipated by inspection of the original expansions. Although i is a small quantity, n may have a large numerical value. Consequently the successive terms in the expansion of $a_{\overline{n}|}$ in powers of i do not necessarily diminish with such rapidity as would admit of a good approximation being obtained from the first two or three terms; in fact, the terms may even increase in value up to a certain point in the expansion, and it might, therefore, be necessary to proceed to an approximation of a high order to get a good result.

6. The conclusion to be drawn from the investigation of the last article is that the method of approximation, by direct expansion, without the aid of interest tables, is not one that can be safely applied to the determination of the rate of interest in the case of an annuity. This conclusion will obviously apply with equal force to the general case of a redeemable security or of a loan payable by instalments—or, in fact, of any series of payments or financial transaction in which the annuity-element predominates. There is, however, one case, involving the annuity-element to a comparatively small extent, in which the method gives a fairly accurate result. This case—which is of sufficient practical importance to repay special investigation—is that of a debenture or other security bearing a fixed rate of dividend and redeemable in one sum at the expiration of a fixed number of years. Let it be required to find the rate of interest realized on a debenture redeemable in n years, carrying a dividend at the rate of g per annum (payable annually) per unit of its redemption-price, and bought at a premium of k per unit on its redemption-price. Let i be the required rate of interest. Then, by formula (17) of Chapter V,

$$k=(g-i)a_{\overline{n}|}$$

$$\therefore\ g-i=ki[1-(1+i)^{-n}]^{-1}=\frac{k}{n}\left[1-\frac{n+1}{2}i+\frac{(n+1)(n+2)}{6}i^2-\ldots\right]^{-1}$$

$$=\frac{k}{n}\left[1+\frac{n+1}{2}i+\frac{n^2-1}{12}i^2-\frac{n^2-1}{24}i^3+\ldots\right]$$

If the terms involving powers of i above the first be neglected, this equation gives, as a first approximation,

$$i=\frac{g-\dfrac{k}{n}}{1+\dfrac{n+1}{2n}k} \quad \cdots\cdots\cdots \quad (5)$$

In this formula the numerator = the balance of the year's dividend after deduction therefrom of $\frac{1}{n}$th of the premium paid on purchase, and the denominator

$$=\frac{1}{n}\left[(1+k)+\left(1+\frac{n-1}{n}k\right)+\left(1+\frac{n-2}{n}k\right)+\ .\ .\ .+\left(1+\frac{1}{n}\cdot k\right)\right],$$

so that the approximation really amounts to taking the rate which the purchaser of the debenture would realize on his *average* invested capital if he were to write off an equal proportionate part of the premium each year out of the annual dividend and to take the balance of the dividend as interest for the year. This is not a theoretically correct way of dealing with the investment, but it is obvious that, if the term of the debenture were short, it might be expected to give an average yield differing only slightly from the true yield. On inspection of the algebraical expansion from which the approximation is obtained, it will appear that this is the case, for if $\frac{n-1}{6}i$ be small as compared with 1—that is, in general, if n be not large—the value of the first term neglected, namely, $\frac{n^2-1}{12}i^2$, will be small as compared with that of $\frac{n+1}{2}i$.

As an example of the use of the formula, let it be required to find, without reference to tables, the approximate yield on a bond, bearing interest at $4\frac{1}{2}$ per-cent, payable half-yearly, redeemable in 25 years at $112\frac{1}{2}$, and bought just after payment of the half-yearly dividend, at a price of 120. Here the half-yearly dividend per unit of the redemption price $=\cdot 02$; $k=\frac{7\cdot 5}{112\cdot 5}$; and $n=50$. Hence, by the formula,

$$\text{the approximate half-yearly yield } =\frac{\cdot 02-\frac{1}{50}\cdot\frac{1}{15}}{1+\frac{51}{100}\cdot\frac{1}{15}}=\frac{28}{1551}=\cdot 018053.$$

The true half-yearly yield, to six places of decimals, is ·017968. The approximation is slightly in excess of the true value, and it will be seen, on consideration of the method by which formula (5) was obtained, that the effect of neglecting terms involving powers of i above the first will, in general, be to give to i too *large* a value if k is positive—that is, in the case of a bond bought at a *premium* —and too *small* a value if k is negative—that is, in the case of a bond bought at a *discount*. It must, of course, be borne in mind that the application of the formula to redeemable securities bought at a *discount* will be limited to those cases in which there is a definite contract to redeem at the expiration of a fixed period. A security, redeemable merely at the option of the debtor *on or after* a fixed date, and bought at a discount on the redemption-price, should be regarded [for a similar reason to that set forth in Chap. V, Art. 4 (iii)] as a perpetuity of the periodical dividend, and the yield would accordingly be determined by dividing the periodical dividend by the purchase-price; for example, the effective yield on a debenture bearing interest at 5 per-cent per annum, payable annually, redeemable at 110 on or after a given date at the option of the debtor, and bought at 105 would be $\frac{5}{1{\cdot}05}$ or 4·7619 . . . per-cent.

7. It has been pointed out that the impracticability of obtaining a reliable approximation by direct expansion, without the aid of interest tables, is due to the fact that, although the successive powers of i form a rapidly-decreasing series of quantities, the coefficients by which they are multiplied may increase for a certain number of terms with equal or even greater rapidity, so that the early terms in the expansion will not necessarily exhibit rapid convergency. It is obvious, therefore, that if the unknown quantity i could be replaced, in the expansion, by some very much smaller unknown quantity, without any corresponding increase in the coefficients, the series would be rendered much more rapidly convergent, and the error resulting from neglecting the terms involving the higher powers of the unknown quantity would be correspondingly minimized. This is the expedient adopted in the second of the methods of approximation mentioned in Article 3. Suppose that the equation to be solved reduces to the form

$$A = b_0 + b_1 i + b_2 i^2 + \dots$$

in which all the quantities except i are known. By reference to the conditions of the problem, or by actual trial, it will be easy to find a rate of interest which very nearly satisfies the equation. Let this rate be i', and let $i = i' + \rho$. Then, by substitution, the equation becomes

$$A = b_0 + b_1(i' + \rho) + b_2(i' + \rho)^2 + \dots$$

$$= B_0 + B_1\rho + B_2\rho^2 + \dots$$

where
$$B_0=b_0+b_1i'+b_2i'^2+\ldots$$
$$B_1=b_1+2b_2i'+3b_3i'^2+\ldots$$
$$B_2=b_2+3b_3i'+\ldots$$

The successive terms of this modified equation will generally decrease rapidly, since ρ is necessarily small. Hence an approximately accurate result may be expected to be obtained from the first two or three terms. As a first approximation,

$$\rho=\frac{A-B_0}{B_1} \text{ and } i=i'+\frac{A-B_0}{B_1} \quad . \quad . \quad . \quad . \quad . \quad (6)$$

A second approximation may be obtained by substituting $B_2\rho\cdot\frac{A-B_0}{B_1}$ for $B_2\rho^2$ in the original equation, whence

$$A=B_0+\left(B_1+B_2\cdot\frac{A-B_0}{B_1}\right)\rho$$

$$\rho=\frac{B_1(A-B_0)}{B_1^2+AB_2-B_0B_2} \quad . \quad . \quad . \quad . \quad . \quad . \quad . \quad . \quad (7)$$

and
$$i=i'+\frac{B_1(A-B_0)}{B_1^2+AB_2-B_0B_2} \text{ approximately.}$$

But a better approximation may, in general, be obtained by repeating the original process, that is to say, by putting $i=i''+\rho'$, where $i''=i'+\frac{A-B_0}{B_1}$, and finding a first approximation to ρ' in the same way as for ρ. This process may be repeated until any desired degree of accuracy is obtained.

In the foregoing investigation the problem has been expressed in general terms, and it may appear that it would be a matter of some difficulty to calculate the numerical values of the quantities B_0, B_1, B_2, &c. In practice, however, it is not necessary to obtain an expansion in terms of i before putting $i=i'+\rho$. The simpler and more convenient plan of procedure, in any given problem, will be to substitute $i'+\rho$ for i before expanding, and then to expand directly in powers of ρ, and it will usually be found that the coefficients required in the approximation assume such a form that they can be easily evaluated with the aid of interest tables. The process will be exemplified by the following investigations of the cases of an annuity and a loan repayable by instalments.

8. Take, first, the case of the annuity. Let a, as before, be the given present value of an annuity of 1 per annum payable annually for n years, let i be the unknown rate of interest, and suppose that, on reference to a table of the present values of an annuity at various rates of interest, it is found that $a_{\overline{n}|}$ at rate $i'=a'$, which differs by only a small quantity from the given present value a. Assume that $i=i'+\rho$, where ρ will be a small quantity—positive or negative—relatively to i'. Then

$$a=\frac{1-v^n}{i}=\frac{1-(1+i'+\rho)^{-n}}{i'+\rho}$$

$$=\frac{1}{i'}\left[1-v'^n(1+\rho v')^{-n}\right]\left[1+\frac{\rho}{i'}\right]^{-1}$$

$$=\frac{1}{i'}\left[1-v'^n+n\rho v'^{n+1}-\frac{n(n+1)}{2}\rho^2v'^{n+2}+\ldots\right]\left[1-\frac{\rho}{i'}+\frac{\rho^2}{i'^2}-\ldots\right]$$

$$=a'-\frac{\rho}{i'}(a'-nv'^{n+1})+\frac{\rho^2}{i'^2}\left[a'-nv'^{n+1}-\frac{n(n+1)}{2}i'v'^{n+2}-\ldots\right]$$

Hence, as a first approximation,

$$\rho=i'\frac{a'-a}{a'-nv'^{n+1}} \quad \text{and} \quad i=i'+i'\frac{a'-a}{a'-nv'^{n+1}} \quad . \quad . \quad . \quad (8)$$

and, for a second approximation,

$$a=a'-\frac{\rho}{i'}(a'-nv'^{n+1})+\frac{\rho}{i'}(a'-a)\left[1-\frac{n(n+1)}{2}\cdot\frac{i'v'^{n+2}}{a'-nv'^{n+1}}\right]$$

whence
$$\rho=i'\frac{a'-a}{a-nv'^{n+1}+\dfrac{n(n+1)}{2}\cdot\dfrac{(a'-a)i'v'^{n+2}}{a'-nv'^{n+1}}}$$

and
$$i=i'+i'\frac{a'-a}{a-nv'^{n+1}+\dfrac{n(n+1)}{2}\cdot\dfrac{(a'-a)i'v'^{n+2}}{a'-nv'^{n+1}}} \quad . \quad . \quad . \quad (9)$$

Similarly, if the *amount* of the annuity were given as s, and the value of $s_{\overline{n}|}$ at rate i' were found to be s', a quantity differing only slightly from s, the resulting approximations would be

$$i=i'+i'\frac{s'-s}{s'-n(1+i')^{n-1}} \quad . \quad . \quad . \quad . \quad . \quad . \quad . \quad . \quad . \quad . \quad (10)$$

and
$$i=i'+i'\frac{s'-s}{s-n(1+i')^{n-1}-\dfrac{n(n-1)}{2}\cdot\dfrac{(s'-s)i'(1+i')^{n-2}}{s'-n(1+i')^{n-1}}} \quad . \quad . \quad (11)$$

Formulas (9) and (11) are not of any practical importance. If a more accurate approximation than that given by formula (8) or formula (10) were required, the best course to adopt would be to repeat the process by which those formulas were obtained. Thus, if the present value of the annuity were given, let $i'+i'\dfrac{a'-a}{a'-nv'^{n+1}}=i''$, and let $a_{\overline{n}|}$ at rate i'' be a''.

Then for a more accurate approximation,

$$i \doteq i''+i''\frac{a''-a}{a''-nv''^{n+1}} \quad . \quad . \quad . \quad . \quad . \quad . \quad (12)$$

To evaluate this expression it would merely be necessary to calculate the values a'' and v''^{n+1} by means of logarithms.

9. In order to test the formulas deduced in the last article, let $n=30$, and $a=20$—to take the same data as in Art. 5. On reference to Spitzer's Interest Tables, it will be found that $a_{\overline{30}|}=20{\cdot}24930$ at $2\frac{3}{4}$ per-cent, and 19·92097 at $2\frac{7}{8}$ per-cent. The latter value is the nearer to the given present value, and it will, therefore, be proper to assume that $i=\cdot02875+\rho$, where ρ will be a small negative quantity Also v^{31} at $2\frac{7}{8}$ per-cent$=\cdot4153313$.

$$\text{Formula (8) gives } i=\cdot02875-\frac{\cdot07903\times\cdot02875}{19{\cdot}92097-12{\cdot}45994}$$

$$=\cdot0284455$$

and, since v^{32} at $2\frac{7}{8}$ per-cent$=\cdot40372$

$$\text{Formula (9) gives } i=\cdot02875-\frac{\cdot07903\times\cdot02875}{20-12{\cdot}45994-\cdot05716}$$

$$=\cdot0284464$$

If ·0284455—the result given by the first approximation—be taken as a new trial rate, it will be found that $a_{\overline{30}|}$ at this rate$=20{\cdot}00035$, and $v^{31}=\cdot419160$. Hence, by formula (12),

$$i=\cdot0284455+\frac{\cdot00023\times\cdot0284455}{20{\cdot}000-12{\cdot}575}$$

$$=\cdot0284464.$$

The true value of i, correct to seven places of decimals, is ·0284464. It will be seen, therefore, that in the particular example under consideration either the second application of the first approximation or a single application of the second approximation gives the required rate accurately to the seventh place of decimals.

10. It may appear that a simpler method of dealing with the equation $a=\dfrac{1-(1+i'+\rho)^{-n}}{i'+\rho}$ would have been to multiply up by $i'+\rho$ before expanding. It may be shown, however, that this would not give so good an approximation. For, suppose that

$$\frac{1-(1+i'+\rho)^{-n}}{i'+\rho}=b_0+b_1\rho+b_2\rho^2+\ldots$$

then $$a(i'+\rho)=(b_0+b_1\rho+b_2\rho^2+\ldots)(i'+\rho)$$

or $$a=b_0+\rho\left(b_1+\frac{b_0-a}{i'}\right)+\frac{b_1}{i'}\rho^2+\left(1+\frac{\rho}{i'}\right)(b_2\rho^2+\ldots).$$

Hence the first approximation given by multiplying up by $i'+\rho$ and then expanding would be obtained by neglecting

$$\frac{b_1}{i'}\rho^2+\left(1+\frac{\rho}{i'}\right)(b_2\rho^2+\ldots)$$

whereas the approximation given by the method of Art. 8 is obtained by neglecting simply

$$b_2\rho^2+b_3\rho^3+\ldots\ldots$$

A comparison of these two expressions will indicate at once that the better approximation might be expected to be obtained by the method followed in Art. 8.

11. In the case of a loan repayable by instalments, the method may be applied in precisely the same way as in the case of the annuity. Let it be required to find the effective rate of interest realized on the purchase, at the price of A, of a loan redeemable by instalments of the total amount of C, and bearing an annual dividend at the rate g reckoned on C, let the successive instalments be C_1, C_2, C_3, &c., repayable certainly on the expiration of n_1, n_2, n_3, &c., years respectively; let i' be a rate (found by trial) which brings out a price not differing greatly from A, and let $i=i'+\rho$, where ρ is unknown; also, as in Art. 24 of Chapter V, let $K=C_1v^{n_1}+C_2v^{n_2}+\ldots.$ Then

$$A=K+\frac{g}{i}(C-K)$$

$$=[C_1(1+i'+\rho)^{-n_1}+\ldots]+\frac{g}{i'}\left[1+\frac{\rho}{i'}\right]^{-1}[C-C_1(1+i'+\rho)^{-n_1}-\ldots]$$

$$=[C_1v'^{n_1}-n_1\rho C_1v'^{n_1+1}+\ldots]+\frac{g}{i'}\left[1-\frac{\rho}{i'}\right][C-C_1v'^{n_1}+n_1\rho C_1v'^{n_1+1}\ldots]$$

$$+\text{terms involving higher powers of } \rho$$

$$=K'+\frac{g}{i'}[C-K']-\frac{\rho}{i'}\left[\frac{g}{i'}(C-K')+(i'-g)(n_1C_1v'^{n_1+1}+\ldots)\right]$$

$$+\text{terms involving higher powers of } \rho$$

$$=A'-\frac{\rho}{i'}[A'-K'+(i'-g)\Sigma n_1C_1v'^{n_1+1}]$$

$$+\text{terms involving higher powers of } \rho.$$

Hence, as a first approximation,

$$\rho=i'\frac{A'-A}{A'-K'+(i'-g)\Sigma n_1C_1v'^{n_1+1}}$$

and

$$i=i'+i'\frac{A'-A}{A'-K'+(i'-g)\Sigma n_1C_1v'^{n_1+1}}\quad . \quad . \quad . \quad . \quad (13)$$

where A′ and K′ respectively denote the value of the loan, and the value of the capital repayable, at the trial rate i'. As applied to a debenture repayable in one sum, the formula reduces to

$$i=i'+i'\frac{A'-A}{A'-K'+(i'-g)nCv'^{n+1}}\quad . \quad . \quad . \quad . \quad . \quad (14)$$

As an example of the use of this formula, let it be required to find, as in Art. 6, the approximate yield on a $4\frac{1}{2}$ per-cent debenture, redeemable in 25 years at $112\frac{1}{2}$, and bought just after payment of the half-yearly dividend at 120. If ·0175 be taken as a trial half-yearly yield, the values of the various quantities occurring in the formula will be as follows:

$$i'=\cdot 0175;\quad A'=112\tfrac{1}{2}v'^{50}+2\tfrac{1}{4}a'_{\overline{50}|}=121\cdot 821$$

$$A=120;\quad K'=112\tfrac{1}{2}v'^{50}=47\cdot 253$$

$$i'-g=\cdot 0175-\cdot 02=-\cdot 0025;\quad \text{and } nCv'^{n+1}=2322\cdot 0$$

Hence $$i=\cdot 0175+\cdot 0175\frac{1\cdot 821}{68\cdot 763}=\cdot 017963$$

This result differs by 5 only in the sixth place from the true value, and by repeating the process—·017963 being taken as a new trial rate—it would, of course, be easy to obtain a very much closer approximation.

12. If the trial rate i' be taken $=g$, then $A'=C$; $i'-g=0$; and formulas (13) and (14) reduce to the simple form

$$i=g+g\frac{C-A}{C-K'} \quad \ldots\ldots\ldots \quad (15)$$

where K′ is to be calculated at rate g. This is a very convenient formula for a first approximation, as it entails the calculation of only one quantity, namely, K′; but it has not, of course, the generality of formulas (13) and (14). The value of formulas (13) and (14) consists in the fact that they afford a means of obtaining an approximation to any desired degree of accuracy, since the rate obtained by any particular application of the formula may be used as a new trial rate for the purpose of obtaining a closer approximation.

Formula (15), applied to the case of the debenture taken as an example in the last preceding Article, gives

$$i=\cdot02-\cdot02\frac{7\cdot5}{112\cdot5-41\cdot797}$$

$$=\cdot02-\cdot002122=\cdot017878$$

which is not quite so good a result as that obtained, without the assistance of Interest Tables, by formula (5).

13. The method discussed in the last few articles may, of course, be applied, as indicated by the general investigation of Art. 7, to any description of annuity, or more generally to any series of payments.

Thus, in the case of an n-year annuity payable p times a year, and of the given present value of $a^{(p)}$, it may be easily shown that, as a first approximation,

$$i=i'+p[(1+i')^{\frac{1}{p}}-1]\frac{a'^{(p)}_{\overline{n}|}-a^{(p)}}{v'^{\frac{p-1}{p}}a'^{(p)}_{\overline{n}|}-nv'^{n+1}} \quad \ldots\ldots \quad (16)$$

and, again, in the case of an n-year annuity of the *second* order of the present value of a_2, that, as a first approximation,

$$i=i'+i'\frac{a'_{\overline{n}|\overline{2}|}-a_2}{a'_{\overline{n}|\overline{2}|}+\frac{1}{i'}(a'_{\overline{n}|}-nv'^{n+1})-n^2v'^{n+1}} \quad \ldots \quad (17)$$

Formula (16) is of no practical use, because, as has already been pointed out, the best course in the case of an annuity payable p times a year would be to determine the effective rate for $\frac{1}{p}$th of a year by formula (8), but it may serve as an instructive example in the application of the method.

14. It remains now to consider the third of the methods of approximation mentioned in Art. 3, namely, the method of approximation by interpolation between two or more trial rates giving nearly correct results. For the most general development of this method, the Calculus of Finite Differences is required. In practice, however, it is usual to employ what is technically called a *first-difference interpolation*—that is, to interpolate between two trial rates only. An interpolation of this nature—which alone will be considered here—rests merely upon the simple assumption that the differences between the values of an interest-function at various rates of interest are directly proportional to the differences in the corresponding rates. In the case of a function involving in its algebraical expression only the first power of the rate of interest this assumption is strictly correct. For example:—

The amount of 100	in a year	at	2	per-cent is	102
„	„	„	$2\frac{1}{2}$	„	102·5
„	„	„	$3\frac{1}{8}$	„	103·125
„	„	„	$4\frac{1}{2}$	„	104·5

and it will be seen, on inspection, that the difference between any of two of these amounts is directly proportional to the difference in the corresponding rates; for instance, the difference of ·625, between the amounts at $3\frac{1}{8}$ and $2\frac{1}{2}$ per-cent, bears the same ratio to the difference of 2·5 between the amounts at $4\frac{1}{2}$ and 2 per-cent as the difference between $3\frac{1}{8}$ and $2\frac{1}{2}$ per-cent bears to the difference between $4\frac{1}{2}$ and 2 per-cent. Hence, if it were required to find the rate i at which 100 would amount in a year to 102·9, and it were given that at 2 and $4\frac{1}{2}$ per-cent 100 would amount to 102 and 104·5 respectively, the result obtained by the first-difference interpolation formula,

$$\frac{i-\cdot 02}{\cdot 045-\cdot 02}=\frac{102\cdot 9-102}{104\cdot 5-102}$$

(which, on reduction, gives $i=\cdot 029$), would be strictly correct.

But most interest functions are of a much more complex character, and in such cases the assumption upon which the method of first difference interpolation rests is only approximately correct. In general, the smaller the differences between the trial rates and the true rate the more nearly accurate will be the resulting approximation; for example, if it were found that a given annuity-value fell between the values at $2\frac{1}{2}$ and $2\frac{5}{8}$ per-cent, a better result would be obtained by interpolating between these near rates than by interpolating between 2 and 3 per-cent. In general, also, an *inter*polation—that is, an approximation by reference to two trial rates of which one is greater and the other less than the true rate—will give a better result than an *exter*polation—that is, an approximation based upon two trial rates of which both are greater or both less than the true rate.

The application of the method of first-difference interpolation presents no analytical difficulties, but it will be convenient to deduce, as in the case of each of the two methods of approximation previously discussed, the formulas appropriate to the annuity and the redeemable security.

15. In the case of the annuity, suppose it to have been ascertained—by reference to tables or by actual trial—that the given present value a of an n-year annuity lies between a' and a'', the respective values of an n-year annuity at rates i' and i''. Then, on the assumption involved in the method of first-difference interpolation, it follows that, approximately,

$$\frac{i-i'}{i''-i'}=\frac{a-a'}{a''-a'}$$

whence

$$i=i'+\frac{a-a'}{a''-a'}(i''-i') \quad . \quad . \quad . \quad . \quad . \quad . \quad (18)$$

To test this formula, let $a=20$ and $n=30$, as before. On reference to the tables, it is found that $a_{\overline{30}|}=20{\cdot}24930$ at $2\frac{3}{4}$ per-cent and $19{\cdot}92097$ at $2\frac{7}{8}$ per-cent. Hence, by formula (18),

$$i={\cdot}0275+\frac{24930}{32833}\times{\cdot}00125={\cdot}0284491$$

which, it will be seen, differs only in the sixth place of decimals from the true value of i. A more accurate approximation might be readily obtained by calculating $a_{\overline{30}|}$ at the rate ·02845 and employing formula (18) to interpolate between this rate and ·02875.

16. In the case of a redeemable security, several different methods of interpolation may be followed.

(i) Let A′ and A″ be the present values of the security to pay i' and i'' respectively, these values being found by the formulas

$$A' = K' + \frac{g}{i'}(C - K') \quad \text{and} \quad A'' = K'' + \frac{g}{i''}(C - K'').$$

Then, A being the given present value of the security and i being the true yield which it is required to determine, it follows, as in the case of the annuity, that

$$i = i' + \frac{A - A'}{A'' - A'}(i'' - i') \text{ approximately} \quad . \quad . \quad . \quad (19)$$

If g—the rate of dividend (calculated on C) payable on the security—be taken as the second trial rate in place of i'', then, since A″ becomes $= C$ and $A' = K' + \frac{g}{i'}(C - K')$, formula (19) reduces to the form

$$i = i' + \frac{A - K' - \frac{g}{i'}(C - K')}{C - K' - \frac{g}{i'}(C - K')}(g - i')$$

$$= g + i'\frac{C - A}{C - K'} \quad . \quad . \quad . \quad . \quad . \quad . \quad . \quad . \quad . \quad . \quad . \quad (20)$$

a very simple and convenient approximate formula, involving the calculation of only one quantity, namely, K′, that is, the present value of the capital at rate i'.

The reciprocals of A, A′, and A″ may obviously be substituted for A, A′, and A″ in the foregoing argument. The interpolation between i' and i'' then gives

$$i = i' + \frac{\frac{1}{A} - \frac{1}{A'}}{\frac{1}{A''} - \frac{1}{A'}}(i'' - i') \text{ approximately} \quad . \quad . \quad . \quad (19)a$$

which reduces, if g be taken as the second trial rate in place of i'', to

$$i = g + i'\frac{\frac{C - A}{A}}{\frac{C - K'}{A'}} \quad . \quad . \quad . \quad . \quad . \quad . \quad . \quad . \quad . \quad (20)a$$

In the case of a security redeemable in n years at par and bought at a premium of k per unit, formulas (20) and (20)a become

$$i = g - \frac{k}{a'_{\overline{n}|}}$$

and
$$i = \frac{g - \dfrac{k}{s'_{\overline{n}|}}}{1+k}$$

respectively. The second expression gives the common rule for finding the yield on a redeemable security bought at a premium:—Deduct from the periodical dividend the sinking fund which would provide for the replacement of the premium at the date of redemption, and divide the remainder by the price. In the application of this rule the rate of interest employed in calculating the sinking fund should, of course, be a rate differing not greatly from the actual yield on the security.

(ii) By a simple transformation, the equation $A = K + \frac{g}{i}(C-K)$ may be written in the form $i = g\frac{C-K}{A-K}$. Hence, if it were possible to correctly guess the unknown rate i, the result of calculating K and inserting its value in the expression $g\frac{C-K}{A-K}$ (in which all the remaining quantities g, C, and A, are known), should be to exactly reproduce the rate employed in the calculation. Suppose now the value of $g\frac{C-K}{A-K}$ to be successively calculated at the trial rates i' and i'', and the respective results to be I' and I''. If the true unknown rate i had been employed, the result, as explained above, would have been i. Hence, by interpolation, an approximate value of i is given by the equation

$$\frac{i-i'}{i''-i'} = \frac{i-I'}{I''-I'}$$

whence
$$i = \frac{i'(I''-I') - I'(i''-i')}{I''-I'-i''+i'}$$

$$= \frac{i'I'' - I'i''}{I''-I'-i''+i'} \quad . \; . \; . \; . \; . \; . \; . \; . \; . \quad (21)$$

(iii) If the original equation be written in the form $g=i\frac{A-K}{C-K}$, another approximation to the value of i may be obtained by a precisely similar process to that followed in (ii)—that is, by calculating the values of $i'\frac{A-K'}{C-K'}$ and $i''\frac{A-K''}{C-K''}$ at the trial rates i' and i'' respectively, and interpolating between the results.

Suppose that i' gives as a result G',
and „ i'' „ „ G'',
The true rate i would give „ g.

Hence, approximately,

$$\frac{i-i'}{i''-i'}=\frac{g-G'}{G''-G'}$$

whence
$$i=\frac{i'G''-G'i''+g(i''-i')}{G''-G'} \quad . \quad . \quad . \quad . \quad . \quad (22)$$

17. To test the accuracy of the various approximations obtained in the preceding article, it will be useful to take, as before, the example of a $4\frac{1}{2}$ per-cent debenture, redeemable in 25 years at $112\frac{1}{2}$, and bought just after the payment of a half-yearly dividend for 120, so that $g=\cdot02$; $C=112\cdot5$; and $A=120$. If i' be taken as $\cdot0175$, and i'' as $\cdot01875$, then A'—already calculated in Art. 11— $=121\cdot821$; $A''=117\cdot037$; $K'=47\cdot253$; $K''=44\cdot440$;

$$I'=g\frac{C-K'}{A-K'}=\cdot02\times\frac{65\cdot247}{72\cdot747}=\cdot017938;$$

$$I''=g\frac{C-K''}{A-K''}=\cdot02\times\frac{68\cdot060}{75\cdot560}=\cdot018015;$$

$$G'=i'\frac{A-K'}{C-K'}=\cdot0175\times\frac{72\cdot747}{65\cdot247}=\cdot019512;$$

$$G''=i''\frac{A-K''}{C-K''}=\cdot01875\times\frac{75\cdot560}{68\cdot060}=\cdot020816;$$

Hence, formula (19) gives $i = \cdot 0175 + \dfrac{1 \cdot 821}{4 \cdot 784} \times \cdot 00125 = \cdot 017976$

" " (20) " $i = \cdot 02 - \cdot 0175 \times \dfrac{7 \cdot 5}{65 \cdot 247} = \cdot 017988$

" " (21) " $i = \dfrac{\cdot 000021075}{\cdot 001173} = \cdot 017967$

" " (22) " $i = \dfrac{\cdot 00002343}{\cdot 001304} = \cdot 017968$

It will be observed that in this case formula (22) gives the true value of i, but this is an accidental result of the fact that only a small number of places of decimals have been retained in the calculations. For most practical purposes any one of the formulas will give a sufficiently accurate result, but it will generally be advisable to *re-calculate* the value of the security at the rate obtained by the first approximation, whether with the object merely of checking the result, or in order to obtain a final and closer approximation by formula (20). In practice it will usually be found more convenient to work with the original equations from which the approximate formulas for i have been obtained than to use the formulas themselves. For example, the relation $\dfrac{i-i'}{i''-i'} = \dfrac{i-\mathrm{I}'}{\mathrm{I}''-\mathrm{I}'}$ is easier to remember than formula (21), inasmuch as it follows at once from the principle upon which the method is based; and it is also a better working formula, since it involves the *differences* instead of the *products* of the quantities, and consequently entails less arithmetic.

18. In the foregoing Articles the *methods* of approximation have been successively discussed, and the resulting formulas applicable to the annuity and the redeemable security have been deduced incidentally. For purposes of comparison it will be convenient to bring together in the following Table the formulas relating to the annuity and those relating to the redeemable security.

Approximate Formulas for the Rate of Interest.

ANNUITY				REDEEMABLE SECURITY			
Given n and a			*Example* $n=30$ $a=20$	Given C_1, C_2, &c., n_1, n_2, &c., g, and A			*Example* $C=112{\cdot}5$ $n=50$ $g={\cdot}02$ $A=120$
Method	Approximate Formula for i	No. of Formula	Approximate Value of i	Method	Approximate Formula for i	No. of Formula	Approximate Value of i
I	None of practical utility	...	...	I	(Applicable only to a Debenture redeemable in one sum) $\dfrac{g-\dfrac{k}{n}}{1+\dfrac{n+1}{2n}k}$ where $k=\dfrac{A-C}{C}$.	5	·018053
I	$i'+i'\dfrac{a'-a}{a'-nv'^{n+1}}$	8	·0284455	II	(a) $i'+i'\dfrac{A'-A}{A'-K'+(i'-g)\Sigma n_1 C_1 v'^{n_1+1}}$	14	·017963
	" (2nd application)	12	·0284464		(b) $g+g\dfrac{C-A}{C-K'}$	15	·017878
I	$i'+\dfrac{a-a'}{a''-a'}(i''-i')$	18	·0284491	III	(a) $i'+\dfrac{A-A'}{A''-A'}(i''-i')$	19	·017976
					(b) $g+i'\dfrac{C-A}{C-K'}$	20	·017988
					(c) $\dfrac{i'I''-I''i'}{I''-I'-i''-i'}$	21	·017967
					(d) $\dfrac{i'G''-i''G'+g(i''-i')}{G''-G'}$	22	·017968
ıe value of i to seven places			·0284464	True value of i to six places			·017968

NOTE.—Any of the approximate rates obtained by the formulas may be used as a new trial rate for the purpose of obtaining a more accurate approximation.

19. It will be convenient to conclude this chapter with a few illustrative examples:

(*a*) A debenture stock, redeemable at par on 1 October 1922, and bearing interest at 6 per-cent per annum, payable half-yearly on

1 April and 1 October, is quoted on 1 August 1900 at 117. What rate of interest does it yield?

The corresponding quotation on 1 October 1900, after payment of the half-year's interest then due, would obviously be about 115 (*i.e.*, 117 + two months' interest − 3). Hence, as a rough guide to the yield, formula (5) gives $i = \dfrac{3-\dfrac{15}{44}}{100+\dfrac{45}{88}\times 15} = \cdot 0247\ldots$ from which it appears that $2\frac{1}{2}$ and $2\frac{3}{8}$ per-cent would be suitable trial rates to employ for the purpose of obtaining a more accurate approximation.

Now the price of the stock per-cent on 1 August 1900 to yield the half-yearly effective rate i would be

$$v^{\frac{1}{3}}[100v^{44}+3(1+a_{\overline{44}|})]$$

and the values of this expression at $2\frac{1}{2}$ and $2\frac{3}{8}$ per-cent will be found to be 115·299 and 119·012 respectively. Hence, the approximate half-yearly yield $= \cdot 025 - \dfrac{1\cdot 701}{3\cdot 713}\times\cdot 00125 = \cdot 02443$. The required yield is therefore, approximately, £4. 17*s.* 9*d.* per-cent, convertible half-yearly.

In practice, it is usual to estimate the *ex interest* price as at the next following dividend date by simply deducting accrued dividend from the quotation, and to calculate the yield on the net price so obtained. Thus, in the case under consideration, the net price, after deduction of four months' accrued dividend, would be 115, which would give as at 1 October 1900 a yield of £4. 17*s.* 7*d.* per-cent, convertible half-yearly. By this method the proportion of the dividend from the date of purchase to the next following dividend date is allocated wholly to interest, instead of partly to interest and partly to reduction of principal, and, consequently, the yield for the remaining term of the investment is slightly reduced.

In the foregoing solution no allowance has been made for the fact that the whole of the dividend would be subject to income tax. This fact could, however, be taken into account by a very trifling modification of the work. For let the rate of tax be 1*s.* in the £. Then the price of the stock per-cent to yield the net half-yearly rate i *after deduction of tax* would be $v^{\frac{1}{3}}[100v^{44}+2\cdot 85(1+a_{\overline{44}|})]$, from which it will be found—by interpolation between $2\frac{3}{8}$ and $2\frac{1}{4}$ per-cent

—that $i = \cdot 02303$ approximately. The yield would therefore be approximately £4. 12*s.* 2*d.* per-cent, convertible half-yearly *net*, or £4. 17*s.* 0*d.* subject to tax. The adjustment for income tax consequently makes a difference of 9*d.* in this case in the yield.

(*b*). Given the values of $a_{\overline{n}|}$ at rates i' and i respectively, find approximately the yield on an annuity payable annually for n years and bought at a price to yield interest at rate i' on the *whole* purchase-money for the term of n years, and to admit of the replacement of principal by a sinking-fund invested at the lower rate i.

Let I be the required rate. Then to yield rate I the annual rent of the annuity for each unit invested $= \dfrac{1}{a_{\overline{n}|}} + i' - i$.

Also to yield the effective rate i' the annual rent per unit invested would be $\dfrac{1}{a'_{\overline{n}|}}$;

and to yield the effective rate i the annual rent per unit invested would be $\dfrac{1}{a_{\overline{n}|}}$.

Hence
$$\frac{\mathrm{I} - i}{i' - i} = \frac{\dfrac{1}{a_{\overline{n}|}} + i' - i - \dfrac{1}{a_{\overline{n}|}}}{\dfrac{1}{a'_{\overline{n}|}} - \dfrac{1}{a_{\overline{n}|}}}$$

whence
$$\mathrm{I} = i + \frac{(i' - i)^2}{\dfrac{1}{a'_{\overline{n}|}} - \dfrac{1}{a_{\overline{n}|}}} \quad \ldots\ldots\ldots \quad (23)$$

This is an example of *exterpolation*, for I must obviously be greater than either i or i'. In practice, if interest tables were available, it would be better to interpolate between the two rates of interest at which the ordinary 20-year annuity-values were respectively just greater and just less than the annuity-value on the special basis.

For example, let it be required to find the yield on a 20-year annuity bought to pay $3\frac{1}{2}$ per-cent for 20 years on the whole sum invested, and to admit of the replacement of principal by a $2\frac{1}{2}$ per-cent sinking-fund.

Since $\dfrac{1}{a_{\overline{20}|}}$ at $2\frac{1}{2}$ per-cent$= \cdot 064147$, and $\dfrac{1}{a_{\overline{20}|}}$ at $3\frac{1}{2}$ per-cent$= \cdot 070361$,

formula (23) gives $\quad \mathrm{I} = \cdot 025 + \dfrac{\cdot 0001}{\cdot 006214} = \cdot 04109.$

Now $a_{\overline{20}|}$ at $3\frac{1}{2}$ and $2\frac{1}{2}$ per-cent$=\dfrac{1}{\dfrac{1}{a_{\overline{20}|}}^{2\frac{1}{2}\%}+{\cdot}01}=13{\cdot}487$,

and on reference to Oakes's Interest Tables it appears that $a_{\overline{20}|}$ at 4 per-cent$=13{\cdot}590$, and $a_{\overline{20}|}$ at $4\frac{1}{8}$ per-cent$=13{\cdot}441$. Hence, by simple interpolation, the required yield$={\cdot}04087$ approximately.

(*c*). A Government Stock bearing interest at $3\frac{1}{2}$ per-cent payable half-yearly for eight years, at the end of which period holders will have the option of accepting repayment or of exchanging their holdings for equal amounts of an existing stock bearing interest at 3 per-cent payable half-yearly and redeemable at par 20 years from the present time, is quoted at 110 per-cent. A half-year's interest on each stock has just been paid. What should be the present quotation of the 3 per-cent stock to give the same yield as the $3\frac{1}{2}$ per-cent?

A present purchaser of the $3\frac{1}{2}$ per-cent stock would obviously realize less than 3 per-cent on his investment if he were to accept repayment at the end of eight years. Hence it must be assumed that the option to exchange will be exercised.

The first step is to determine the yield on the $3\frac{1}{2}$ per-cent stock, allowing for the option to exchange. Since the extra $\frac{1}{2}$ receivable for the first eight years would only suffice, if applied to write down principal, to write off 4 of the premium it is obvious that the yield is considerably under 3 per-cent. If $2\frac{1}{2}$ per-cent convertible half-yearly be taken as a trial rate, then

$100v^{40}$	at $1\frac{1}{4}$	per-cent	=	60·841
$1\frac{1}{2}a_{\overline{40}|}$	,,	,,	=	46·990
$\frac{1}{4}a_{\overline{16}|}$	,,	,,	=	3·605
Value of Stock to pay $1\frac{1}{4}$ per-cent half-yearly			=	111·436

Hence $1\frac{1}{4}$ per-cent proves to be less than the true yield. If now $1\frac{3}{8}$ per-cent be taken as a second trial rate, then

$100v^{40}$	at $1\frac{3}{8}$	per-cent	=	57·912
$1\frac{1}{2}a_{\overline{40}|}$	,,	,,	=	45·915
$\frac{1}{4}a_{\overline{16}|}$	,,	,,	=	3·569
Value of Stock to pay $1\frac{3}{8}$ per-cent half-yearly			=	107·396

Hence by interpolation, the half-yearly yield is approximately

$$\cdot 0125+\frac{1\cdot 436}{4\cdot 040}\times\cdot 00125=\cdot 012944\ldots$$

It only remains to calculate the value of the 3 per-cent Stock at this rate.

$100v^{40}$ at $1\cdot 2944\ldots$ per-cent $=$ (by logarithms) $59\cdot 784$

$$\therefore \text{Value of Stock per-cent} = 59\cdot 784+\frac{\cdot 015}{\cdot 012944\ldots}(100-59\cdot 784)$$

$$=106\cdot 4.$$

The 3 per-cent Stock should therefore be quoted at $106\frac{1}{2}$ approximately.

(*d*). A 5 per-cent loan was issued on 1 July 1895 at the price of 95 per-cent. Interest is payable half-yearly on 1 January and 1 July, and the principal is repayable at par in 20 equal instalments, by annual drawings commencing on 1 July 1901. Determine approximately (i) the rate of interest paid by the borrowers on the whole loan; (ii) the rate realized by an original subscriber on a bond drawn for repayment on 1 July 1901.

(i). In addition to paying $2\cdot 5$ half-yearly for each 95 borrowed —that is, $2\cdot 631\ldots$ per-cent half-yearly on the issue price—the borrowers have to pay a bonus of 5 on redemption, which (as the average term of the loan is 15 years) might be roughly equivalent to an additional $\frac{1}{8}$th per-cent interest half-yearly. Hence, $2\frac{3}{4}$ per-cent would appear to be a suitable half-yearly trial rate.

In terms of a half-yearly rate of interest,

$$K'=\cdot 025\left(a_{\overline{50}|}^{(\frac{1}{2})}-a_{\overline{10}|}^{(\frac{1}{2})}\right) \text{ per unit repayable}$$

$$=\cdot 025\times\frac{a_{\overline{50}|}-a_{\overline{10}|}}{1+\frac{i}{2}}$$

$$=\text{at } 2\tfrac{3}{4} \text{ per-cent } \frac{\cdot 458927}{1\cdot 01375} \text{ or } \cdot 45270.$$

Also $C=1$; $A=\cdot 95$; and $g=\cdot 025$. Hence, by formula (20),

$$i=\cdot 025+\cdot 0275\frac{\cdot 05}{\cdot 5473}$$

$$=\cdot 02751 \text{ approximately.}$$

In this case it turns out that the true yield is very close to the assumed rate. In fact, at $2\frac{3}{4}$ per-cent the value of the loan per unit, by the formula $A=K+\frac{g}{i}(C-K)$,

$$=\cdot 45270+\frac{\cdot 025}{\cdot 0275}\times\cdot 54730=\cdot 95025.$$

And the value to pay $2\frac{1}{2}$ per-cent half-yearly would clearly be unity. Hence, by interpolation, the half-yearly yield at the issue-price of $95=\cdot 0275+\dfrac{\cdot 00025}{\cdot 05}\times\cdot 0025$,

$$=\cdot 02751 \ldots \text{ as before.}$$

(ii). The rate realized on a bond drawn for repayment on 1 July 1901 may be approximately calculated by formula (5).

Here $g=\cdot 025$; $k=-\cdot 05$; $n=12$. Hence the half-yearly yield

$$=\frac{\frac{1}{40}+\frac{1}{240}}{1-\frac{13}{480}}=\cdot 03 \text{ very nearly.}$$

The true yield is, in fact, slightly over 3 per-cent half-yearly, for the value of the bond at the time of issue, to yield this rate, would have been $100v^{12}+2\frac{1}{2}a_{\overline{12}|}$ at 3 per-cent, which $=95\cdot 023$. The bond in this case being bought at a *discount*, formula (5) gives, as explained in Art. 6, rather too small a value for i.

(*e*). The Revenue Account of an assurance company shows that the fund increased from A at the beginning of the year to B at the end of the year, and that the net interest earnings (after deduction of income tax) were I. Find approximately (i) the effective rate of interest; (ii) the force of interest, earned on the fund in the year.

(i). In order to find the effective rate, it is usual to consider the interest earnings as received at the end of the year and the other income and the outgo as uniformly distributed over the year. On this basis the balance of other income (exclusive of interest earnings) and outgo, amounting to B−A−I, must be treated as received continuously throughout the year. Hence, if i be the required effective rate,

$$A(1+i)+(B-A-I)\bar{s}_{\overline{1}|}=B.$$

Now, $$\bar{s}_{\overline{1}|} = \frac{i}{\log_e(1+i)} = \frac{1}{1-\frac{i}{2}+\frac{i^2}{3}-\ldots} = 1+\frac{i}{2}-\frac{i^2}{12}\ldots$$

$$\therefore \quad A(1+i)+(B-A-I)\left(1+\frac{i}{2}-\frac{i^2}{12}\ldots\right)=B,$$

whence (if powers of i above the first be neglected),

$$i=\frac{2I}{A+B-I} \text{ approximately.}$$

(ii). The force of interest, *i.e.*, the nominal rate of interest convertible momently, is measured by the ratio of the interest received during an indefinitely short interval to the principal bearing interest during that interval. Its value will vary slightly from moment to moment, but, on the assumption that income (including interest earnings) and outgo are uniformly distributed over the year, its *average* value may be taken to be the ratio of the interest earnings to the mean fund. Hence, if δ be the required force of interest,

$$\delta=\frac{2I}{A+B} \text{ approximately.}$$

It is easy to show that these values of i and δ approximately correspond. For

$$i=\frac{2I}{A+B-I}=\frac{2I}{A+B}\left(1-\frac{I}{A+B}\right)^{-1}$$

$$=\frac{2I}{A+B}+\frac{2I^2}{(A+B)^2}+\ldots$$

$$=\delta+\frac{\delta^2}{2!}+\ldots$$

which, to the second power, is the correct relation between the effective rate of interest and the corresponding force.

(*f*). Consols are bought on 16 June 1900 at $101\frac{5}{8}$. What rate of interest do they yield?

As there is a reduction in the rate of dividend on this security after 5 April 1903, it will be best to proceed by the method of Art. 16.

Let i be the quarterly rate of interest realized by a purchaser. Then since the period elapsed since the last dividend-date is 72 days, the algebraical expression for the value of the stock per-cent on 16 June 1900, will be

$$(1+i)^{\frac{72}{91}}\left[\tfrac{5}{8}a_{\overline{92}|}+\tfrac{1}{16}a_{\overline{12}|}+100v^{92}\right].$$

If $2\frac{1}{2}$ per-cent convertible quarterly be taken as one trial rate, the value of this expression will be $1{\cdot}00625^{\frac{72}{91}}\times 100{\cdot}720=101{\cdot}218$. If 2 per-cent convertible quarterly be taken as a second trial rate, the value of the expression becomes $1{\cdot}005^{\frac{72}{91}}\times 109{\cdot}926=110{\cdot}361$. Hence by formula (19) the approximate quarterly yield $={\cdot}00625-\dfrac{{\cdot}407}{9{\cdot}143}\times{\cdot}00125={\cdot}006194\ldots$, representing an effective yield of just over $2\frac{1}{2}$ per-cent.

(*g*). A Foreign Railway Loan, originally for £2,000,000, bearing interest at 5 per-cent, payable half-yearly on 1 January and 1 July, and redeemable at 105 per-cent by half-yearly drawings (for repayment on 1 January and 1 July) by the operation of an accumulative sinking-fund—£65,000 being applied half-yearly to the service of the loan—is quoted $11\frac{1}{2}$ years after issue at 95 *ex interest*. What rate of interest would the investment yield to a syndicate acquiring the whole of the outstanding bonds.

The investment practically amounts to the purchase of an annuity of £130,000 per annum, payable half-yearly for the remaining term of the loan, at a price equal to 95 per-cent of the nominal amount of the outstanding bonds. Hence it will be necessary in the first instance to find (i) the term which the loan has still to run; (ii) the amount of the outstanding bonds.

Let n be the number of half-years comprised in the original term of the loan—from the date of issue to the date of redemption of the last bond.

Then, since the loan was virtually a loan of £2,100,000, repayable with interest at the rate of $\dfrac{5}{1{\cdot}05}$ per-cent per annum convertible half-yearly, by an annuity of £130,000 per annum, payable half-yearly, it follows that

$$6{\cdot}5\,a_{\overline{n}|}=210,$$

where $a_{\overline{n}|}$ is to be calculated at $\dfrac{2{\cdot}5}{1{\cdot}05}$ per-cent,

whence $$n=\frac{\log 13-\log 3}{\log 43-\log 42}=\frac{{\cdot}6368221}{{\cdot}0102192}=62{\cdot}316.$$

At the date of valuation, therefore, the loan has 39·316 half-years still to run, and the nominal amount of the outstanding bonds is $\frac{1}{1\cdot05} \times 65{,}000 a_{\overline{39\cdot316}|}$ at $\frac{2\cdot5}{1\cdot05}$ per-cent, or 1,569,149, the value of which, at 95 per-cent would be 1,490,692. Hence, the question resolves itself into finding the rate of interest at which $a_{\overline{39\cdot316}|} = \frac{1{,}490{,}692}{65{,}000}$ or 22·934. By reference to a table of the values of $a_{\overline{n}|}$, it will be found that the required rate is very nearly ·03. Hence, the investment would yield, approximately, 6 per-cent convertible half-yearly.

In practice the redemption-schedule would be so adjusted as to provide for the repayment of an exact integral number of bonds at the end of each half-year and for the repayment of the whole of the then outstanding bonds at the end of the 31st year, but this would not materially affect the yield.

CHAPTER VII.

CAPITAL REDEMPTION ASSURANCES.

1. It has been shown in previous chapters that the capital invested in any series of payments may be replaced by means of a sinking-fund. More generally, a sum required at the end of any number of years, whether to replace invested capital or for any other purpose, may be secured, in theory, by the accumulation of an annual sinking-fund of $\frac{1}{s_{\overline{n|}}}$ per unit, where n is the number of years in question. In practice, however, an isolated transaction of this nature presents certain difficulties; it may be found impracticable to invest the requisite sinking-fund and the periodical interest-earnings with the necessary regularity—in fact, this difficulty would almost invariably arise in the case of a sinking-fund of small amount—and, owing to the fluctuations in the rate of interest obtainable upon investments, the accumulation of a fixed periodical sinking-fund will not, as a rule, produce the exact sum required. Consequently, many insurance companies have, of late years, made it part of their business to grant assurances securing the payment of a fixed sum at the expiration of a fixed term of years. These assurances were originally intended to meet the requirements of investors in leasehold properties, and were accordingly called *Leasehold Redemption Assurances*, but they have since been utilized for many other financial purposes—to provide, for example, for the repayment of the principal of a loan or for the redemption of a debenture-issue—and have acquired the alternative names of *Sinking-Fund Assurances* and CAPITAL REDEMPTION ASSURANCES.

2. The consideration for a Capital Redemption Assurance—that is the price paid to the assurance company in consideration of its granting the assurance—usually takes the form of a single payment made at the inception of the assurance, or of a series of uniform periodical payments made at equal intervals throughout the term of the assurance, the first such payment being made at the inception of the assurance and the last at the beginning of the concluding interval in the term. The single payment and the uniform periodical payment are called respectively a *Single Premium*, and an *Annual*, *Half-yearly*, or *Quarterly Premium*, as the case may be. It will be observed that the periodical premium is of precisely the same nature as a sinking-fund, but that it differs from it in being paid at the beginning of each interval, or, in other words, *in advance*, instead of at the *end* of each interval. In fact, the payments of the periodical premium for a Capital Redemption Assurance form an *annuity-due*, whereas the successive sinking-fund contributions form an ordinary annuity.

3. The net Single Premium for a Capital Redemption Assurance of 1, payable at the end of n years—that is, the Single Premium which, if accumulated at the assumed rate of interest, without any deduction for expenses or for the profit of the insurers, would amount to 1 at the end of n years—is denoted by the symbol $A_{\overline{n}|}$. The net periodical premium for a similar assurance is denoted by the symbols $P_{\overline{n}|}$, $P^{(2)}_{\overline{n}|}$, $P^{(4)}_{\overline{n}|}$, &c., according as it is payable yearly, half-yearly, quarterly or with any other frequency.

4. The net Single Premium for a Capital Redemption Assurance has been defined to be such a sum as would accumulate to the sum assured by the end of the given term; hence, it follows that, on the basis of a single uniform rate of interest i,

$$A_{\overline{n}|}\times(1+i)^n=1$$

whence
$$A_{\overline{n}|}=v^n \quad \ldots\ldots\ldots \quad (1)$$

On the same basis,

$$P_{\overline{n}|}[(1+i)^n+(1+i)^{n-1}+\ldots(1+i)]=1$$

whence
$$P_{\overline{n}|}=\frac{1}{s_{\overline{n+1}|}-1} \quad \ldots\ldots\ldots \quad (2)$$

Alternative expressions for $P_{\overline{n}|}$ may be obtained as follows:

(i) The net annual premium must clearly be the equivalent, in the form of an annuity-due, of the net single premium; hence it follows that

$$P_{\overline{n}|}\times \mathbf{a}_{\overline{n}|}=A_{\overline{n}|}$$

whence
$$P_{\overline{n}|}=\frac{v^n}{\mathbf{a}_{\overline{n}|}} \quad \ldots\ldots\ldots \quad (3)$$

(ii) Again, the annual rent obtained by the investment of a unit in the purchase of an annuity-due, payable annually for n years, must be equal to interest in advance on the unit, together with a sum sufficient, if accumulated throughout the term of the annuity, to replace the unit at the end of the term. But the interest in advance on 1 is d; and the sum paid annually in advance which will, if duly accumulated, produce 1 at the end of n years is $P_{\overline{n}|}$.

Hence $$\frac{1}{\mathbf{a}_{\overline{n}|}} = d + P_{\overline{n}|}$$

whence $$P_{\overline{n}|} = \frac{1}{\mathbf{a}_{\overline{n}|}} - d \text{ or } \frac{1}{1+a_{\overline{n-1}|}} - d \quad . \quad . \quad . \quad . \quad (4)$$

It may be easily shown that formulas (2), (3), and (4) are algebraically identical. For

$$\frac{1}{s_{\overline{n+1}|}-1} = \frac{1}{(1+i)s_{\overline{n}|}} = \frac{v^n}{(1+i)a_{\overline{n}|}}$$
$$= \frac{v^n}{\mathbf{a}_{\overline{n}|}} = \frac{1-ia_{\overline{n}|}}{\mathbf{a}_{\overline{n}|}} = \frac{1}{\mathbf{a}_{\overline{n}|}} - d$$

5. From the form of the expression obtained in formula (4), it appears that the numerical value of $P_{\overline{n}|}$ for given values of n and i may be found by entering an Annual Premium Conversion Table with the value of $a_{\overline{n-1}|}$. The subject of Conversion Tables is fully discussed in Chapter VIII of the Text-Book, Part II, and it will be sufficient to state here that Annual Premium Conversion Tables are tables giving at various rates of interest the values of $\frac{1}{1+X} - d$ for values of X proceeding by small equal differences throughout the range of practicable annuity-values. Hence, if the table based on the rate of interest i be entered with the value of $a_{\overline{n-1}|}$ at that rate, the result will be

$$\frac{1}{1+a_{\overline{n-1}|}} - d, \text{ or } P_{\overline{n}|}.$$

Let it be required, for example, to find the value of $P_{\overline{20}|}$ at 3 per-cent. The value of $a_{\overline{19}|}$ at 3 per-cent is, to three places of decimals, 14·324, and the tabulated value corresponding to 14·324 in the 3 per-cent Annual Premium Conversion Table is ·03613. Hence $P_{\overline{20}|}$ at 3 per-cent = ·03613. Of course, this result might also have been obtained by taking the reciprocal of $(s_{\overline{21}|}-1)$ or 27·676.

6. The values of $P^{(2)}_{\overline{n|}}$, $P^{(4)}_{\overline{n|}}$, &c., may be readily obtained by any of the methods employed in finding an expression for $P_{\overline{n|}}$. In general,

$$P^{(m)}_{\overline{n|}} = \frac{1}{\frac{1}{m}(1+i)^n + s^{(m)}_{\overline{n|}} - \frac{1}{m}} = \frac{v^n}{a^{(m)}_{\overline{n|}}}$$

$$= \frac{1}{a^{(m)}_{\overline{n|}}} - m(1-v^{\frac{1}{m}}) \quad . \quad . \quad . \quad . \quad . \quad . \quad . \quad . \quad (5)$$

The third expression is given for purposes of comparison with the corresponding expression for $P_{\overline{n|}}$, but from its form it will be seen that the Annual Premium Conversion Table affords no facilities for the evaluation of $P^{(m)}_{\overline{n|}}$.

In the special case in which m is made infinite $P^{(m)}_{\overline{n|}}$ becomes the premium per annum payable continuously, by infinitely small instalments, for an assurance of 1 payable at the end of n years, and is denoted by the special symbol $\overline{P}_{\overline{n|}}$.

Formula (5) then becomes

$$\overline{P}_{\overline{n|}} = \frac{1}{\bar{s}_{\overline{n|}}} = \frac{v^n}{\bar{a}_{\overline{n|}}} = \frac{1}{\bar{a}_{\overline{n|}}} - \delta \quad . \quad . \quad . \quad . \quad . \quad (6)$$

The numerical value of $\overline{P}_{\overline{n|}}$ may be found by entering with $\bar{a}_{\overline{n|}}$ an Annual Premium Conversion Table constructed on a *continuous* basis (that is, a table in which X is the argument and $\frac{1}{X} - \delta$ the result).

7. It will be seen that the sole difference between the net annual premium for a Capital Redemption Assurance and the net premium per annum payable at more frequent intervals consists in the fact that the former is payable in one sum at the beginning of the year, while the latter is payable by instalments spread over the year. The second method of payment entails a loss of interest to the assurer as compared with the first, and consequently necessitates a corresponding increase in the premium per annum payable at more frequent intervals as compared with the annual premium. In the case of a premium payable m times a year, the loss of interest, valued at the beginning of the year, is

$$\frac{1}{m} P^{(m)}_{\overline{n|}} [(1-v^{\frac{1}{m}}) + (1-v^{\frac{2}{m}}) + \ldots + (1-v^{\frac{m-1}{m}})]$$

$$= P^{(m)}_{\overline{n|}} (1 - a^{(m)}_{\overline{1|}})$$

Hence, it follows that

$$P_{\overline{n}|}^{(m)} = P_{\overline{n}|} + P_{\overline{n}|}^{(m)}(1 - a_{\overline{1}|}^{(m)})$$

whence

$$P_{\overline{n}|}^{(m)} = \frac{P_{\overline{n}|}}{a_{\overline{1}|}^{(m)}} = P_{\overline{n}|} \cdot \frac{j_{(m)}}{d\left(1 + \frac{j_{(m)}}{m}\right)}$$

This relation may be readily obtained from formula (5). For, since

$$a_{\overline{n}|}^{(m)} = a_{\overline{n}|} \cdot a_{\overline{1}|}^{(m)}$$

it follows that

$$P_{\overline{n}|}^{(m)} = \frac{v^n}{a_{\overline{n}|}} \cdot \frac{1}{a_{\overline{1}|}^{(m)}} = P_{\overline{n}|} \frac{j_{(m)}}{d\left(1 + \frac{j_{(m)}}{m}\right)}$$

As a special case,

$$\bar{P}_{\overline{n}|} = P_{\overline{n}|} \frac{\delta}{d}.$$

8. At the expiration of the term of a Capital Redemption Policy, the net premiums paid in respect of the Policy, accumulated at the rate of interest assumed in the calculation of the premium, will amount, by definition, to the sum assured. Further, at any given time during the currency of the Policy, the net premiums paid up to that time will clearly amount to such a sum as will suffice, with the remaining premiums and interest, to provide the sum assured on the expiration of the term of the Policy. This sum is called the *Value of the Policy*, or the *Policy-Value*. It will be seen, therefore, that the Value of a Capital Redemption Policy, at any time during its currency, may be determined in two ways, namely, either (i) by a *retrospective* process, as the accumulated amount of the net premiums paid, or (ii) by a *prospective* process, as the difference between the discounted value of the sum assured and the discounted value of the remaining net premiums. These two methods of determining the Policy-Value must obviously produce identical results.

9. The Value, at the end of t years, of a Capital Redemption Policy assuring 1 at the expiration of n years, at a net annual premium of $P_{\overline{n}|}$, is denoted by the symbol ${}_tV_{\overline{n}|}$; the value, after t years, of a similar policy, at a net premium of $P_{\overline{n}|}^{(m)}$ per annum payable m times a year, is denoted by the symbol ${}_tV_{\overline{n}|}^{(m)}$.

It will be convenient to consider separately the two cases in which t is (i) integral, and (ii) partly integral and partly fractional—the first case being that of a policy which has been an exact number of years in force, and the second that of a policy which has been in force an integral number of years and a fraction of a year.

(i) Let t be integral. In this case it will be proper to assume that t years' premiums have been paid and that the next premium is about to fall due.

Considered *retrospectively* the policy-value may be regarded, as already explained, as the accumulated amount of the net premiums paid. From this point of view, therefore,

$$_tV_{\overline{n}|}=P_{\overline{n}|}(s_{\overline{t+1}|}-1)=\frac{s_{\overline{t+1}|}-1}{s_{\overline{n+1}|}-1}=\frac{s_{\overline{t}|}}{s_{\overline{n}|}} \quad . \quad . \quad . \quad . \quad (7)$$

Considered *prospectively* the policy-value is such a sum as will, with the remaining premiums and interest, suffice to provide the sum assured at the expiration of the term of the policy; that is to say, it is the present value of the sum assured *less* the present value of the remaining premiums. Hence, from this point of view,

$$_tV_{\overline{n}|}=v^{n-t}-P_{\overline{n}|}\,\mathrm{a}_{\overline{n-t}|}$$

Now
$$v^{n-t}=1-ia_{\overline{n-t}|}=1-d\,\mathrm{a}_{\overline{n-t}|}$$

$$\therefore \quad _tV_{\overline{n}|}=1-(P_{\overline{n}|}+d)\mathrm{a}_{\overline{n-t}|}$$

And by formula (4),
$$P_{\overline{n}|}+d=\frac{1}{\mathrm{a}_{\overline{n}|}}$$

$$\therefore \quad _tV_{\overline{n}|}=1-\frac{\mathrm{a}_{\overline{n-t}|}}{\mathrm{a}_{\overline{n}|}} \quad . \quad . \quad . \quad . \quad . \quad . \quad . \quad . \quad . \quad . \quad (8)$$

From this expression the algebraical identity of the formulas obtained by the retrospective and prospective methods may be readily established. For

$$1-\frac{\mathrm{a}_{\overline{n-t}|}}{\mathrm{a}_{\overline{n}|}}=\frac{\mathrm{a}_{\overline{n}|}-\mathrm{a}_{\overline{n-t}|}}{\mathrm{a}_{\overline{n}|}}=\frac{v^{n-t}\mathrm{a}_{\overline{t}|}}{\mathrm{a}_{\overline{n}|}}=\frac{s_{\overline{t}|}}{s_{\overline{n}|}}\,.$$

In the case of a policy subject to a premium payable m times a year, each year's premium is the exact equivalent, after allowance for loss of interest, of the annual premium for a similar policy. Hence it follows that the policy-value at the end of any integral number of years will be the same as that of a similar policy subject to annual premiums. This result may be readily established by algebra. For

$$ {}_{t}V^{(m)}_{\overline{n}|} = P^{(m)}_{\overline{n}|}.(1+i)^{\frac{1}{m}}s^{(m)}_{\overline{t}|} $$

$$ = \frac{(1+i)^{\frac{1}{m}}s^{(m)}_{\overline{t}|}}{(1+i)^{\frac{1}{m}}s^{(m)}_{\overline{n}|}} = \frac{s^{(m)}_{\overline{t}|}}{s^{(m)}_{\overline{n}|}} = \frac{s_{\overline{t}|}}{s_{\overline{n}|}} = {}_{t}V_{\overline{n}|}. $$

(ii). Let t be partly integral and partly fractional. In this case $(r+1)$ premiums will have been paid on a policy subject to annual premiums, where r is the greatest integer in t, while r premiums and one or more instalments of an additional full year's premium will have been paid on a policy subject to premiums payable m times a year.

Take first the case of a policy subject to annual premiums, and let $t=r+\frac{1}{p}$. Then by the retrospective method

$$ {}_{r+\frac{1}{p}}V_{\overline{n}|} = P_{\overline{n}|}s_{\overline{r+1}|}(1+i)^{\frac{1}{p}} = (1+i)^{\frac{1}{p}}({}_{r}V_{\overline{n}|} + P_{\overline{n}|}) $$

$$ = v^{1-\frac{1}{p}}{}_{r+1}V_{\overline{n}|} \quad . \quad . \quad . \quad . \quad . \quad . \quad . \quad . \quad . \quad . \quad . \quad . \quad (9) $$

and by the prospective method

$$ {}_{r+\frac{1}{p}}V_{\overline{n}|} = v^{n-r-\frac{1}{p}} - v^{1-\frac{1}{p}}P_{\overline{n}|}\mathbf{a}_{\overline{n-r-1}|} $$

$$ = v^{1-\frac{1}{p}}[v^{n-r-1} - P_{\overline{n}|}\mathbf{a}_{\overline{n-r-1}|}] $$

$$ = v^{1-\frac{1}{p}}{}_{r+1}V_{\overline{n}|} \text{ as before.} $$

In the case of a policy subject to a premium payable m times a year, let $t=r+\frac{l}{m}+\frac{1}{qm}$. There will then have been paid on the policy r full years' premiums and $(l+1)$ instalments of an additional year's premium. Hence

$$ {}_{r+\frac{l}{m}+\frac{1}{qm}}V^{(m)}_{\overline{n}|} = (1+i)^{\frac{1}{qm}}P^{(m)}_{\overline{n}|}s^{(m)}_{\overline{r+\frac{l+1}{m}}|} $$

$$ = (1+i)^{\frac{1}{qm}}P^{(m)}_{\overline{n}|}v^{1-\frac{l+1}{m}}(s^{(m)}_{\overline{r+1}|} - s^{(m)}_{\overline{1-\frac{l+1}{m}}|}) $$

$$ = v^{1-\frac{l}{m}-\frac{1}{qm}}{}_{r+1}V_{\overline{n}|} - (1+i)^{\frac{1}{qm}}P^{(m)}_{\overline{n}|}a^{(m)}_{\overline{1-\frac{l+1}{m}}|} $$

$$ = {}_{r+\frac{l}{m}+\frac{1}{qm}}V_{\overline{n}|} - (1+i)^{\frac{1}{qm}}P^{(m)}_{\overline{n}|}a^{(m)}_{\overline{1-\frac{l+1}{m}}|} \quad . \quad . \quad . \quad (10) $$

This relation shows that at the end of any fractional period the value of a Capital Redemption Policy, subject to premiums payable m times a year, falls short of the value of a similar policy at annual premiums by the value of the unpaid portion of the full year's premium —a result which might have been deduced from the consideration that at the end of the year the two policies have the same value.

If $\frac{1}{q}$ be put=0 in formula (10) the resulting expression gives the policy-value *just after* payment of the $(l+1)$th instalment of the full year's premium, and in order to obtain the value *just before* payment of that instalment—that is, at the end of $r+\frac{l}{m}$ years—it would be necessary to deduct $\frac{1}{m}P^{(m)}_{\overline{n}|}$. The required result may, however, be more simply obtained by putting $q=1$, whence

$$_{r+\frac{l+1}{m}}V^{(m)}_{\overline{n}|} = {}_{r+\frac{l+1}{m}}V_{\overline{n}|} - P^{(m)}_{\overline{n}|}\,a^{(m)}_{\overline{1-\frac{l+1}{m}}|}$$

and, by writing $(l-1)$ for l,

$$_{r+\frac{l}{m}}V^{(m)}_{\overline{n}|} = {}_{r+\frac{l}{m}}V_{\overline{n}|} - P^{(m)}_{\overline{n}|}\,a^{(m)}_{\overline{1-\frac{l}{m}}|} \quad . \quad . \quad . \quad . \quad . \quad . \quad . \quad (11)$$

Thus the value of a policy subject to a half-yearly premium, just before payment of the second half-year's premium, is given by the formula

$$_{r+\frac{1}{2}}V^{(2)}_{\overline{n}|} = {}_{r+\frac{1}{2}}V_{\overline{n}|} - \tfrac{1}{2}P^{(2)}_{\overline{n}|}.$$

From the foregoing analysis it appears that Capital Redemption Policies subject to premiums payable at half-yearly or shorter intervals may be valued, with approximate accuracy, as policies at annual premiums subject to deduction of the unpaid instalments (if any) of the current year's premium.

10. Since $P_{\overline{n}|} = \frac{1}{(1+i)s_{\overline{n}|}}$ and $s_{\overline{n}|} = (1+i)^{n-1} + (1+i)^{n-2} + \ldots + 1$, it is clear that the lower the rate of interest assumed in the calculation of the premium, the larger will be the premium. On the other hand, the lower the rate of interest employed in accumulating the premiums, the smaller will be their accumulated amount. A decrease in the assumed rate of interest affects the policy-value, therefore, in two opposite ways, and the question arises whether the net result is to increase or decrease the value.

Since ${}_1V_{\overline{n}|}=(1+i)P_{\overline{n}|}=\dfrac{1}{s_{\overline{n}|}}$, it is evident that a decrease in the rate of interest *increases* the value of a policy of one year's duration, provided n be >1.

Now

$$1-{}_tV_{\overline{n}|}=\frac{\mathbf{a}_{\overline{n-t}|}}{\mathbf{a}_{\overline{n}|}}$$

$$=\frac{\mathbf{a}_{\overline{n-1}|}}{\mathbf{a}_{\overline{n}|}}\cdot\frac{\mathbf{a}_{\overline{n-2}|}}{\mathbf{a}_{\overline{n-1}|}}\cdot\ldots\cdot\frac{\mathbf{a}_{\overline{n-t}|}}{\mathbf{a}_{\overline{n-t+1}|}}$$

$$=(1-{}_1V_{\overline{n}|})(1-{}_1V_{\overline{n-1}|})\ldots(1-{}_1V_{\overline{n-t+1}|})$$

and since ${}_1V_{\overline{n}|}$, ${}_1V_{\overline{n-1}|}$, &c., being the values of policies of one year's duration, are all *increased* by a decrease in the rate of interest, it follows that $1-{}_tV_{\overline{n}|}$ is decreased, and, therefore, that ${}_tV_{\overline{n}|}$ is increased. Hence, the lower the assumed rate of interest the greater will be the policy-value.

11. The net annual premium for a Capital Redemption Assurance of 1, payable at the expiration of $n-t$ years, is $P_{\overline{n-t}|}$. Hence, when an n-year policy for 1, at a net annual premium of $P_{\overline{n}|}$, has been t years in force, the remaining $(n-t)$ premiums of $P_{\overline{n}|}$ would assure the sum of $\dfrac{P_{\overline{n}|}}{P_{\overline{n-t}|}}$, and the accumulations of the t premiums already paid must be sufficient to secure the balance of the sum assured, namely, $1-\dfrac{P_{\overline{n}|}}{P_{\overline{n-t}|}}$. It follows, therefore, that at the end of t years an n-year policy for 1 could be converted into a *Free* or *Paid-up Policy* (that is, a policy free from any further payments of premium) for $1-\dfrac{P_{\overline{n}|}}{P_{\overline{n-t}|}}$. The Paid-up equivalent of an n-year Capital Redemption Policy at the end of t years is denoted by the symbol ${}_tW(A_{\overline{n}|})$.

Hence, in the case of an n-year Capital Redemption Policy for 1, subject to an annual premium of $P_{\overline{n}|}$, which has been t years in force

$${}_tW(A_{\overline{n}|})=1-\frac{P_{\overline{n}|}}{P_{\overline{n-t}|}}=1-\frac{s_{\overline{n-t}|}}{s_{\overline{n}|}}$$

$$=\frac{(1+i)^{n-t}s_{\overline{t}|}}{s_{\overline{n}|}}=\frac{a_{\overline{t}|}}{a_{\overline{n}|}}\quad\ldots\ldots\quad(12)$$

Also, since $$\frac{s_{\overline{t}|}}{s_{\overline{n}|}} = {}_t\text{V}_{\overline{n}|}$$

$${}_t\text{W}(\text{A}_{\overline{n}|}) = \frac{{}_t\text{V}_{\overline{n}|}}{v^{n-t}} = \frac{{}_t\text{V}_{\overline{n}|}}{\text{A}_{\overline{n-t}|}}$$

This result shows that, as must clearly be the case, the amount of the Paid-up Policy is the sum which the policy-value, if applied as a single premium, would assure at the expiration of the term of the original policy.

In practice, a Capital Redemption Policy may usually be converted into a Paid-up Policy for an amount bearing the same proportion to the full sum assured as the number of premiums paid bears to the total number payable.

On this basis, an n-year policy for 1 would be convertible at the end of t years into a paid-up policy for $\frac{t}{n}$. This amount is less than the theoretical paid-up equivalent; for, since the Arithmetical Mean of the n quantities $v, v^2, \ldots v^n$, is obviously less—n being $>t$—than that of the t quantities $v, v^2 \ldots v^t$, it follows that $\frac{a_{\overline{n}|}}{n}$ is $< \frac{a_{\overline{t}|}}{t}$, and therefore that $\frac{a_{\overline{t}|}}{a_{\overline{n}|}}$ is $> \frac{t}{n}$ or that ${}_t\text{W}(\text{A}_{\overline{n}|})$ is $> \frac{t}{n}$.

12. Of the numerous practical questions that arise in connection with Capital Redemption Assurances the following may be taken as examples:

(i) A Capital Redemption Policy for a term of 40 years, subject to an annual premium at the rate of £1. 8*s*. per-cent, is offered for sale just before the 11th annual premium falls due. What would be its value as an investment to pay 4 per-cent interest, and how would the value be affected (*a*) if the policy were convertible, at the option of the holder, into a Paid-up Policy for a reduced amount bearing the same proportion to the full sum assured as the number of premiums paid bears to the total number originally payable, (*b*) if it carried a guaranteed surrender-value of 95 per-cent of the premiums paid accumulated at 2 per-cent compound interest?

If the policy be regarded simply as a contract securing the payment of the sum assured at the expiration of the original term of 40 years in consideration of the due payment of the annual premium, its investment-value at the end of 10 years to pay 4 per-cent, would be the present value of the sum assured at 4 per-cent interest *less* the present value of the future premiums at the same rate. Hence, on this basis the required value per 100 assured$=100v^{30}-1{\cdot}4\mathbf{a}_{\overline{30}|}$ at 4 per-cent $=30{\cdot}832-25{\cdot}177=5{\cdot}655$.

Consider now the effect of assumptions (*a*) and (*b*):

On assumption (*a*) the Policy could be converted into a Paid-up Policy of 25 per 100 originally assured, and the value of this reduced Policy at 4 per-cent would be $25v^{30}$ which$=7{\cdot}708$.

On assumption (*b*) the policy could be surrendered at the end of 10 years for $\cdot 95\times 1{\cdot}4(s_{\overline{11}|}-1)$ per 100 assured, where $s_{\overline{11}|}$ is to be calculated at 2 per-cent, that is, for 14·854.

In this case, therefore, the surrender-value would be nearly twice the 4 per-cent value of the Paid-up Policy, while the latter would be considerably in excess of the 4 per-cent investment-value of the original Policy on the basis of its being kept in force for the full sum assured until maturity.

These results indicate the importance of Paid-up Policy and Surrender-Value options in connection with Capital Redemption Policies.

(ii) A loan is made at 4 per-cent payable annually, and the principal is to be repaid by means of a 20-year Capital Redemption Policy, subject to an annual premium calculated on a net 3 per-cent basis. What is the actual rate of interest paid by the borrower on the entire transaction?

The value of $\mathrm{P}_{\overline{20}|}$ at 3 per-cent is ·03613. Hence, in respect of each 100 advanced, the borrower pays 3·613 at the *beginning* of each year for a term of 20 years, by way of a premium to secure the repayment of the principal, and 4·000 at the *end* of each year, for the same period, by way of interest. The actual rate of interest which he pays on the whole transaction is consequently the value of i given by the equation

$$100=4a_{\overline{20}|}+3{\cdot}613\,\mathbf{a}_{\overline{20}|}\,.$$

On solution of this equation by trial, it will be found that the required rate of interest is 4·64 per-cent approximately.

(iii) Required the value, to pay interest at rate i on the basis of a Capital Redemption Assurance being effected to replace capital, of a leasehold property of the estimated net value of R per annum for an unexpired term of n years.

Let K denote the required value.

The investment may be covered by a Policy maturing in either n or $n+1$ years.

(a). Suppose an n-year assurance to be effected, and let S_1 denote the sum to be assured, and $P'_{\overline{n}|}$ the office rate of premium per unit assured. Then, since the premium on the assurance is payable in advance, the investor's total initial outlay will be $K+S_1.P'_{\overline{n}|}$. The annual income from the property must suffice to pay interest on the total outlay and the renewal premium on the assurance.

Hence $$R=(K+S_1P'_{\overline{n}|})i+S_1P'_{\overline{n}|}.$$

At the end of the nth year, interest only will be payable (the last premium on the assurance having been paid at the beginning of the year out of the income received at the end of the $(n-1)$th year), and there will consequently be a balance of income, amounting to $S_1P'_{\overline{n}|}$, available, with the proceeds of the policy, to replace the total outlay; whence

$$S_1P'_{\overline{n}|}+S_1=K+S_1P'_{\overline{n}|}$$

and $$S_1=K.$$

It follows, therefore, from the first equation, that

$$K=S_1=\frac{R}{P'_{\overline{n}|}(1+i)+i}=\frac{Rv}{P'_{\overline{n}|}+d}.$$

(b). Suppose an $(n+1)$-year assurance to be effected, and let S_2 denote the sum to be assured, and $P'_{\overline{n+1}|}$ the office rate of premium per unit assured. Here, also, the total outlay is $K+S_2P'_{\overline{n+1}|}$, and

$$R=(K+S_2P'_{\overline{n+1}|})i+S_2P'_{\overline{n+1}|}$$

but at the end of the $(n+1)$th year, the proceeds of the policy must provide a year's interest in addition to replacing the total outlay; whence

$$S_2=(1+i)(K+S_2P'_{\overline{n+1}|}).$$

These equations lead to the results

$$K=R\left(\frac{1}{P'_{\overline{n+1}|}+d}-1\right)$$

and $$S_2=\frac{R}{P'_{\overline{n+1}|}+d}.$$

From the results obtained in (*a*) and (*b*), it appears that the price to be paid for an n-year annuity of 1 per annum to yield interest at rate i, on the basis of a Capital Redemption Policy being effected to replace the invested capital, will be $\frac{v}{P'_{\overline{n}|}+d}$ or $\frac{1}{P'_{\overline{n+1}|}+d}-1$ according as an assurance for n or $n+1$ years is effected, and that the sum to be assured will be, in the first case, the price paid, and in the second case the price paid increased by a year's rent of the annuity. The expressions $\frac{v}{P'_{\overline{n}|}+d}$ and $\frac{1}{P'_{\overline{n+1}|}+d}-1$ will not, *in general*, be equal for office-values of $P'_{\overline{n}|}$ and $P'_{\overline{n+1}|}$. If, however, both premiums be net premiums calculated at the rate of interest i, then the two expressions become $\frac{v}{P_{\overline{n}|}+d}$ and $\frac{1}{P_{\overline{n+1}|}+d}-1$ respectively, and it may easily be shown that each is $=a_{\overline{n}|}$. It is clear that this is as it should be, for, under the special conditions contemplated, the assurances become merely sinking-funds, calculated and accumulated at the rate of interest employed in valuing the annuity.

As a numerical example, let it be required to find the price to be paid (allowing for income tax at 1*s*. in the £) for an improved ground rent of £100 per annum payable annually for 20 years, the investment being made to yield interest at 4 per-cent (less tax) and to admit of the replacement of capital by means of a 20-year Capital Redemption Assurance at an annual premium of £3. 12*s*. 3*d*. per-cent.

In this case the formula obtained in (*a*) will be the one to be employed, and $i=\cdot038$; $R=95$; and $P'_{\overline{20}|}=\cdot036125$. Hence the price to be paid = the sum to be assured $=\frac{95}{1\cdot038\times\cdot036125+\cdot038}=1{,}258\cdot316$

The annual premium on the policy $=1{,}258\cdot316\times\cdot036125=$ 45·457

Total initial outlay = 1,303·773

Net income from ground rent, less tax=		95
Interest on 1,303·773 at 4 per-cent, less tax	=49·543	
Annual premium on policy	=45·457	
		95

13. Throughout this chapter it has been assumed that the net premium for a Capital Redemption Assurance would be calculated on the basis of a single uniform rate of interest. This, however, would not always be the case. In view of the difficulty of forecasting, with any certainty, the rate of interest likely to be obtainable on investments throughout the long periods over which many Capital Redemption Assurances extend, it is considered by some authorities that a decreasing rate of interest should be employed in the calculation of net premiums for such assurances. The assumption of an annual decrease in the rate leads to inconveniently complex formulas, and for practical purposes it is more usual to take a uniform rate of, say, 3 per-cent for the first ten or twenty years, a rate $\frac{1}{8}$, $\frac{1}{4}$, or $\frac{1}{2}$ per-cent lower for the next ten or twenty years, and so on, until a minimum of, say, 2 per-cent is reached.

Let it be required, for example, to calculate the annual premium for a Capital Redemption Assurance on the basis of 3 per-cent for the first twenty years, $2\frac{1}{2}$ per-cent for the following twenty years, and 2 per-cent thereafter. Clearly for values of n less than 21, the value of $P_{\overline{n}|}$ will be given by the ordinary formula $\frac{1}{s_{\overline{n+1}|}-1}$, where $s_{\overline{n+1}|}$ is taken at 3 per-cent. For values of n between 21 and 40,

$$P_{\overline{n}|}=\frac{1}{\overset{3\%}{s_{\overline{21}|}}(1\cdot025)^{n-20}+\overset{2\frac{1}{2}\%}{s_{\overline{n-20}|}}-1}$$

and, finally, for values of n exceeding 40,

$$P_{\overline{n}|}=\frac{1}{\overset{3\%}{s_{\overline{21}|}}(1\cdot025)^{20}(1\cdot02)^{n-40}+\overset{2\frac{1}{2}\%}{s_{\overline{20}|}}(1\cdot02)^{n-40}+\overset{2\%}{s_{\overline{n-40}|}}-1}$$

The net *value* of a policy subject to a premium calculated on this basis would, of course, be found by accumulating the premiums paid at 3 per-cent up to twenty years from the inception of the assurance, at $2\frac{1}{2}$ per-cent during the following twenty years, and at 2 per-cent thereafter.

CHAPTER VIII.

Interest Tables.

1. In the solution of Compound Interest problems—whether in the simpler problems involving merely the calculation, at a specified rate of interest, of the present value or amount of a given capital sum or annuity, or in those of a more complex description, such, for example, as questions involving the determination of the rate of interest in a given financial transaction—much time and labour may often be saved by the use of Interest Tables, *i.e.*, prepared tables showing the values of the elementary interest functions at various rates of interest. Many such tables are already in existence, but it may occasionally be necessary, for some practical purpose, to construct a table of some special function or to tabulate the values of one of the elementary functions at a special rate of interest or to a greater number of places of decimals than has been retained in any existing table. In studying the subject of Interest Tables it is necessary, therefore, to investigate the methods that may be employed in the construction of such tables, as well as to acquire a knowledge of the nature and extent of the principal existing tables.

2. The functions whose values have been most generally tabulated are $(1+i)^n$, v^n, $s_{\overline{n|}}$, $a_{\overline{n|}}$, $\frac{1}{s_{\overline{n|}}}$ and $\frac{1}{a_{\overline{n|}}}$ for various values of i and n. The values of both $\frac{1}{s_{\overline{n|}}}$ and $\frac{1}{a_{\overline{n|}}}$ are given in some tables, but this has usually been considered unnecessary, since the values of either function can be readily obtained from those of the other by reference to the simple relation $\frac{1}{a_{\overline{n|}}} = \frac{1}{s_{\overline{n|}}} + i$.

Among other functions of which tables have been published may be mentioned $\log(1+i)$, $\log\frac{i}{j_{(m)}}$, $\log j_{(m)}$, $\log(1+i)^n$, $\log v^n$, $\log\frac{1}{a_{\overline{n}|}}$, $\frac{s_{\overline{n}|}}{1+i's_{\overline{n}|}}$, $(g-i)a_{\overline{n}|}$.

3. In regard to the practical utility of any given set of tables of the elementary functions, the following points present themselves for consideration:—(i) the range and subdivision of the rates of interest for which the results are tabulated, (ii) the range of the values of n, (iii) the number of decimal places given in the results, (iv) the arrangement of the tables.

(i) The rates of interest of practice are usually nominal rates convertible half-yearly or quarterly. Now the present value or amount of 1 at rate j convertible m times a year is equal to the present value or amount of 1 at the effective rate $\frac{j}{m}$ for m times the given number of years, and, similarly, the present value or amount of an annuity of 1 per annum payable m times a year for n years at the nominal rate j convertible m times a year is equal to the present value or amount of an annuity of $\frac{1}{m}$ per annum payable annually for nm years at the effective rate $\frac{j}{m}$. Hence it follows that, in practice, tables of the elementary functions are required for values of i ranging by small differences of $\frac{1}{8}$th, or even $\frac{1}{16}$th, from say ·005 upwards.

In some tables the rates of interest range by larger differences, of say $\frac{1}{2}$ or $\frac{1}{4}$, from a minimum rate of 2 or 3 per-cent, but the values of the functions are given for each rate convertible half-yearly and quarterly as well as annually—the annuity payments, in the case of the functions $a_{\overline{n}|}$ $s_{\overline{n}|}$ and $\frac{1}{a_{\overline{n}|}}$ or $\frac{1}{s_{\overline{n}|}}$, being assumed to be made with corresponding frequency. Such tables answer much the same purpose as those constructed for a more extensive range of annual rates, except that they give the values only for integral numbers of years and not for integral numbers of half-years or quarters, unless, as in Corbaux's Tables, the values are specially given for each half-year in the case of a rate of interest convertible half-yearly, and for each quarter in the case of a rate convertible quarterly. For the valuation of Stock Exchange securities, and in the determination of the yield on such securities, it is convenient to have the values of the elementary functions for each integral number of half-years or quarters. In general, tables constructed upon the first-mentioned plan, *i.e.*, for effective rates ranging from a low initial value by very small differences, are probably the most useful.

(ii) The values of n generally range from 1 to 50, 60 or 100. Financial transactions do not, as a rule, extend over so long a period as 100 years. Hence, for tables at the higher rates of interest, say $3\frac{1}{2}$ per-cent and upwards, the utility of which is practically limited to transactions in which a *yearly* rate of interest is involved, a range of 1 to 60 in the values of n is sufficient. But, as regards the tables at the lower rates (representing in practice half-yearly or quarterly rates), in which n will generally denote a number of half-years or quarters, a more extensive range is desirable; for example, in the valuation of Consols as at 5th April, 1900, at 2 per-cent convertible quarterly, the value of v^{92} or $a_{\overline{92}|}$ for $i=\cdot005$ would be required. It will be obvious that a range of 1 to 100 in the values of n covers a period of 50 years for a nominal rate convertible half-yearly, and a period of 25 years for a nominal rate convertible quarterly. The value of any one of the elementary functions for a value of n beyond the limits of a given table may sometimes be conveniently found with the aid of the table. Suppose, for example, that it is required to find the value of v^{195} or $a_{\overline{195}|}$ at a quarterly rate of interest, for the purpose of finding the yield on India 3 per-cent Stock as at 5th January, 1900, and that the available tables only go up to $n=100$. The required values may then be obtained by means of the relations

$$v^{195}=v^{100}\times v^{95}\,;\;\; a_{\overline{195}|}=v^{100}a_{\overline{95}|}+a_{\overline{100}|}.$$

The results obtained in this way may not, of course, be correct to as many places of decimals as the values upon which they are based. Frequently, it will be found more convenient to calculate the required values from the appropriate formulas by logarithms.

(iii) For many practical purposes, tables giving the values of v^n to five places of decimals and those of $a_{\overline{n}|}$ to three or four places are sufficient But when large sums are involved, and it is required to obtain results correct to the nearest penny, greater accuracy is necessary. Suppose, for example, that it were required to find the annuity (payable half-yearly) to redeem a loan of £100,000 in 50 years, with interest at 4 per-cent, convertible half-yearly. The value of $\dfrac{1}{a_{\overline{100}|}}$ at 2 per-cent to eight places of decimals is ·02320274, so that the half-yearly annuity-payment to the nearest penny would be £2,320. 5*s*. 6*d*. The value of $\frac{1}{a_{\overline{100}|}}$ to five places is ·02320. Hence the half-yearly payment, if calculated by a table giving the values of $\frac{1}{a_{\overline{n}|}}$ to five places only, would be £2,320, which differs by 5*s*. 6*d*. from the correct result.

(iv) The principal objects to be attained in the arrangement of tables are (*a*) facility and celerity in use when numerous values have to be extracted, (*b*) minimization of the risk of error from the use of the wrong table, in case of an isolated reference.

The most important distinction in regard to arrangement is that in some tables the values of the several functions at each rate of interest are exhibited in parallel columns, whereas in others the values of each function at the various rates of interest are brought together. In the determination of an unknown rate of interest the latter arrangement is more convenient.

4. In calculations in which great accuracy is required it may be necessary to determine the requisite values from the elementary formulas by means of logarithms. For this purpose the table of the values of $\log(1+i)$ to 15 places of decimals originally prepared by the late Mr. Peter Gray for the first edition of this work will be found useful, in conjunction with an extended logarithm table.

In order to minimize any risk of error from mistakes in printing or other causes, it is desirable to use independent tables for calculation and for checking. When only one table is available, it may sometimes be advisable to check independently by logarithms any values taken from the tables.

5. In the construction of Interest Tables it is usual to employ, when practicable, what is known as the *Continued Process*, *i.e.*, a process by which each value of the function is obtained from the value next preceding or next following it. The advantages of this method of procedure are (i) that, in general, it entails much less labour than would be involved in the calculation of the values independently; (ii) that it admits of the whole of the results up to any given point being checked by the verification of the value last obtained, since that value depends on all those that precede it. On the other hand, an error in the calculation of any given value is carried forward by the Continued Process to every subsequent value, so that it is desirable to verify the results by an independent check at short intervals—say, for every tenth value. Further, an error may be introduced by the accumulation of a small error resulting from the limitation of the number of decimal places retained in the calculations, but this can in many cases be obviated by a systematic adjustment; for example, in the construction of a table of $\log(1\cdot04)^n$ by repeated addition of ·01703—this being the value of $\log 1\cdot04$ to five places of decimals, while the value to seven places is 0170333—an error of, approximately, 1 in defect in the fifth place will arise in every three additions, but this may be eliminated by the addition of 1 at every third operation.

6. In the application of the Continued Process to the tabulation of the values of a given function it is necessary to have (i) an *Initial Value*—upon which the subsequent values are based—(ii) a *Working Formula, i.e.*, a formula connecting one value of the function with the next, (iii) a *Verification* or *Check* Formula.

Thus, in the tabulation of the values of $a_{\overline{n}|}$ for values of n from 1 to 100, $a_{\overline{100}|}$ may be taken as the *Initial Value*, $a_{\overline{n-1}|}=(1+i)a_{\overline{n}|}-1$ as the *Working Formula*, and $a_{\overline{n}|}=\dfrac{1-v^n}{i}$ as the *Verification Formula*, to be applied to check every 10th or 20th value.

7. The principle that a series of values tabulated by a Continued Process may be checked by the verification of the value last obtained depends upon the assumption that each value is employed in the calculation of the next succeeding one. It must be remembered, therefore, that the efficacy of a check of this nature, as applied to a series of final values, is restricted to those cases in which each final value is actually used in the calculation of the next. For example, in the tabulation of $(1+i)^n$, by forming $\log(1+i)^n$ by repeated addition of $\log(1+i)$, and taking the antilogarithms of the results, the accuracy of the final value, say $(1+i)^{100}$, would not be any proof of the accuracy of the preceding values. It would prove only that the values of $\log(1+i)^n$ were correct. The values of $(1+i)^n$, having been separately obtained by taking antilogarithms, and not being employed in the *Working Formula*, would have to be checked by some other method; in fact, the Continued Process in this case is really used only in the calculation of the subsidiary values of $\log(1+i)^n$.

8. A very useful check, when the nature of the tabulated function is such as to admit of its being employed, is that obtained by the verification of the *sum* of the tabulated values. This check has the

advantages of being equally efficacious, whether the values have been calculated separately or by a Continued Process, and of being applicable to the detection of mistakes in copying (or printer's errors in a proof), as well as to actual mistakes in calculation. When available, it may generally be applied to verify small sections of the resulting values, as well as the final total.

In the tabulation, for example, of the values of v^n, the accuracy of any series of r successive values, beginning, say, with v^{m+1}, may be verified by seeing that their sum $=v^{m+1}+\ldots+v^{m+r}$, that is, $a_{\overline{m+r}|}-a_{\overline{m}|}$ or $\dfrac{v^m-v^{m+r}}{i}$. In the application of this check formula, the values of v^m and v^{m+r} should, of course, be independently calculated.

In this connection, the following relations will be useful:—

$$\sum_{m+1}^{m+r}(1+i)^n=s_{\overline{m+r+1}|}-s_{\overline{m+1}|}$$

$$\sum_{m+1}^{m+r}v^n=a_{\overline{m+r}|}-a_{\overline{m}|}$$

$$\sum_{m+1}^{m+r}\log(1+i)^n=\frac{r}{2}(2m+r+1)\log(1+i)$$

$$\sum_{m+1}^{m+r}\log v^n=\frac{r}{2}(2m+r+1)\log v.$$

$$\sum_{m+1}^{m+r}s_{\overline{n}|}=\sum_{m+1}^{m+r}\frac{(1+i)^n-1}{i}=\frac{s_{\overline{m+r+1}|}-s_{\overline{m+1}|}-r}{i}$$

$$\sum_{m+1}^{m+r}a_{\overline{n}|}=\sum_{m+1}^{m+r}\frac{1-v^n}{i}=\frac{r-a_{\overline{m+r}|}+a_{\overline{m}|}}{i}.$$

The functions $\dfrac{i}{(1+i)^n-1}$ and $\dfrac{i}{1-v^n}$ do not admit of algebraical summation. Consequently, a check of this nature cannot be applied to tables of $\dfrac{1}{s_{\overline{n}|}}$ and $\dfrac{1}{a_{\overline{n}|}}$—except for the purpose of verifying a copy or a printed proof, when the original calculations have been previously checked by some other method.

9. An approximate check, which will sometimes be found useful, is afforded by an inspection of the differences of the tabulated results. The differences between the successive values of any function should, in general, form a regular series, and as they will, as a rule, be comparatively small quantities, any error of importance in the tabulated values will

usually give rise to an obvious irregularity. Suppose, for example, that the amounts of an annuity of 1 per annum for 62 to 67 years at 4 per-cent were erroneously printed as 259·451, 270·829, 282·662, 295·968, 308·767, and 321·078. An inspection of the differences—11·378, 11·833, 13·306, 12·799, 12·311—would show at once that the difference between the third and fourth value is too large, while that between the fifth and sixth is too small, and on investigation it would be found that the fourth and fifth values should be 294·968 and 307·767, thus altering the differences to the regular series 11·378, 11·833, 12·306, 12·799, and 13·311.

10. Tables of the values of $(1+i)^n$, v^n, $s_{\overline{n}|}$, and $a_{\overline{n}|}$ may, as a rule, be most easily constructed by actual multiplication, by means of the Working Formulas

$$(1+i)^n=(1+i)^{n-1}\times(1+i);\quad v^{n-1}=v^n\times(1+i);$$
$$s_{\overline{n}|}=s_{\overline{n-1}|}+(1+i)^{n-1};\quad \text{or}\quad (1+i)s_{\overline{n-1}|}+1;$$
$$a_{\overline{n}|}=a_{\overline{n-1}|}+v^n;\quad \text{or}\quad (1+i)a_{\overline{n+1}|}-1;$$

the first or second formulas for $s_{\overline{n}|}$ and $a_{\overline{n}|}$ being applicable according as the functions $(1+i)^n$ and v^n have or have not been already tabulated.

If, however, the value of i be such that the operation of multiplying by $1+i$ would be unduly laborious, it may be more convenient to tabulate the *logarithms* of the functions by means of the Working Formulas

$$\log(1+i)^n=\log(1+i)^{n-1}+\log(1+i)$$
$$\log v^n=\log v^{n-1}-\log(1+i)$$
$$\log s_{\overline{n}|}=\log\{(1+i)s_{\overline{n-1}|}+1\}$$
$$\log a_{\overline{n}|}=\log(1+a_{\overline{n-1}|})-\log(1+i).$$

In applying the last two formulas it will be convenient—in order to save the labour of taking antilogarithms at each operation—to use a table of Gauss's logarithms, in which the value of $\log(1+x)$ is found by entering the table with $\log x$. In the case of $\log s_{\overline{n}|}$, the *modus operandi* will be as follows:—Begin with $\log s_{\overline{1}|}$, the value of which is 0, since $s_{\overline{1}|}=1$ for all values of i; obtain $\log(1+i)s_{\overline{1}|}$ by adding $\log(1+i)$ to $\log s_{\overline{1}|}$, and enter the table of Gauss's logarithms; the result will be $\log\{(1+i)s_{\overline{1}|}+1\}$ or $\log s_{\overline{2}|}$; again add $\log(1+i)$, obtaining $\log(1+i)s_{\overline{2}|}$, and enter the table, which will give $\log\{(1+i)s_{\overline{2}|}+1\}$ or $\log s_{\overline{3}|}$; and so on. In the case of $\log a_{\overline{n}|}$, begin with $\log a_{\overline{1}|}$, *i.e.*, $\log v$; obtain $\log(1+a_{\overline{1}|})$ by entering the table, and deduct $\log(1+i)$, which will give

$\log(1+a_{\overline{1}|})-\log(1+i)$ or $\log a_{\overline{2}|}$; enter the table with this result, and deduct $\log(1+i)$, thus obtaining $\log(1+a_{\overline{2}|})-\log(1+i)$ or $\log a_{\overline{3}|}$, and so on.

In each case the work may be facilitated by writing the constant quantity $\log(1+i)$ at the top of a moveable card for convenience in adding or subtracting at each operation, and a periodical adjustment must be made, as explained in Art. 5, to eliminate the error resulting from the fact that the value of $\log(1+i)$ will be correct to the number of decimal places retained only.

11. The values of $\frac{1}{s_{\overline{n}|}}$ and $\frac{1}{a_{\overline{n}|}}$ may be tabulated either from the values of $s_{\overline{n}|}$ and $a_{\overline{n}|}$ by taking reciprocals, or from $\log s_{\overline{n}|}$ and $\log a_{\overline{n}|}$ by taking the antilogarithms of the complementary logarithms. If the values of $\frac{1}{s_{\overline{n}|}}$ and $\frac{1}{a_{\overline{n}|}}$ were calculated independently, the relation $\frac{1}{a_{\overline{n}|}}=\frac{1}{s_{\overline{n}|}}+i$ would afford the most obvious and convenient method of checking the results. As already stated, however, it is not usual to tabulate both $\frac{1}{s_{\overline{n}|}}$ and $\frac{1}{a_{\overline{n}|}}$, since the value of one can be so easily obtained from that of the other, and the check in question would not, therefore, in general be applicable. In these circumstances the calculated values of $\frac{1}{s_{\overline{n}|}}$ or $\frac{1}{a_{\overline{n}|}}$, as the case might be, could be verified either by taking their reciprocals and comparing the results with the values of $s_{\overline{n}|}$ or $a_{\overline{n}|}$, or by dividing i on the arithmometer by $(1+i)^n-1$ or $1-v^n$.

The values of $\frac{1}{s_{\overline{n}|}}$ and $\frac{1}{a_{\overline{n}|}}$ could also be tabulated directly, with the aid of Gauss's logarithms, by means of the relations

$$\log\frac{1}{s_{\overline{n}|}}=\log\frac{1}{s_{\overline{n-1}|}}-\log(1+i)-\log\left[1+\frac{1}{(1+i)s_{\overline{n-1}|}}\right]$$

$$\log\frac{1}{a_{\overline{n}|}}=\log\frac{1}{a_{\overline{n-1}|}}+\log(1+i)-\log\left(1+\frac{1}{a_{\overline{n-1}|}}\right).$$

12. A table of the values of $P_{\overline{n}|}$ at a given rate of interest may be constructed, as explained in Chap. VII, either by taking the reciprocals of $(s_{\overline{n+1}|}-1)$ or by entering an Annual Premium Conversion Table with $a_{\overline{n-1}|}$. In this connection it may be noticed that a Single Premium Conversion Table would, in theory, afford a simple means of checking a table of the values of $a_{\overline{n}|}$, since the result of entering the Conversion

Table with $a_{\overline{n}|}$ should be v^{n+1}; in practice, however, this check would be of little value owing to the limitations of the Conversion Table in the matter of decimal places.

13. The values of $(1+i)^{\frac{r}{m}}$ and $v^{\frac{r}{m}}$, or of $s^{(m)}_{\overline{n}|}$ and $a^{(m)}_{\overline{n}|}$ at the *effective* rate i are not often required, but they could be tabulated, if necessary, by the continued methods indicated by the following formulas:—

$$\log (1+i)^{\frac{r+1}{m}} = \log (1+i)^{\frac{r}{m}} + \frac{1}{m}\log (1+i)$$

$$\log v^{\frac{r}{m}} = \log v^{\frac{r+1}{m}} + \frac{1}{m}\log (1+i)$$

$$s^{(m)}_{\overline{n}|} = s^{(m)}_{\overline{n-1}|} + \frac{1}{m}\sum_{r=(n-1)m}^{r=nm-1} (1+i)^{\frac{r}{m}}$$

or

$$\log s^{(m)}_{\overline{n}|} = \log s^{(m)}_{\overline{1}|} + \log\left[1 + \frac{(1+i)s^{(m)}_{\overline{n-1}|}}{s^{(m)}_{\overline{1}|}}\right]$$

$$a^{(m)}_{\overline{n}|} = a^{(m)}_{\overline{n-1}|} + \frac{1}{m}\sum_{r=(n-1)m+1}^{r=nm} v^{\frac{r}{m}}$$

or

$$\log a^{(m)}_{\overline{n}|} = \log a^{(m)}_{\overline{1}|} + \log\left[1 + \frac{v a^{(m)}_{\overline{n-1}|}}{a^{(m)}_{\overline{1}|}}\right].$$

The formulas given above for $\log s^{(m)}_{\overline{n}|}$ and $\log a^{(m)}_{\overline{n}|}$ are adapted to the application of a table of Gauss's logarithms—the table being entered in the one case with $\log s^{(m)}_{\overline{n-1}|} + \log (1+i) - \log s^{(m)}_{\overline{1}|}$, and in the other with $\log a^{(m)}_{\overline{n-1}|} - \log (1+i) - \log a^{(m)}_{\overline{1}|}$. In the case of each of the four functions $(1+i)^{\frac{r}{m}}$, $v^{\frac{r}{m}}$, $s^{(m)}_{\overline{n}|}$, and $a^{(m)}_{\overline{n}|}$, a summation formula could easily be obtained to check the tabulated values.

Although the methods indicated above are of some interest as generalisations of the methods applicable to the functions $(1+i)^n$, v^n, $s_{\overline{n}|}$, and $a_{\overline{n}|}$, the most convenient method of constructing tables of $s^{(m)}_{\overline{n}|}$ and $a^{(m)}_{\overline{n}|}$ in practice would probably be to multiply the values of $s_{\overline{n}|}$ and $a_{\overline{n}|}$ (supposing these to have been already tabulated) by the factor $\frac{i}{j_{(m)}}$. The value of this function would generally be such as to admit of the values of $s^{(m)}_{\overline{n}|}$ and $a^{(m)}_{\overline{n}|}$ being obtained by direct multiplication with the aid of an extended multiplication table, but if the logarithms of $s_{\overline{n}|}$ and $a_{\overline{n}|}$ had been already tabulated, it might be found more convenient to construct $\log s_{\overline{n}|}^{(m)}$ and $\log a_{\overline{n}|}^{(m)}$ by the addition of the constant $\log \frac{i}{j_{(m)}}$, and to take antilogarithms. The logarithms could be verified by the relations $\Sigma s_{\overline{n}|}^{(m)} = \frac{i}{j_{(m)}} \Sigma s_{\overline{n}|}$, $\Sigma a_{\overline{n}|}^{(m)} = \frac{i}{j_{(m)}} \Sigma a_{\overline{n}|}$, and the final results by summation formulas.

14. The amounts and present values of annuities at any given *force of interest* may be conveniently found by means of a table of the values of $\log \frac{e^x - 1}{x}$. The application of such a table will be sufficiently indicated by the following relations:

$$\log \bar{s}_{\overline{n}|} = \log \frac{e^{n\delta} - 1}{\delta} = \log \frac{e^{n\delta} - 1}{n\delta} + \log n$$

$$\log s_{\overline{n}|}^{(m)} = \log \frac{e^{n\delta} - 1}{m\left[e^{\frac{\delta}{m}} - 1\right]} = \log \frac{e^{n\delta} - 1}{n\delta} - \log \frac{e^{\frac{\delta}{m}} - 1}{\frac{\delta}{m}} + \log n$$

$$\log s_{\overline{n}|} = \log \frac{e^{n\delta} - 1}{e^{\delta} - 1} = \log \frac{e^{n\delta} - 1}{n\delta} - \log \frac{e^{\delta} - 1}{\delta} + \log n$$

$$\log \bar{a}_{\overline{n}|} = \log e^{-n\delta} \bar{s}_{\overline{n}|} = \log \frac{e^{n\delta} - 1}{n\delta} + \log n - n\delta \log e$$

&c. &c. &c.

15. As an example of the construction of a table, let it be required to tabulate the values of $\frac{1}{a_{\overline{n}|}}$ at 3·1 per-cent.

In this case the working formula

$$\log \frac{1}{a_{\overline{n}|}} = \log \frac{1}{a_{\overline{n-1}|}} + \log(1+i) - \log\left(1 + \frac{1}{a_{\overline{n-1}|}}\right)$$

may conveniently be employed with the aid of Wittstein's Table of Gaussian logarithms, from which the values of $\log(1+x)$ may be found, with approximate accuracy, to seven places of decimals for all values of $\log x$ from $\bar{7}\cdot0000000$ to 4·0000000. The value of log 1·031 to eight places is ·01325867. Hence, in working to seven places, it will be necessary to take the seventh figure as 7 in two cases out of every three, and as 6 in the remaining case. Also, since the initial value $\log \frac{1}{a_{\overline{1}|}}$ is $\log(1+i)$, which must be taken as ·0132587, it will be best to take the seventh figure of $\log(1+i)$ in the working formula as successively 6, 7, 7. The value of $\log\left(1+\frac{1}{a_{\overline{1}|}}\right)$ will be found by entering Wittstein with $\log\frac{1}{a_{\overline{1}|}}$ or ·0132587, and that of $\log\frac{1}{a_{\overline{2}|}}$ by adding $\log(1+i)$ to $\log\frac{1}{a_{\overline{1}|}}$ and deducting $\log\left(1+\frac{1}{a_{\overline{1}|}}\right)$ from the result. The addition and subtraction may be performed in a single operation, by a cross cast, the values of $\log\frac{1}{a_{\overline{n}|}}$ and $\log\left(1+\frac{1}{a_{\overline{n}|}}\right)$ being placed in adjacent columns, and the value of $\log(1+i)$ being written at the edge of a moveable card. The values of $\frac{1}{a_{\overline{n}|}}$ will finally be obtained by taking the antilogarithms of the tabulated values of $\log\frac{1}{a_{\overline{n}|}}$. The logarithmic work may be checked by a periodical calculation of $\log\frac{1}{a_{\overline{n}|}}$ from the formula $\log i - \log(1-v^n)$, and the final values by reciprocation and summation, or by comparison of their logarithms with the values of $\log\frac{1}{a_{\overline{n}|}}$ from which they were obtained. The whole process is shown in the following specimen of the work:—

n	$\log\frac{1}{a_{\overline{n}\|}}$	$\log\left(1+\frac{1}{a_{\overline{n}\|}}\right)$	$\frac{1}{a_{\overline{n}\|}}$	$a_{\overline{n}\|}$
1	·0132587	·3077099	1·031000	·96993
2	$\bar{1}$·7188074	·1828049	·523368	1·91070
3	$\bar{1}$·5492612	·1316861	·354210	2·82318
4	$\bar{1}$·4308338	·1036911	·269671	3·70822
5	$\bar{1}$·3404013	·0859960	·218978	4·56667
6	$\bar{1}$·2676640	·0737952	·185210	5·39928
7	$\bar{1}$·2071275	·0648740	·161112	6·20686
8	$\bar{1}$·1555121	·0580682	·143058	6·99017
9	$\bar{1}$·1107026	·0527068	·129034	7·74990
10	$\bar{1}$·0712545	...	·117830	8·48680
				48·81171

$\log(1\cdot031)^{-10}=\bar{1}\cdot8674133$, whence $v^{10}=\cdot7369080$;

$$\log\frac{1}{a_{\overline{10}|}}=\log i-\log(1-v^{10})=\bar{2}\cdot4913617-\bar{1}\cdot4201076=\underline{\underline{\bar{1}\cdot0712541}}$$

whence $a_{\overline{10}|}=8\cdot486833$ and $\sum_{n=1}^{n=10} a_{\overline{n}|}=\frac{10-a_{\overline{10}|}}{i}$ . . . $=\underline{\underline{48\cdot8118}}$

It will be observed that the values of $\log \frac{1}{a_{\overline{10}|}}$, as obtained by the working formula and the check formula respectively, differ in the seventh place of decimals. The discrepancy does not, however, affect the accuracy of the tabulated value of $\frac{1}{a_{\overline{10}|}}$ to the sixth place. The more serious discrepancy between the values of $\Sigma a_{\overline{n}|}$, as obtained by actual summation and the summation formula respectively, is due mainly to the fact that the values of $\frac{1}{a_{\overline{n}|}}$ have been cut down to six places before reciprocation, which throws out the values of $a_{\overline{n}|}$ in the fifth place.

If it had been required to tabulate the values of $a_{\overline{n}|}$ from an 8-figure value of $\log 1{\cdot}031$, it would have been better to use the formula $a_{\overline{n-1}|}=(1+i)a_{\overline{n}|}-1$, and to set out the work as follows:—

n	$a_{\overline{n}|}$	$a_{\overline{n}|}\times{\cdot}03$	$a_{\overline{n}|}\times{\cdot}001$	$a_{\overline{n}|}$ to five places
10	8·486833	·254605	·008487	8·48683
9	7·749925	·232498	·007750	7·74993
8	6·990173	·209705	·006990	6·99017
7	6·206868	·186206	·006207	6·20687
6	5·399281	·161978	·005399	5·39928
5	4·566658	·137000	·004567	4·56666
4	3·708225	·111247	·003708	3·70823
3	2·823180	·084695	·002823	2·82318
2	1·910698	·057321	·001911	1·91070
1	·969930	...	...	·96993
				48·81178

Here the total agrees to the fourth place with the result obtained by the summation formula.

16. As a further example, let it be required to tabulate $P_{\overline{n}|}$, for values of n up to 20, on the basis of a rate of interest falling by equal annual decrements from ·035 in the 1st year to ·0255 in the 20th year. Let i_1, i_2, &c., denote the rates of interest for the 1st, 2nd, &c., years, so that $i_1={\cdot}035$, $i_2={\cdot}0345$, $i_3={\cdot}034$, &c. Then

$$P_{\overline{n}|}[(1+i_n)+(1+i_n)(1+i_{n-1})+\ldots+(1+i_n)(1+i_{n-1})\ldots(1+i_1)]=1$$

Hence $\log\frac{1}{P_{\overline{n}|}}=\log(1+i_n)+\log(1+\frac{1}{P_{\overline{n-1}|}})$. A table of Gaussian logarithms may, therefore, be conveniently employed, with $\log \frac{1}{P_{\overline{1|}}}$, that is, $\log(1+i_1)$, as the initial value. The results obtained by the working formula may be checked by an independent calculation of $\log \frac{1}{P_{\overline{20|}}}$, but the values of $\log(1+i_n)$ and the final values of $P_{\overline{n|}}$ must be individually checked. The work will be as follows:—

n	$\log(1+i_n)$	$\log\left(1+\frac{1}{P_{\overline{n-1|}}}\right)$	$\log \frac{1}{P_{\overline{n|}}}$	$P_{\overline{n|}}$	$\log(1+i_n)\ldots(1+i_{20})$	$(1+i_n)\ldots(1+i_{20})$
1	·01494035	...	·0149404	·96618	·25881844	1·814757
2	·01473049	·3085644	·3232949	·47501	·24387809	1·753389
3	·01452054	·4920906	·5066111	·31145	·22914760	1·694914
4	·01431048	·6243630	·6386735	·22979	·21462706	1·639182
5	·01410032	·7285036	·7426039	·18088	·20031658	1·586049
6	·01389006	·8148105	·8287006	·14835	·18621626	1·535382
7	·01367970	·8887761	·9024561	·12518	·17232620	1·487052
8	·01346923	·9536791	·9671483	·10786	·15864650	1·440942
9	·01325867	1·0116323	1·0248910	·09443	·14517727	1·396939
10	·01304800	1·0640789	1·0771269	·08373	·13191860	1·354936
11	·01283723	1·1120474	1·1248846	·07501	·11887060	1·314833
12	·01262635	1·1562969	1·1689233	·06778	·10603337	1·276537
13	·01241537	1·1974035	1·2098189	·06169	·09340702	1·239961
14	·01220430	1·2358147	1·2480190	·05649	·08099165	1·205013
15	·01199311	1·2718849	1·2838780	·05201	·06878735	1·171622
16	·01178183	1·3058996	1·3176814	·04812	·05679424	1·139710
17	·01157044	1·3380921	1·3496625	·04470	·04501241	1·109206
18	·01135895	1·3686554	1·3800144	·04169	·03344197	1·080045
19	·01114736	1·3977510	1·4088984	·03900	·02208302	1·052163
20	·01093566	1·4255154	1·4364511	·03661	·01093566	1·025500
	·25881844					$\frac{1}{P_{\overline{20|}}} = 27·318132$

$$\log \frac{1}{P_{\overline{20|}}} = 1·4364510$$

In the first column are written the values of log 1·035, log 1·0345, log 1·034, &c. The *initial value*, ·0149404, is then placed at the head of the third column; the result of entering Wittstein with ·0149404 is ·3085644, which is placed in the second column, and a cross addition gives ·3232949—the value of $\log \frac{1}{P_{\overline{2|}}}$. This process is repeated to the end of the column. The values of $P_{\overline{n|}}$ are then obtained by taking the antilogarithms of the values of $\log P_{\overline{n|}}$, the latter being read off mentally from the values of $\log \frac{1}{P_{\overline{n|}}}$ by deduction of the first six decimals in $\log \frac{1}{P_{\overline{n}|}}$ from 9 and of the seventh from 10. The numbers in the fifth column are obtained by continuous addition of those in the first from the bottom upwards, and those in the final column by taking antilogarithms. Finally, the cast of the final column gives $\frac{1}{P_{\overline{20}|}}$, and the logarithm of this—being found to agree with the last number in the third column—checks the work of the second and third columns. The logarithms of the first column and the antilogarithms of the fourth column must be checked, as already stated, by individual verification.

17. It remains now to give some account of existing Interest Tables. For this purpose it will be convenient to specify some of the more important tables, in order of date, and to indicate, so far as may appear necessary, their extent or special utility.

JOHN LAURIE.—"Tables of Simple and Compound Interest." 1776.

This work contains, *inter alia,* tables of $\frac{1}{a_{\overline{n}|}}$ to 7 places of decimals for rates of interest proceeding by $\frac{1}{2}$ from 3 to 5 per-cent and for values of n from 1 to 50.

FRANCIS CORBAUX. 1825.

These tables (which appear in the author's work on the "Doctrine of Compound Interest") give—in addition to results which will be found in a more convenient form in later works—the values of $\left(1+\frac{j}{4}\right)^{4n}$, $\left(1+\frac{j}{4}\right)^{-4n}$, $\frac{\left(1+\frac{j}{4}\right)^{4n}-1}{j}$, $\frac{1-\left(1+\frac{j}{4}\right)^{-4n}}{j}$, and $\frac{j}{1-\left(1+\frac{j}{4}\right)^{-4n}}$ for values of j proceeding by $\frac{1}{4}$ per-cent from 3 to 6 per-cent, and for values of n proceeding by $\frac{1}{4}$ from $\frac{1}{4}$ to 16 and by 1 from 16 to 100. They practically give, therefore, for $n=1$ up to $n=64$, the values of the elementary functions at rates of interest proceeding by $\frac{1}{16}$ from $\frac{3}{4}$ to $1\frac{1}{2}$ per-cent. These results are given to 7 places of decimals in the case of the 1st, 2nd, and 5th functions, 7 decreasing to 6 in the case of the 3rd, and 6 decreasing to 5 in that of the 4th.

D. JONES.—"On Annuities and Reversionary Payments." 1844.

Vol. I of this work contains tables of $(1+i)^n$ and v^n to 8 places, $s_{\overline{n}|}$ and $a_{\overline{n}|}$ to 6 places, $\frac{1}{a_{\overline{n}|}}$ to 8 places, and $\log v^n$ to 7 places, for all values of n from 1 to 100, and for rates of interest proceeding by $\frac{1}{2}$ from 2 to 5 per-cent and thence by 1 to 10 per-cent.

P. A. VIOLEINE.—"Nouvelles Tables pour les calculs d'Intérêts Simple e' Composés, &c." Deuxième édition. 1854.

Some of the tables which were first published in this work have been reproduced in Spitzer's later and more extensive collection; the following, however, call for notice:—

Table No.	Function tabulated	n	$100i$
XVI	$s_{\overline{n}\vert}$	1 to 100	1 by $\frac{1}{8}$ and $\frac{1}{6}$ up to 6, and thereafter by $\frac{1}{4}$ and $\frac{1}{3}$ to 10
XVII	$s_{\overline{n}\vert}$	1 to 12	$\frac{1}{12}$ by $\frac{1}{24}$ to $\frac{11}{12}$ (except $\frac{13}{24}$, $\frac{17}{24}$ and $\frac{19}{24}$)
XVIII	$(1+i)s_{\overline{n}\vert}$	Do.	Do.
XX	$\frac{1}{a_{\overline{n}\vert}}$	1 to 100	Do.

The results are given generally to 8 places of decimals.

Lieut.-Col. W. H. OAKES.—"Loans Payable by Drawings and Debenture Interest Tables." 1870.

These tables give to 3 places of decimals the half-yearly rate of interest realised on a Debenture bearing interest at 3, 4, 5 . . . 9 per-cent per annum payable half-yearly, to be redeemed at par in any number of half-years from 1 to 60, and issued (or bought) at a discount of from 1 to 30 per-cent.

F. VINTEJOUX ET J. DE REINACH.—"Tables d'Intérêt." 1874.

The only feature of these tables that calls for notice is the range of the values of n. The values of $(1+i)^n$ are tabulated for all values of n from 1 to 160 and thence by 4 to 300; those of v^n for all values of n from 1 to 100 and thence by 5 to 200; and those of $\frac{1}{a_{\overline{n}\vert}}$ for all values of n from 1 to 200. The rates of interest proceed by $\frac{1}{4}$ from $\frac{3}{4}$ to $2\frac{1}{4}$ per-cent, and the results are given to 6 or 7 places.

T. G. RANCE.—"Compound Interest Tables." 1876.

These tables give the values of $(1+i)^n$, v^n, $s_{\overline{n}\vert}$ and $a_{\overline{n}\vert}$ to 7 places, for all values of n from 1 to 100, at rates of interest proceeding by $\frac{1}{4}$ from $\frac{1}{4}$ to 10 per-cent.

Lieut.-Col. W. H. OAKES.—"Tables of Compound Interest." 1877.

These tables give the values of $(1+i)^n$, v^n, $s_{\overline{n}\vert}$ and $a_{\overline{n}\vert}$ to 5 places, for all values of n from 1 to 100, at rates of interest proceeding by $\frac{1}{8}$ from $\frac{3}{4}$ to 10 per-cent.

FÉDOR THOMAN.—"Theory of Compound Interest and Annuities" (translated) 1887.

In this work the functions $\log(1+i)^n$ and $\log\frac{1}{a_{\overline{n}\vert}}$ are tabulated to 7 places, foi all values of n from 1 to 100, at rates of interest proceeding by $\frac{1}{8}$ to $1\frac{1}{2}$, thence by $\frac{1}{8}$ to 6, by $\frac{1}{4}$ to 7, by $\frac{1}{2}$ to 8, and finally by 1 to 12 per-cent. The values of $\log i$, $\log(1+i)$, $\log^2(1+i)$, and $\frac{1}{j_{(m)}}$ ($m=2$, 4, 6, and 12), are also given to 7 or 10 places for an extensive range of rates of interest.

These tables $\left(\text{except the table of } \frac{1}{j_{(m)}}\right)$ are reprinted in an Appendix to INWOOD'S Tables (25th edition, 1899), in which will be found tables of the elementary functions—generally to 5 places of decimals—and also tables of the values of $\frac{v^n}{i}$, $a^{\left(\frac{1}{n}\right)}_{\infty}$, ${}_{m|}a_{\overline{n-m}|}$, $\frac{s_{\overline{n}|}}{1+i's_{\overline{n}|}}$, and $\frac{i}{j_{(m)}}$.

H. D. HOSKOLD.—"The (Mining) Engineer's Valuing Assistant." 1877.

This work contains, *inter alia*, a table of $(1+i)^n$ to 10 places, for all values of n from 1 to 100, at rates of interest proceeding by $\frac{1}{4}$ from $\frac{1}{2}$ to 3, by $\frac{1}{2}$ from 3 to 6, and by 1 from 6 to 9 per-cent; also tables of $\frac{1}{\frac{1}{s_{\overline{n}|}}+i'}$ for various combinations of i and i'.

T. K. STUBBINS.—"Annuity Tables for Building Societies and General Use." 1881.

The tables in this work give to 4 places the present values of annuities of 1 per month, quarter, or half-year, payable monthly, quarterly, or half-yearly, at rates of interest proceeding by $\frac{1}{2}$ from 3 to 8 per-cent, and convertible with corresponding frequency. The values of n range from 1 to 300 in the monthly table, from 1 to 200 in the quarterly table, and from 1 to 100 in the half-yearly table.

E. PEREIRE.—"Tables de l'Intérêt Composé." 1882.

This work gives the values of $(1+i)^n$, v^n, $s_{\overline{n+1}|}-1$, $a_{\overline{n}|}$, and $\frac{1}{a_{\overline{n}|}}$, to 7 or 8 places, for a fairly extensive range of rates of interest; also $(1+i)^{\frac{n}{12}}$ to 5 places for $n=1$ to 11, and $\frac{\log 2}{\log(1+i)}$ (the time in which a sum of money will double itself at compound interest), $\frac{\log 3}{\log(1+i)}$, &c.

FLEMING'S "Sinking Fund and Loan Repayment Tables." 1886.

This work contains, in addition to various tables of the values of the elementary functions, a table of the values of $\frac{s_{\overline{r}|}}{s_{\overline{n}|}}$ (or ${}_r\mathrm{V}_{\overline{n}|}$) to 8 places, for $n=1$ to 60 and $r=1$ to n, at rates of interest proceeding by $\frac{1}{4}$ from $2\frac{1}{2}$ to 4 per-cent.

Lieut.-Col. W. H. OAKES.—"Tables for finding the Intermediate Rates of Interest in an Annuity-Certain." 1887.

These tables are designed to facilitate the calculation of the unknown rate of interest by the first-difference interpolation formula $i=i'-(i'-i'')\frac{a-a'}{a''-a'}$. For each value of n from 1 to 100 the values of $a'_{\overline{n}|}$ and $\frac{\cdot 125}{a''_{\overline{n}|}-a'_{\overline{n}|}}$ are given in parallel columns for each value of i' proceeding by $\frac{1}{8}$ from $\frac{3}{4}$ to 10 per-cent. The values of $a'_{\overline{n}|}$ are given to 5 places up to $n=13$, 4 places from $n=13$ to 15, and 3 places from $n=26$ to 100; those of the multiplier generally to 3 places, but in certain sections of the table to 4 places.

Lieut.-Col. W. H. OAKES.—"Tables for finding the Half-yearly Rate of Interest from $1\frac{1}{4}$ per-cent upwards, realized on Stock or Bonds, bearing $1\frac{1}{2}$, $1\frac{3}{4}$, 2, $2\frac{1}{4}$, $2\frac{1}{2}$, $2\frac{3}{4}$, and 3 per-cent Half-yearly Interest, issued at any premium and redeemable at par in any number of half-years not exceeding 60." 1889.

These tables give, to the nearest 1*d.*, the values of £100 $(g-i)a_{\overline{n}|}$ for $g=\cdot015$, ·0175, ·02, ·0225, ·025, ·0275 and ·03, $i=\cdot0125$, ·013125, ·01375, ... $(g-\cdot00625)$, and $n=3, 4, 5, \ldots\ldots 60$, together with the additions to the tabulated values corresponding to an increase of 1*d.*, 2*d.*, 3*d.*, ... 1*s.* 3*d.* per-cent in the value of i. In the case of a security bearing interest at one of the specified rates, redeemable at par within 30 years, and bought at a premium falling within the range of tabulated values, the yield may therefore be found—practically by inspection—to within a halfpenny (in most cases) of its true value.

W. M. J. WERKER.—"Die zusammengesetze Zinsen und Zeitrenten oder Annuitätenrechnung." Utrecht and Berlin, 1893.

Appended to this work are tables of the values of $(1+i)^n$, v^n, $s_{\overline{n+1}|}-1$, $a_{\overline{n}|}$, and $\frac{1}{a_{\overline{n}|}}$, all to 8 places of decimals, for values of i proceeding by $\frac{1}{8}$ from 0 to 10 per-cent for $n=1$ to 100, also for values of i proceeding by $\frac{1}{8}$ from 0 to 5 per-cent for $n=101$ to 200.

J. A. ARCHER.—"Tables for the Repayment of Loans." 3rd edition. 1897.

These tables give (*a*) the values of $\frac{1}{a_{\overline{n}|}}$ for all values of n from 1 to 60 at rates of interest proceeding by $\frac{1}{8}$ from 2 to 5 per-cent, (*b*) the values of $\frac{1}{a_{\overline{n}|}}$ for *even* values of n from 2 to 120 at rates of interest proceeding by $\frac{1}{16}$ from 1 to $2\frac{1}{2}$ per-cent, (*c*) the values of $s_{\overline{n}|}$ for all values of n from 1 to 60 at rates of interest proceeding by $\frac{1}{4}$ from 2 to $3\frac{1}{2}$ per-cent, also at 4 and 5 per-cent, (*d*) the values of $\frac{1}{2}s_{\overline{n}|}$ for *even* values of n from 1 to 120 at rates of interest proceeding by $\frac{1}{8}$ from 1 to $1\frac{3}{4}$ per-cent, also at 2 and $2\frac{1}{2}$ per-cent.

All the results are given to 7 places of decimals, and also for (*a*) and (*b*) in money to the nearest farthing per-cent.

S. SPITZER.—"Tabellen für die Zinses-Zinsen und Renten-Rechnung. 4th edition. 1897.

These tables give (*a*) the values of $(1+i)^n$, v^n, $s_{\overline{n+1}|}-1$, $a_{\overline{n}|}$ and $\frac{1}{a_{\overline{n}|}}$ for all values of n from 1 to 100, at rates of interest proceeding by $\frac{1}{8}$ and $\frac{1}{6}$ from 0 to 6 per-cent, and thence by $\frac{1}{4}$ and $\frac{1}{3}$ to 10 per-cent, also at $3\frac{17}{21}$ per-cent (being 4 per-cent on 105), and at the rates of interest corresponding to the following rates of discount: 1, 2, $2\frac{1}{4}$, $2\frac{1}{2}$, $2\frac{5}{8}$, $2\frac{3}{4}$, $2\frac{7}{8}$, 3, $3\frac{1}{4}$, $3\frac{1}{2}$, $3\frac{3}{4}$, $4\frac{1}{2}$, 5, $5\frac{1}{2}$, and 6 per-cent (122 rates in all); (*b*) the values of $\frac{1}{a_{\overline{n}|}}$ at the rates of interest corresponding to the rates of discount specified in (*a*), with the addition of 4 per-cent.

All the results are given to 8 places of decimals.

In addition to the foregoing, the following special tables may be mentioned:—

W. S. B. WOOLHOUSE'S Tables of the values of δ and $\log \delta$, to 5 places of decimals, for values of i proceeding by $\frac{1}{2}$ from $\frac{1}{2}$ to 10 per-cent. *J.I.A.*, xv, 125.

W. H. MAKEHAM'S Table of the values of $\log \frac{e^x - 1}{x}$ to 7 places of decimals for values of x proceeding by ·01 from 0 to 10·4 with supplementary columns by which the values of the function for intermediate values of x may be calculated. *J.I.A.*, xv, 437.

D. J. McG. McKENZIE'S Tables of the values of $\log \frac{mi}{j_{(m)}}$ (to 7 places) and $\frac{j_{(m)}}{m}$ (to 8 increasing to 10 places) for $m = 2, 4, 12, 26, 52$ and ∞, at rates of interest proceeding by $\frac{1}{8}$ from $2\frac{1}{2}$ to 10 per-cent. *J.I.A.*, xxiii, 183–4.

P. GRAY'S Table of the values of $\log_{10}(1+i)$ to 15 places of decimals for values of i proceeding by $\frac{1}{16}$ from 0 to 10 per-cent. First Edition of this Work, pp. 166–7.

Interest Tables of limited extent will be found in many text-books and works of reference. A few tables, taken mainly from the "Short Collection of Actuarial Tables", printed by the Institute of Actuaries for examination purposes, are appended to this work for the convenience of students.

CHAPTER IX.

FORMULAS OF THE INFINITESIMAL CALCULUS.

1. In the investigations of the following chapter an elementary knowledge of the notation and methods of the Calculus of Finite Differences and the Infinitesimal Calculus will be required. For the elements of the Calculus of Finite Differences, reference may be made to Part II of the *Text-Book;* in the present chapter it is proposed to give some account of the elementary methods of the Infinitesimal Calculus.

2. The Infinitesimal Calculus is practically restricted in its applications to functions which possess (it may be within certain limits) the property of *continuity*, and it will be necessary, therefore, to consider in the first instance the nature of a continuous function.

3. A quantity or magnitude is said to admit of *continuous variation* between certain limits when any intermediate value may be assigned to it between those limits. Thus, in the expression v^t, denoting the present value, at the effective rate of interest i, of 1 receivable at the end of t years (where t may be either integral or partly integral and partly fractional), the index t admits of continuous variation between 0 and any positive finite value, and over any given range of say n years an infinite number of different values may be assigned to it, each successive value differing from the preceding one by an infinitely small quantity.

4. A quantity which does not admit of variation is called a *constant* quantity. Thus, in the illustration given in the preceding article, if in a given problem the rate of interest be fixed, the quantity v will be a constant for the purposes of that problem. On the other hand, the expression v^t might, for the purposes of some other problem, be used to denote the present value, at any effective rate of interest within certain limits, of 1 receivable at the end of a fixed term of t years; in that case t would be a constant, and v would admit of continuous variation within the specified limits.

5. One variable quantity is said to be a *function* of another when, if any other quantities involved in the expression of the former in terms of the latter remain unchanged, the value assigned to the latter determines the value of the former. Thus, v^t is a function of t, because for a given constant rate of interest i its value is determined by the value of t. Similarly, v^t is a function of v or i, because for a given constant value of t its value is determined by the value assigned to v or i.

6. When one variable quantity is a function of another, the latter is called the *independent variable*, and the former the *dependent variable.* In investigations of a general character, the independent and dependent variables are usually denoted by x and y respectively, and the relation between them is expressed in some such form as $y=f(x)$, $y=F(x)$, or $y=\phi(x)$. Here x is the *independent* variable, and y is the *dependent* variable, and the value of the latter can be determined for any given value of the former, if the form of the function f, F, or ϕ, be known.

7. A function $f(x)$ is said to be a *continuous* function of x for all values of x between the limits a and b when, for each value of x between those limits, (i) $f(x)$ has a finite value, and (ii) an infinitely small change in the value of x produces an infinitely small change in the value of $f(x)$.

For example, v^t is a continuous function of t between any finite limits, for it assumes a finite value for any assigned finite value of t, and, further, the change of $v^t(v^h-1)$, produced in its value by a change of h in the value of t, becomes infinitely small when h is indefinitely diminished.

8. If $f(x)$ be a continuous function of x for all values of a between $x=a$ and $x=b$, then, since each infinitely small change in the value of x produces an infinitely small change in the value of $f(x)$, it follows that as x changes from a to b, $f(x)$ must assume at least once every intermediate value between $f(a)$ and $f(b)$. It may be noted also, as a necessary consequence of this, that if $f(a)$ and $f(b)$ have *different signs*, there must be some value of x between

a and b for which $f(x)=0$, for in changing from a positive to a negative value the function must pass through zero.

9. A continuous function may be represented *geometrically* in the following way:—

Let OA and OB be measured to the right along OX to represent a and b respectively, and let the ordinates AM and BN be erected at right angles to OX to represent (on a proportionate scale) $f(a)$ and $f(b)$ respectively. Then, if $f(x)$ be a continuous function of x from $x=a$ to $x=b$, it follows from the definition in Art. 7 that $f(x)$ has a *finite* value for each value of x intermediate between a and b. Hence, if OC represent any such intermediate value of x, an ordinate CQ may be drawn to represent (on the same scale as before) the corresponding value of $f(x)$. Suppose an infinitely large number of such ordinates to be drawn to represent the successive values assumed by $f(x)$ as x passes by infinitely small increments from the value a to the value b. Then it is clear from what has been said in Art. 8 that the ends of these ordinates would form a continuous chain of points from M to N. This chain of points, or *curve*, forms a geometrical representation of the function $f(x)$ from $x=a$ to $x=b$.

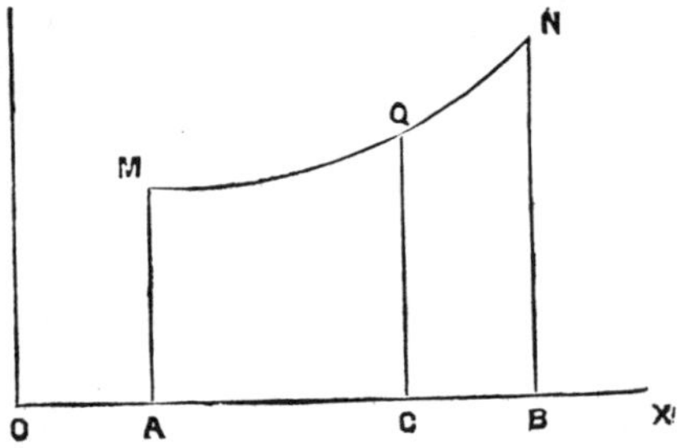

10. It would not, of course, be possible to actually construct the curve representing any given function by the method just indicated. There are, however, certain special functions—such, for example, as those represented by a straight line, a circle, and an ellipse—for which a continuous curve may be drawn by some mechanical contrivance. Moreover, the general course of any function may often be indicated with sufficient accuracy for practical purposes by erecting a number of ordinates for various values of the independent variable, and drawing a *freehand* curve through their ends.

Take, for example, the function $(1+i)^t$.

At the point O in the line $X'OX$ erect an ordinate OB to represent unity—or, what is the same thing $(1+i)^0$. Take OA_1, A_1A_2, A_2A_3, &c., to the right along OX, and Oa_1, a_1a_2, a_2a_3, &c., to the left along OX' each $= OB$ or unity, and erect the ordinates

$A_1 B_1$, $A_2 B_2$, $A_3 B_3$, &c., to represent $(1+i)$, $(1+i)^2$, $(1+i)^3$, &c., respectively, and the ordinates $a_1 b_1$, $a_2 b_2$, $a_3 b_3$, &c., to represent v, v^2, v^3, &c., respectively. Then the points . . . . b_3, b_2, b_1, B, B_1, B_2, B_3, ... lie on the chain of points, or curve, representing the function $(1+i)^x$, and some idea of the *general course* of the function may be gathered by drawing a freehand curve through these points as shown in the diagram.

It will be readily seen that the ordinate of the curve tends, ultimately, to become zero in the direction $O X'$ and infinitely great in the direction $O X$.

11. The diagram given in the last article may be further utilized for the purpose of obtaining a geometrical representation of the functions $s_{\overline{n}|}$, $s^{(m)}_{\overline{n}|}$, $\bar{s}_{\overline{n}|}$, $a_{\overline{n}|}$, $a^{(m)}_{\overline{n}|}$, and $\bar{a}_{\overline{n}|}$. For, let perpendiculars $B K_1$, $B_1 K_2$, $B_2 K_3$, &c., be drawn from B, B_1, B_2, &c., to $A_1 B_1$, $A_2 B_2$, $A_3 B_3$, &c., and let perpendiculars $b_1 k$, $b_2 k_1$, $b_3 k_2$, &c., be drawn from b_1, b_2, b_3, &c., to $O B$, $a_1 b_1$, $a_2 b_2$, &c. Then, since $O A_1$, $A_1 A_2$, $A_2 A_3$, &c., $O a_1$, $a_1 a_2$, $a_2 a_3$, &c., are all equal to unity, and the ordinates $O B$, $A_1 B_1$, $A_2 B_2$, &c., $a_1 b_1$, $a_2 b_2$, $a_3 b_3$, &c., respectively represent 1, $(1+i)$, $(1+i)^2$, &c., v, v^2, v^3, &c., it is clear that the rectangles $K_1 O$, $K_2 A_1$, $K_3 A_2$, &c., represent geometrically the products of unity, and 1, $(1+i)$, $(1+i)^2$, &c., and that the rectangles $k\, a_1$, $k_1 a_2$, $k_2 a_3$, &c., represent geometrically the products of unity and v, v^2, v^3, &c.

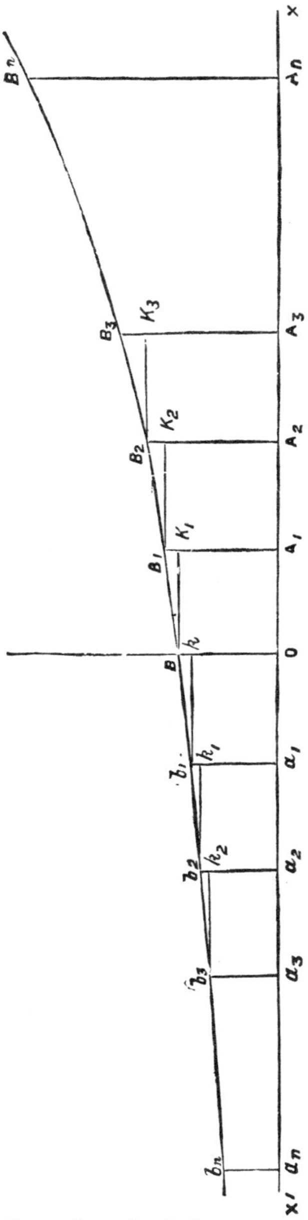

Hence, if $O\,A_n$ and $O\,a_n$ be measured to the right and left respectively of O, each $= n\,O\,B$ or n, and if a rectangle be constructed on each unit of the bases $O\,A_n$ $O\,a_n$ in the same manner as those constructed in the diagram, the total area contained by the n rectangles constructed on $O\,A_n$ will represent $1 + (1+i) + (1+i)^2 + \ldots + (1+i)^{n-1}$ or $s_{\overline{n}|}$, and the total area contained by the n rectangles constructed on $O\,a_n$ will represent $v+v^2+v^3+\ldots+v^n$ or $a_{\overline{n}|}$.

Next, let each of the bases $O\,A_1$, $A_1\,A_2$, $O\,a_1$, $a_1\,a_2$, &c., be divided into m equal parts, let ordinates be drawn to the curve from the points of sub-division, and let a new series of rectangles be constructed by drawing perpendiculars from the point at which each ordinate meets the curve to the next succeeding ordinate to the right. Then the ordinates to the right of $O\,B$ will be respectively equal to $(1+i)^{\frac{1}{m}}$, $(1+i)^{\frac{2}{m}}$, $(1+i)^{\frac{3}{m}}$, &c.... $(1+i)^{n-\frac{1}{m}}$, and those to the left of $O\,B$ will be respectively equal to $v^{\frac{1}{m}}$, $v^{\frac{2}{m}}$, $v^{\frac{3}{m}}$, &c. ... v^n. Hence, since the bases of the new series of rectangles are all $= \frac{1}{m}$, the total area contained by the new rectangles now constructed on the base $O\,A_n$ will represent

$$\frac{1}{m}[1+(1+i)^{\frac{1}{m}}+(1+i)^{\frac{2}{m}}+\ldots+(1+i)^{n-\frac{1}{m}}] \text{ or } s^{(m)}_{\overline{n}|},$$

and the total area contained by the new rectangles constructed on $O\,a_n$ will represent

$$\frac{1}{m}(v^{\frac{1}{m}}+v^{\frac{2}{m}}+\ldots+v^n) \text{ or } a^{(m)}_{\overline{n}|}.$$

If now m be indefinitely increased, the area contained by the resulting series of rectangles on the base $O\,A_n$ will ultimately coincide with the figure contained by $O\,B$, $O\,A_n$, $A_n\,B_n$, and the intercepted portion of the curve, and, similarly, the area contained by the rectangles on the base $O\,a_n$ will ultimately coincide with the figure contained by $O\,B$, $O\,a_n$, $a_n\,b_n$, and the intercepted portion of the curve. But, if m be indefinitely increased, $s^{(m)}_{\overline{n}|}$ becomes $\bar{s}_{\overline{n}|}$, and $a^{(m)}_{\overline{n}|}$ becomes $\bar{a}_{\overline{n}|}$. Hence, the area bounded by $O\,B$, $O\,A_n$, $A_n\,B_n$ and the curve geometrically represents $\bar{s}_{\overline{n}|}$, and the area bounded by $O\,B$, $O\,a_n$, $a_n\,b_n$ and the curve geometrically represents $\bar{a}_{\overline{n}|}$.

12. The foregoing explanation of the nature of a continuous function may assist the student to understand the general character of the problems to which the methods of the Infinitesimal Calculus are more particularly adapted.

The ordinary arithmetical or algebraical Calculus and the Calculus of Finite Differences furnish methods of dealing with the values of a function corresponding to any specified values of the independent variable, and with the changes in the value of the function resulting from any *finite* changes in the value of the independent variable. The Infinitesimal Calculus, on the other hand, affords a means of dealing with problems in which account has to be taken of *all* the values assumed by a function in passing from the value corresponding to one value of the independent variable to that corresponding to another, or of the change in the value of the function corresponding to an infinitely small change in the value of the independent variable. The Differential Calculus deals primarily with the latter class of problems, the Integral Calculus with the former.

13. When a variable quantity changes from one value to another, the amount by which the latter value exceeds the former is called the *increment* of the quantity. An increment in the value of the independent variable x is frequently denoted by h, Δx, or δx, and the corresponding increment in the value of the dependent variable y by k, Δy, or δy.

14. Let y be a continuous function of x for all values of x between certain limits; within those limits let x receive an increment h, and let the corresponding increment in y be k, so that, if $y=f(x)$,

$$y+k=f(x+h),$$

and

$$k=f(x+h)-y=f(x+h)-f(x).$$

Then it is clear that the *rate of change* of y corresponding to an infinitely small increment of x will be measured by the limiting value, when $h=0$, of $\frac{k}{h}$ or $\frac{f(x+h)-f(x)}{h}$. This limiting value is called the *first derived function* or *differential coefficient* of y according to x, and is denoted by $f'(x)$, or $\frac{dy}{dx}$, or $\frac{df(x)}{dx}$.

Thus, $f'(x)$ or $\frac{dy}{dx} = \text{Lt}_{h=0}\frac{f(x+h)-f(x)}{h}$.

The identity $\frac{dy}{dx}=f'(x)$ may be written in the form

$$dy=f'(x)dx.$$

with the meaning that the limiting value of the ratio of Δy to $f'(x)\Delta x$ is unity.

15. A geometrical interpretation of the differential coefficient of a function may be obtained in the following way:—Let the curve in the annexed diagram be the curve representing the function $f(x)$, and let $OA=x$, so that the ordinate AM represents y or $f(x)$. Take $AB=h$ and draw the ordinate BN. Then $BN=y+k$ or $f(x+h)$. Draw MQ perpendicular to BN, join NM and produce it to cut

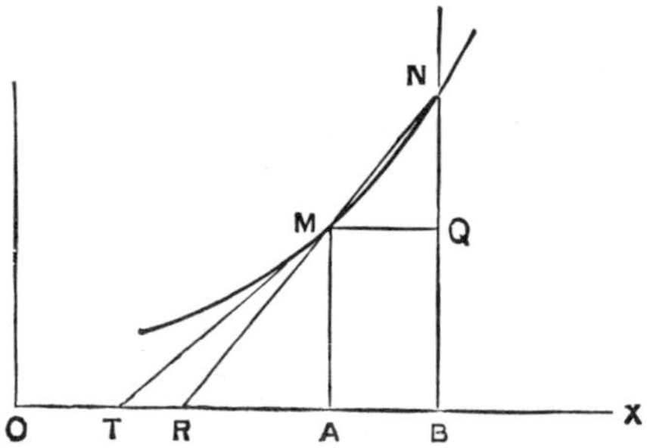

OX in R. Then $NQ=k$, and $\dfrac{NQ}{MQ}$ or $\dfrac{NB}{BR}=\dfrac{k}{h}$ or $\dfrac{f(x+h)-f(x)}{h}$

Now suppose h to be indefinitely diminished. Then the points B and N move up to the points A and M respectively, and the line NMQ tends towards a limiting position MT, say, and becomes a tangent to the curve at the point M. Hence, the limiting value of $\dfrac{f(x+h)-f(x)}{h}$ is $\dfrac{AM}{AT}$, where MT is a tangent to the curve at the point M. In symbols $\dfrac{dy}{dx}$ or $f'(x)=\dfrac{AM}{AT}$.

16. The greater the value of $f'(x)$, the greater will be the ratio $\dfrac{AM}{AT}$, and the greater, consequently, the angle which the tangent to the curve makes with OX. It appears, therefore, that the differential coefficient affords a measure of the gradient or *steepness* of the curve at any given point.

It is evident, also, that a small increment in the value of x will produce an increment or decrement in the value of y according as $f'(x)$ is positive or negative. Hence, if $f'(x)$ is positive for all values of x over a given range, then $f(x)$ increases with x throughout that range, and, conversely, if $f'(x)$ is negative for all values of x over a given range, then throughout that range $f(x)$ decreases as x increases. Again, if $f'(x)$ is positive for all values of x throughout a certain range up to $x=a$, and negative for all greater values of x throughout a certain range, or, in other words, if $f'(x)$ changes from *positive* to *negative* as x passes through the value a, then $f(x)$ *increases* with x up to $x=a$, and then *decreases*. Similarly, if $f'(x)$ changes from *negative* to *positive*, as x passes through the value a, then $f(x)$ *decreases* as x increases up to $x=a$ and then *increases*. Now, as explained in Art. 8, in changing from positive to negative, or from negative to positive, $f'(x)$ must pass through zero. Hence, if $f(x)$ increase with x up to $x=a$ and thereafter decrease, or *vice versa*, $f'(a)=0$. When a function increases up to a certain value of the independent variable and then decreases, it is said to have a *maximum* value, or to be a maximum for that value of the variable; and when it decreases as the variable increases up to a certain value and then increases, it is said to have a *minimum* value, or to be a minimum for that value of the variable. The result just obtained may, therefore, be expressed in the statement that, if $f(x)$ is a *maximum* or *minimum* for $x=a$, $f'(a)=0$. It will be shown hereafter, analytically, that this is a necessary condition, although not the only necessary condition, for the existence of a maximum or minimum.

Geometrically, it will be obvious that the equation $f'(a)=0$ expresses the condition that the tangent to the curve at the point corresponding to the value a of x should be parallel to OX, and it is clear that this will be the case at any point at which the curve attains a maximum or minimum distance from OX, at which, that is to say, $f(x)$ is a maximum or minimum.

17. The operation of finding the differential coefficient of a function is called *differentiating* the function. Any given function which admits of differentiation may be differentiated from first principles by finding the limit of the expression $\dfrac{f(x+h)-f(x)}{h}$ when $x=0$, but the process may in many cases be simplified by the aid of the following general rules:—

(i) The differential coefficient of a constant is zero.

This is obvious, since a change in the independent variable does not produce any corresponding change in a constant.

Hence, *additive* or *subtractive* constants (as distinguished from constants involved as coefficients or indices of variable quantities) disappear on differentiation.

(ii) The differential coefficient of the algebraic sum of a number of functions is the sum of the differential coefficients of the several functions.

Let $y=u+v+w\ldots$, where $u, v, w\ldots$ are functions of x.

Then, if Δy, Δu, Δv, $\Delta w\ldots$ are the increments of $y, u, v, w\ldots$ corresponding to an increment of Δx in x,

$$y+\Delta y=u+\Delta u+v+\Delta v+w+\Delta w+\ldots$$

whence $$\Delta y=\Delta u+\Delta v+\Delta w+\ldots$$

and $$\frac{\Delta y}{\Delta x}=\frac{\Delta u}{\Delta x}+\frac{\Delta v}{\Delta x}+\frac{\Delta w}{\Delta x}+\ldots$$

which becomes in the limit, when Δx is indefinitely diminished,

$$\frac{dy}{dx}=\frac{du}{dx}+\frac{dv}{dx}+\frac{dw}{dx}+\ldots$$

(iii) The differential coefficient of the product of two functions is the sum of the products of each function and the differential coefficient of the other.

Let $$y=uv,$$

where u and v are both functions of x.

Then $$\begin{aligned}\Delta y&=(u+\Delta u)(v+\Delta v)-uv\\&=u\Delta v+v\Delta u+\Delta u\,.\,\Delta v\\&=u\Delta v+(v+\Delta v)\Delta u\end{aligned}$$

and $$\frac{\Delta y}{\Delta x}=u\frac{\Delta v}{\Delta x}+(v+\Delta v)\frac{\Delta u}{\Delta x},$$

whence, in the limit, since $v+\Delta v$ becomes v,

$$\frac{dy}{dx}=u\frac{dv}{dx}+v\frac{du}{dx}.$$

If v be a constant, C say, so that $y=\mathrm{C}u$, then by rule (i) its differential coefficient vanishes, and $\frac{dy}{dx}=\mathrm{C}\frac{du}{dx}$.

(iv) The differential coefficient of the product of any number of functions is the sum of the products of the differential coefficient of each function and the remaining functions.

Let $$y = uvw.$$

Put $vw = z$. Then $y = uz$

and $$\frac{dy}{dx} = u\frac{dz}{dx} + z\frac{du}{dx}.$$

But since $$z = vw,\ \frac{dz}{dx} = v\frac{dw}{dx} + w\frac{dv}{dx}.$$

$$\therefore\quad \frac{dy}{dx} = uv\frac{dw}{dx} + vw\frac{du}{dx} + wu\frac{dv}{dx}.$$

This result may be written in the form—

$$\frac{1}{y}\frac{dy}{dx} = \frac{1}{u}\frac{du}{dx} + \frac{1}{v}\frac{dv}{dx} + \frac{1}{w}\frac{dw}{dx}$$

and can obviously be extended to the product of any number of functions.

(v) The differential coefficient of the quotient of two functions is the result obtained by deducting the product of the numerator and the differential coefficient of the denominator from the product of the denominator, and the differential coefficient of the numerator, and dividing by the square of the denominator.

Let $$y = \frac{u}{v}.$$

Then $$\Delta y = \frac{u + \Delta u}{v + \Delta v} - \frac{u}{v} = \frac{v\Delta u - u\Delta v}{v(v + \Delta v)},$$

whence $$\frac{\Delta y}{\Delta x} = \frac{v\dfrac{\Delta u}{\Delta x} - u\dfrac{\Delta v}{\Delta x}}{v(v + \Delta v)}$$

and, in the limit, $$\frac{dy}{dx} = \frac{1}{v^2}\left(v\frac{du}{dx} - u\frac{dv}{dx}\right).$$

This result may be written in the symmetrical form—

$$\frac{1}{y}\frac{dy}{dx} = \frac{1}{u}\frac{du}{dx} - \frac{1}{v}\frac{dv}{dx}.$$

(vi) The differential coefficient of y according to x, where y is a function of u and u is a function of x, is the product of the differential coefficients of y according to u and u according to x.

For let Δy and Δu be the increments of y and u corresponding to an increment of Δx in x.

Then $$\frac{\Delta y}{\Delta x}=\frac{\Delta y}{\Delta u}\cdot\frac{\Delta u}{\Delta x} \text{ identically,}$$

whence, in the limit,

$$\frac{dy}{dx}=\frac{dy}{du}\cdot\frac{du}{dx}.$$

18. It is now necessary to determine the differential coefficients of those functions which occur most commonly, alone or in combination, in practice. Most of these must be deduced from first principles.

(i) To find the differential coefficient of a rational power.

Let $y=x^n$, and first let n be integral.

Then $$\frac{dy}{dx}=\text{Lt}_{h=0}\frac{(x+h)^n-x^n}{h}$$

$$=\text{Lt}_{h=0}\left[nx^{n-1}+\frac{n(n-1)}{2!}hx^{n-2}+\ldots+h^{n-1}\right]$$

The terms after the first, being finite in number, vanish when h becomes infinitely small.

Hence, if n be integral, $\dfrac{dy}{dx}=nx^{n-1}$. Next, let n be fractional, and $=\dfrac{r}{s}$ where r and s are both integral. Then $y^s=x^r$.

Now, by the result just obtained,

$$\frac{d(y^s)}{dy}=sy^{s-1}=sx^{\frac{r(s-1)}{s}} \text{ and } \frac{d(x^r)}{dx}=rx^{r-1},$$

and, by Art. 17 (vi), $$\frac{d(y^s)}{dx}=\frac{d(y^s)}{dy}\cdot\frac{dy}{dx}.$$

Hence $$\frac{dy}{dx}=\frac{1}{sx^{\frac{r(s-1)}{s}}}\cdot rx^{r-1}=\frac{r}{s}\cdot x^{\frac{r}{s}-1}.$$

Lastly, let n be negative and $=-t$.

Then $y=\dfrac{1}{x^t}$.

Now, by Art. 17 (v), $$\frac{d\left(\frac{1}{x^t}\right)}{dx}=\frac{-\frac{d(x^t)}{dx}}{x^{2t}},$$

which, since t is positive, $=\frac{-tx^{t-1}}{x^{2t}}=-tx^{-(t+1)}$;

$$\therefore \quad \frac{dy}{dx}=-tx^{-(t+1)}.$$

Hence, if n be any rational quantity, positive, negative, or fractional,

$$\frac{d(x^n)}{dx}=nx^{n-1}.$$

(ii) To find the differential coefficient of an exponential.

Let $y=e^x$.

Then $$\frac{dy}{dx}=\text{Lt}_{h=0}\frac{e^{x+h}-e^x}{h}=e^x\text{Lt}_{h=0}\frac{e^h-1}{h}.$$

Now $$\frac{e^h-1}{h}=1+\frac{h}{2}\left(1+\frac{h}{3}+\frac{h^2}{3.4}+\ldots\right),$$

the limiting value of which, when h becomes infinitely small, is **1**.

Hence $$\frac{dy}{dx}=e^x.$$

Next, let $y=a^x$.

Then $$\log_e y = x\log_e a,$$

and $$y=e^{x\log_e a}=e^u,$$

where $$x\log_e a=u.$$

Now $$\frac{d(e^u)}{dx}=\frac{d(e^u)}{du}\cdot\frac{du}{dx}.$$

Hence $$\frac{dy}{dx}=e^u\cdot\frac{d(x\log_e a)}{dx}$$

$$=e^u.\log_e a$$

$$=a^x.\log_e a.$$

(iii) To find the differential coefficient of a logarithm.

Let $$y=\log_e x.$$

Then $$e^y=x.$$

Now, by Art. 17 (vi), since y is a function of x, and e^y is a function of y,

$$\frac{de^y}{dx}=\frac{de^y}{dy}\cdot\frac{dy}{dx}.$$

But, by example (ii) of this Article,

$$\frac{de^y}{dy}=e^y.$$

Hence $$e^y\frac{dy}{dx}=\frac{dx}{dx}=1,$$

whence $$\frac{dy}{dx}=e^{-y}=\frac{1}{x}.$$

Since $$\log_a x=\frac{\log_e x}{\log_e a},$$

it follows that $$\frac{d(\log_a x)}{dx}=\frac{1}{x\log_e a}.$$

19. In differentiating a function consisting of a number of factors, it is often convenient to take logarithms. For example, let $y=\dfrac{uvw\ldots}{f\phi\theta\ldots}$, where u, v, w, f, ϕ, θ, &c., are all functions of x. Then

$$\log y=\log u+\log v+\log w+\ldots-\log f-\log\phi-\log\theta-\ldots$$

and $$\frac{1}{y}\frac{dy}{dx}=\frac{1}{u}\frac{du}{dx}+\frac{1}{v}\frac{dv}{dx}+\frac{1}{w}\frac{dw}{dx}+\ldots$$
$$-\frac{1}{f}\frac{df}{dx}-\frac{1}{\phi}\frac{d\phi}{dx}-\frac{1}{\theta}\frac{d\theta}{dx}-\ldots$$

whence $$\frac{dy}{dx}=\frac{uvw\ldots}{f\phi\theta\ldots}\left[\frac{1}{u}\frac{du}{dx}+\frac{1}{v}\frac{dv}{dx}+\frac{1}{w}\frac{dw}{dx}+\ldots\right.$$
$$\left.-\frac{1}{f}\frac{df}{dx}-\frac{1}{\phi}\frac{d\phi}{dx}-\frac{1}{\theta}\frac{d\theta}{dx}-\ldots\right]$$

It may be easily seen that this result is identical with that obtained by the application of rules (iv) and (v) of Art. 17.

The same artifice may be conveniently adopted in many other cases. Let it be required, for example, to find the differential coefficient of g^{c^x}.

Here $\log_e y = c^x \log_e g$

hence $\frac{1}{y}\frac{dy}{dx} = c^x \log_e c \log_e g$

and $\frac{dy}{dx} = c^x \log_e c \log_e g \cdot g^{c^x}.$

20. The result of differentiating $\frac{dy}{dx}$ according to x is called the *second differential coefficient* or *second derivative* of y. The second differential coefficient of y is denoted by the symbol $\frac{d^2y}{dx^2}$, or, if $y=f(x)$, by $f''(x)$. Similarly, the result of repeating the operation of differentiation n times in succession is called the nth differential coefficient or derivative, and is denoted by $\frac{d^ny}{dx^n}$, or $f^{(n)}(x)$.

21. If y be a product of two functions of x, u and v, it may be easily shown, by a method similar to that employed in establishing the Binomial Theorem for a positive integral exponent, that

$$\frac{d^ny}{dx^n} = u\frac{d^nv}{dx^n} + n\frac{du}{dx}\cdot\frac{d^{n-1}v}{dx^{n-1}} + \frac{n(n-1)}{2}\frac{d^2u}{dx^2}\cdot\frac{d^{n-2}v}{dx^{n-2}} + \ldots$$
$$+ n\frac{d^{n-1}u}{dx^{n-1}}\cdot\frac{dv}{dx} + \frac{d^nu}{dx^n}\cdot v.$$

22. If $y = a_0 + a_1x + a_2x^2 + \ldots + a_nx^n$,

then $\frac{dy}{dx} = a_1 + 2a_2x + 3a_3x^2 + \ldots + na_nx^{n-1}$

$$\frac{d^2y}{dx^2} = 2a_2 + 2\cdot 3a_3x + \ldots + n(n-1)a_nx^{n-2}$$
$$\vdots$$

and $\frac{d^ny}{dx^n} = n!\,a_n.$

Hence, if y be a rational integral function of x of the nth degree, each derivative is a function of a degree one lower than the preceding derivative, the nth derivative is a constant, and all higher derivatives vanish.

23. Let $f(x)$ be a function of x, which admits of being expanded in a convergent series in powers of x for all values of x within a certain range. Then it may be shown, and will here be assumed, that the function and its successive derivatives are continuous within the specified range of values of x.

Assume that $\quad f(x)=a_0+a_1x+a_2x^2+a_3x^3+\ldots$

Then
$$\begin{aligned} f'(x)&=a_1+2a_2x+3a_3x^2+\ldots \\ f''(x)&=\quad 2a_2+2\,.\,3a_3x+\ldots \\ &\vdots \\ f^{(n)}(x)&=\qquad\qquad n!\,a_n+\ldots \end{aligned}$$

Put $x=0$ in these equations. Then

$$a_0=f(0)\;;\;\; a_1=f'(0)\;;\;\; a_2=\frac{1}{2\,!}f''(0)\;;\;\; \&c.\ \ldots\ a_n=\frac{1}{n\,!}f^{(n)}(0),$$

where $f(0)$, $f'(0)$, $f''(0)$, &c., denote the results obtained by putting $x=0$ in $f(x)$ and its 1st, 2nd, &c., derivatives.

Hence, by substitution of these values in the original expansion, it follows that

$$f(x)=f(0)+xf'(0)+\frac{x^2}{2\,!}f''(0)+\ldots+\frac{x^n}{n\,!}f^{(n)}(0)+\ldots$$

Again, let $f(x)=\phi(a+x)$.

Then $$f'(x)=\phi'(a+x)\,\frac{d(a+x)}{dx}=\phi'(a+x)$$

$$f''(x)=\frac{d}{dx}\,\phi'(a+x)=\phi''(a+x)\,\frac{d(a+x)}{dx}=\phi''(a+x),$$

and so on, whence, if x be put $=0$,

$$f(0)=\phi(a)\;;\;\; f'(0)=\phi'(a)\;;\;\; f''(0)=\phi''(a)\;;\;\; \&c.$$

Hence, by substitution,

$$\phi(a+x)=\phi(a)+x\phi'(a)+\frac{x^2}{2\,!}\,\phi''(a)+\ldots$$

The expansions just obtained are known as Maclaurin's and Taylor's Theorems respectively, and it must be borne in mind that their applicability in any given case depends upon whether the function fulfils the assumed conditions.

As an example of the application of Maclaurin's Theorem, let it be required to expand e^x in powers of x. If $f(x)=e^x$, then $f'(x)=e^x$.

$f''(x)=e^x$, and generally $f^{(n)}(x)=e^x$. Hence $f(0)=1$; $f'(0)=1$; $f''(0)=1$; and $f^{(n)}(0)=1$; whence

$$e^x=1+x+\frac{x^2}{2\,!}+\frac{x^3}{3\,!}+\ldots+\frac{x^n}{n\,!}+\ldots$$

This series is known to be convergent for all values of n.

Again, as an example of the application of Taylor's Theorem, let it be required to expand $(a+x)^n$ in a series of powers of x.

Here $\qquad \phi^{(r)}(a)=n(n-1)\ldots(n-r+1)a^{n-r}$

Hence $\qquad (a+x)^n=a^n+na^{n-1}x+\dfrac{n(n-1)}{2\,!}a^{n-2}x^2+\ldots$

If n be negative or fractional and x be $>a$, this series is divergent, and, in that case, therefore, Taylor's expansion would not hold.

24. It has been shown in Art. 16 that if a continuous function $f(x)$ is a maximum or minimum for the value a of the independent variable, then $f'(a)=0$. It will now be desirable to investigate the conditions for a maximum or minimum analytically. A maximum value of a continuous function is one which is greater, and a minimum value is one which is less than the neighbouring values on either side. In symbols, if $f(x)$ be a maximum for $x=a$, then, for small values of h, $f(a+h)-f(a)$ and $f(a-h)-f(a)$ must both be *negative*, and, similarly, if it be a minimum, then these expressions must both be *positive*. Now, by Taylor's Theorem,

$$f(a+h)-f(a)=hf'(a)+\frac{h^2}{2\,!}f''(a)+\frac{h^3}{3\,!}f'''(a)+\ldots$$

and $\qquad f(a-h)-f(a)=-hf'(a)+\dfrac{h^2}{2\,!}f''(a)-\dfrac{h^3}{3\,!}f'''(a)+\ldots$

If $f'(a)$ be not 0, then $f(a+h)-f(a)$ and $f(a-h)-f(a)$ will have different signs, for, since h may be made indefinitely small, the signs of the right-hand sides of the two equations will be determined by that of $f'(a)$. But, in order that $f(x)$ may be a maximum or minimum for $x=a$, $f(a+h)-f(a)$ and $f(a-h)-f(a)$ must have the *same* sign. Hence, for a maximum or minimum, $f'(a)=0$. If, now, $f''(a)$ be *positive*, then $f(x)$ will be a *minimum* for $x=a$, while, if $f''(a)$ be *negative*, $f(x)$ will be a *maximum*. But, if $f''(a)=0$, then $f'''(a)$ must also be 0, in order that $f(x)$ may be a maximum or minimum for $x=a$, and $f(a)$ will be a maximum or minimum according as $f^{(iv)}(a)$ is negative or positive, and so on. Hence, generally, $f(x)$ will be a maximum or minimum for $x=a$, if the first derivative which is *not* 0 for this value of x is of *even* order, and it will be a maximum or a minimum, according as this derivative is negative or positive. In order, therefore, to find the maxima or minima (if any) of a given function of x, $f(x)$ say, it is necessary (i) to find the values of x which satisfy the equation $f'(x)=0$, and (ii) to examine the corresponding values of the successive derivatives until a derivative is reached which does not vanish.

It may be observed that the maximum values of a function will not all necessarily be greater than its minimum values, for a maximum or minimum value is determined with reference only to the immediately neighbouring values of the function.

25. It has been indicated in Art. 4 that a quantity regarded as a *constant* for the purposes of one problem may become an *independent variable* for the purposes of another. In some problems two or more quantities contained in the expression of a function may have to be regarded as variable, or susceptible of continuous variation. In these circumstances the function would be said to be a function of two, three, &c., variables, as the case might be, and the differential coefficient of the function according to any one of the variables x (the other variables being considered for the moment as constants) is called the *partial differential coefficient* according to x, and is often denoted, for purposes of distinction, by the special symbol $\dfrac{\partial}{\partial x}$.

Thus, if $u=f(x, y)$,

$$\frac{\partial u}{\partial x}=\mathrm{Lt}_{h=0}\frac{f(x+h, y)-f(x, y)}{h}.$$

Let Δu denote the increment of u when *both* x and y are supposed to receive increments, the former of h and the latter of k.

Then
$$\begin{aligned}\Delta u&=f(x+h, y+k)-f(x, y)\\&=f(x+h, y+k)-f(x, y+k)\\&\quad+f(x, y+k)-f(x, y).\end{aligned}$$

Now, as h is indefinitely diminished, $\dfrac{f(x+h, y+k)-f(x, y+k)}{h}$

approaches the limiting value $\frac{\partial f(x, y+k)}{\partial x}$, and when k is indefinitely diminished $\frac{f(x, y+k)-f(x, y)}{k}$ approaches the limiting value $\frac{\partial f(x, y)}{\partial y}$, while $\frac{\partial f(x, y+k)}{\partial x}$ becomes $\frac{\partial f(x, y)}{\partial x}$. Hence, in the limit, the relation $\Delta u = f(x+h, y+k) - f(x, y)$ may be written in the symbolical form

$$du = \frac{\partial f}{\partial x} \cdot dx + \frac{\partial f}{\partial y} \cdot dy.$$

By similar reasoning, this relation can be extended to any number of variables, so that, if $u = f(x, y; z \ldots)$,

$$du = \frac{\partial f}{\partial x} dx + \frac{\partial f}{\partial y} \cdot dy + \frac{\partial f}{\partial z} dz + \ldots$$

Suppose now that $u = f(v, w)$, where both v and w are functions of x. Then, from the above,

$$du = \frac{\partial f}{\partial v} \cdot dv + \frac{\partial f}{\partial w} dw,$$

which may be written in the form

$$du = \frac{\partial f}{\partial v} \cdot \frac{dv}{dx} dx + \frac{\partial f}{\partial w} \cdot \frac{dw}{dx} dx.$$

Hence $$\frac{du}{dx} = \frac{\partial f}{\partial v} \cdot \frac{dv}{dx} + \frac{\partial f}{\partial w} \cdot \frac{dw}{dx}.$$

26. It remains now to explain the notation and elementary methods of the Integral Calculus.

27. Let $\phi(x)$ be a given function of x; then $\phi(a)$ will be the value of the function corresponding to $x = a$, and $\phi(b)$ will be the value corresponding to $x = b$. Now let $b - a = nh$, and let it be required to find the value of $h[\phi(a+h) + \phi(a+2h) + \ldots + \phi(a+nh)]$, that is, the sum of the products of each successive value of the function and the increment in the value of x. The evaluation of this sum, which may be symbolically denoted by $\Sigma_{x=a+h}^{x=a+nh} \phi(x)h$, is a problem in finite summation, and, as such, may be solved by the methods of algebra or finite differences. But suppose h to be indefinitely decreased. The number of terms comprised in Σ will then be indefinitely increased, and as x changes by infinitely small increments from a to b, $\phi(x)$ will assume in succession each corresponding value from $\phi(a)$ to $\phi(b)$. In these circumstances, the limiting value of the sum (if such a value exist) is called the *definite integral* of $\phi(x)$ between the limits a and b, and is denoted by $\int_a^b \phi(x)dx$, the symbol $\int$ being a long *s* (the first letter of the word "sum"), and the dx denoting that the increment h, by which each value of $\phi(x)$ is to be multiplied, is to be indefinitely diminished. The evaluation of this sum is the fundamental problem of the Integral Calculus.

28. A geometrical representation of a definite integral may be obtained in the following way:—

Let the function $\phi(x)$ be represented by the curve shown in the annexed diagram, in the manner explained in Art. 9, so that the ordinate of the curve at any point is the value of $\phi(x)$ corresponding to the value of x represented by the distance along OX from O to the foot of the ordinate. Let $OA=a$ and $OB=b$, let AB be divided into n parts, each $=h$, and on each of these parts let a rectangle be constructed as shown in the diagram. Then

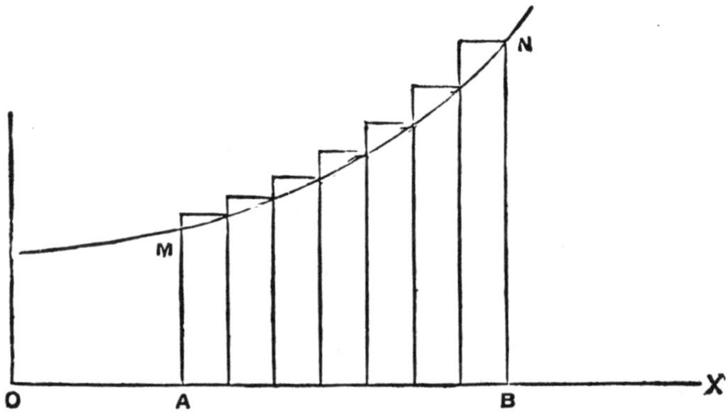

$AM=\phi(a)$, $BN=\phi(b)$, and the area of any one of the rectangles will be $h\phi(a+rh)$. Hence the whole area represented by the rectangles constructed on AB will be $\Sigma_{x=a+h}^{x=a+nh}\phi(x)h$. Now suppose h to be indefinitely diminished. In these circumstances the number of rectangles will become infinitely large, while their bases will become infinitely small, and their total area will ultimately coincide with that contained by AB, AM, BN, and the curve MN. Hence the area contained by the ordinates AM and BN, the base BA and the intercepted portion of the curve forms a geometrical representation of $\int_a^b \phi(x)\,dx$.

29. The applications of the Integral Calculus to the Theory of Compound Interest may now be illustrated. For it has been shown in Art. 11 that if a curve be drawn to represent the function $(1+i)^x$, then the area contained by the base Oa_n drawn to the left along OX' to represent n, the ordinates OB and a_nb_n and the intercepted portion of the curve forms a geometrical representation of $\bar{a}_{\overline{n}|}$. But in the notation of the Integral Calculus, this area is $=\int_0^n v^t dt$.

Hence $$\bar{a}_{\overline{n}|}=\int_0^n v^t dt.$$

Similarly, $$s_{\overline{n}|}=\int_0^n (1+i)^t dt.$$

30. It is now necessary to investigate a method of evaluating the definite integral $\int_a^b \phi(x)dx$.

Let $f(x)$ be a function of x such that $f'(x)=\phi(x)$. Then, since $\phi(x)$ is the limiting value of the expression $\dfrac{f(x+h)-f(x)}{h}$, when h is indefinitely diminished, it follows that $\int_a^b \phi(x)dx$, regarded as the limiting value of $\Sigma_{x=a}^{x=a+(n-1)h}\phi(x)h$, $=$ the limiting value of $\Sigma_{x=a}^{x=a+(n-1)h}[f(x+h)-f(x)]$, that is, of

$$f(a+h)-f(a)+f(a+2h)-f(a+h)+f(a+3h)-f(a+2h)+\dots$$
$$+f(a+nh)-f(a+\overline{n-1}h)$$

which $=f(a+nh)-f(a)$. Now when h is indefinitely diminished, $nh=b-a$, and the expression just given becomes $f(b)-f(a)$.

Hence $$\int_a^b \phi(x)dx=f(b)-f(a)$$

where $$f'(x)=\phi(x).$$

The problem of evaluating the definite integral of $\phi(x)$ resolves itself, therefore, into finding the function whose differential coefficient is $\phi(x)$, that is, into performing a process which is the converse of differentiation. By reference to the object in view, the symbol $\int \phi(x)dx$ is used to denote the process in question, and this symbol is called an *Indefinite Integral* of $\phi(x)$. The process is called *integration.*

31. Although it may be proved that every continuous function has an indefinite integral, no infallible rules can be laid down for finding the integral of any given function. The process rests ultimately on the recognition of the function to be integrated (or of some simpler function upon the integral of which the integral in question may be found to depend), as the differential coefficient of some known function. Hence the requisites for success in integration are (i) a knowledge of the differential coefficients of various standard functions, (ii) a knowledge of the artifices by which indefinite integrals may be resolved into others of a simpler character.

32. It would be beyond the scope of this chapter, or the immediate requirements of students of this work, to attempt to give a complete list of fundamental integrals, or a resumé of methods of reduction Under the first head it will be sufficient to note the following results:—

$$\frac{d}{dx}\cdot x^n = nx^{n-1}. \qquad \text{Hence} \int x^n dx = \frac{x^{n+1}}{n+1}$$

(except for $n=-1$)

$$\frac{d}{dx}\cdot e^x = e^x \qquad \text{,,} \int e^x dx = e^x$$

$$\frac{d}{dx}\cdot a^x = a^x \log_e a \qquad \text{,,} \int a^x dx = \frac{a^x}{\log_e a}$$

$$\frac{d}{dx}\cdot \log_e x = \frac{1}{x} \qquad \text{,,} \int \frac{dx}{x} = \log_e x$$

In all the above results $(x+c)$ may be substituted for x, since the addition of a constant to x does not affect the *form* of the differential coefficient. Similarly, a constant factor may be introduced; thus:—

$\int ce^x dx = ce^x$. Again, since

$$\frac{d}{dx}(u+v+w+\ldots\ ) = \frac{du}{dx} + \frac{dv}{dx} + \frac{dw}{dx} + \ldots$$

it follows that

$$\int (u+v+w+\ldots)dx = \int udx + \int vdx + \int wdx + \ldots$$

For example,

$$\int (a_0 + a_1 x + a_2 x^2 + \ldots + a_n x^n)\,dx$$

$$= a_0 x + a_1 \frac{x^2}{2} + a_2 \frac{x^3}{3} + \ldots + a_n \frac{x^{n+1}}{n+1}.$$

33. Under the second heading mentioned above, two artifices of special utility may be mentioned. The first is the process of *changing the independent variable.*

Let it be required to find $\int \phi(x)\,dx$, and suppose that $\phi(x)$ can be expressed in the form $\psi(u)$, where $u = f(x)$, and that $f'(x) = \chi(u)$, so that $\dfrac{du}{dx} = \chi(u)$. Then $\displaystyle\int \phi(x)\,dx = \int \psi(u)\frac{dx}{du}\,du = \int \frac{\psi(u)}{\chi(u)}\,du.$ If now $\dfrac{\psi(u)}{\chi(u)}$ can be recognized as the differential coefficient of some known function of u, the integral can be expressed as a function of u and hence of x.

For example, let $\phi(x) = c^x g^{c^x}$.

Put $u = c^x$, so that $c^x g^{c^x} = u g^u$,

and $$du = c^x \log_e c\,dx = u \log_e c\,dx.$$

Then $$\int c^x g^{c^x} dx = \int u g^u \cdot \frac{du}{u \log_e c}$$

$$= \int \frac{g^u\,du}{\log_e c} = \frac{1}{\log_e c \log_e g} \cdot g^u$$

$$= \frac{g^{c^x}}{\log_e c \log_e g}.$$

In this case an experienced integrator would at once recognize $c^x g^{c^x}$ as the differential coefficient (except for a constant factor) of g^{c^x}, and would therefore save the trouble of going through the intermediate process of putting $c^x = u$, but the artifice is one that may often be usefully employed to reduce less easily recognized functions.

The second artifice to be noticed is that of *integration by parts*, and is obtained from the well-known formula of the Differential Calculus

$$\frac{d(uv)}{dx} = u\frac{dv}{dx} + v\frac{du}{dx},$$

which gives, on integration,

$$\int u \frac{dv}{dx} dx = uv - \int v \frac{du}{dx}.$$

Hence the rule:—If the function to be integrated consists of two factors, one of which (the second, say, for identification) is recognizable as a differential coefficient, then the required integral = the product of the first factor and the integral of the second, less the integral of the product of the differential coefficient of the first factor and the integral of the second.

For example, required $\int \log x \, dx$.

This may be written $\int \log x \frac{d(x)}{dx} dx$, for the differential coefficient of x is 1. Hence by the formula

$$\int \log x \, dx = x \log x - \int x \cdot \frac{d \log x}{dx} dx$$

$$= x \log x - \int 1 \, . \, dx = x \log x - x.$$

34. In infinitesimal analysis it is sometimes necessary to find the differential coefficient of a Definite Integral.

Let it be required to find $\frac{d}{dc}\int_a^b \phi(x, c) dx$, where a, b, and $\phi(x, c)$ are all functions of c, the c being inserted in ϕ so that its presence in the function may be more clearly indicated.

Assume that

$$\int \phi(x, c) dx = \psi(x, c),$$

Then
$$\int_a^b \phi(x, c) dx = \psi(b, c) - \psi(a, c),$$

and
$$\frac{d}{dc}\int_a^b \phi(x, c) dx = \frac{d\psi(b, c)}{dc} - \frac{d\psi(a, c)}{dc}$$

= by Art. 25

$$\frac{\partial\psi(b, c)}{\partial c} + \frac{\partial\psi(b, c)}{\partial b} \cdot \frac{db}{dc}$$

$$- \frac{\partial\psi(a, c)}{\partial c} - \frac{\partial\psi(a, c)}{\partial a} \cdot \frac{da}{dc}.$$

Now
$$\frac{d\psi(x, c)}{dx} = \phi(x, c).$$

Hence
$$\frac{\partial\psi(b, c)}{\partial b} = \phi(b, c)$$

and
$$\frac{\partial\psi(a, c)}{\partial a} = \phi(a, c).$$

Also
$$\frac{\partial\psi(b, c)}{\partial c} - \frac{\partial\psi(a, c)}{\partial c} = \frac{\partial}{\partial c}[\psi(b, c) - \psi(a, c)]$$
$$= \frac{\partial}{\partial c}\int_a^b \phi(x, c)\,dx$$
$$= \mathrm{Lt}_{h=0}\int_a^b \frac{\phi(x, c+h) - \phi(x, c)}{h}\,dx = \int_a^b \frac{d\phi(x, c)}{dc}\,dx.$$

Hence, finally,
$$\frac{d}{dc}\int_a^b \phi(x, c)dx = \int_a^b \frac{d\phi}{dc}\,dx + \phi(b, c)\frac{db}{dc} - \phi(a, c)\frac{da}{dc}.$$

If neither b nor a be a function of c, then
$$\frac{d}{dc}\int_a^b \phi(x, c)dx = \int_a^b \frac{d\phi(x, c)}{dc}\,dx.$$

35. It has been shown that the evaluation of a Definite Integral depends, in general upon the determination of the Indefinite Integral. Sometimes, however, the value of the Definite Integral between some special limits can be found, when the Indefinite Integral cannot be expressed in finite terms. For example, it may be shown that
$$\int_0^\infty e^{-a^2x^2}dx = \frac{\sqrt{\pi}}{2a}.$$

When a required Definite Integral cannot be found, either by the determination of the Indefinite Integral or otherwise, it is necessary to resort to some one of the various methods of *approximate* integration. These methods (which are of special importance in connection with the subject of Life Contingencies, since most of the functions met with in that subject do not admit of exact integration) consist either (i) in replacing the given Integral by a nearly equivalent Integral of a simpler character or by a series of such Integrals, or (ii) in expanding the given

Integral in a series of equidistant values of the function to be integrated (multiplied by a constant factor) and the successive differential coefficients of the function.

36. The general process adopted in the practical application of the first of the above-mentioned methods of approximation may be indicated by reference to the geometrical representation of a Definite Integral. It has been shown in Art. 28 that the evaluation of the Definite Integral $\int_a^b \phi(x)dx$ comes to the same thing as the determination of the area contained by the base $(b-a)$, the two ordinates $\phi(a)$ and $\phi(b)$, and the intercepted portion of the curve which represents the function $\phi(x)$. Now this area will not be materially altered if the true curve be replaced by another curve following approximately the same course. Hence, if some *integrable* function, $\psi(x)$ say, can be found which, when graphically represented, will occupy nearly the same position as the curve representing $\phi(x)$, then the value of $\int_a^b \psi(x)dx$ will be approximately the same as that of $\int_a^b \phi(x)dx$. Now the function $c_0+c_1x+c_2x^2+\ldots\ldots+c_{n-1}x^{n-1}$ may be made to assume the same values as $\phi(x)$ for n values of x [or, in other words, to pass through n points on the curve representing $\phi(x)$], by assigning to c_0, c_1, &c. . . . c_{n-1} . . . the values given by the simultaneous equations

$$\begin{array}{llll} c_0+c_1x_1+\ldots+c_{n-1}x_1^{n-1} & =\phi(x_1) & \text{or} & y_1 \\ c_0+c_1x_2+\ldots+c_{n-1}x_2^{n-1} & =\phi(x_2) & ,, & y_2 \\ \vdots & \vdots & & \vdots \\ c_0+c_1x_n+\ldots+c_{n-1}x_n^{n-1} & =\phi(x_n) & ,, & y_n. \end{array}$$

If, then, $(n-2)$ equidistant ordinates be drawn to the curve representing $\phi(x)$ between $\phi(a)$ and $\phi(b)$, and c_0, c_1, c_2. . .c_{n-1} be given the values determined by the equations

$$c_0+c_1a+\ldots+c_{n-1}a^{n-1}=\phi(a)$$

$$c_0+c_1\left(a+\frac{b-a}{n-1}\right)+\ldots+c_{n-1}\left(a+\frac{b-a}{n-1}\right)^{n-1}=\phi\left(a+\frac{b-a}{n-1}\right)$$

$$c_0+c_1\left(a+\frac{2\overline{b-a}}{n-1}\right)+\ldots+c_{n-1}\left(a+\frac{2\overline{b-a}}{n-1}\right)^{n-1}=\phi\left(a+\frac{2\overline{b-a}}{n-1}\right)$$

$$\vdots$$

$$c_0+c_1b+\ldots+c_{n-1}b^{n-1}=\phi(b)$$

then the curve representing the function $c_0+c_1x+\ldots+c_{n-1}x^{n-1}$ will coincide with that representing $\phi(x)$ at each end of the section under consideration, and also at $n-2$ intermediate points, and will clearly, therefore, follow more or less the same course. Hence, approximately,

$$\int_a^b \phi(x)\,dx=\int_a^b (c_0+c_1x+\ldots+c_{n-1}x^{n-1})\,dx$$

$$=c_0(b-a)+\frac{c_1}{2}(b^2-a^2)+\ldots+\frac{c_{n-1}}{n}(b^n-a^n).$$

Suppose, for example, that n be taken as 3, and for convenience let x be measured from the foot of the central ordinate, so that the required integral becomes $\int_{-\frac{b-a}{2}}^{\frac{b-a}{2}}\phi(x)\,dx$, and let $\phi\left(-\frac{b-a}{2}\right)$, $\phi(0)$ and $\phi\left(\frac{b-a}{2}\right)$ be denoted by y_{-1}, y_0 and y_1. Then

$$c_0-c_1\frac{b-a}{2}+c_2\frac{(b-a)^2}{4}=y_{-1}$$

$$c_0=y_0$$

and

$$c_0+c_1\frac{b-a}{2}+c_2\frac{(b-a)^2}{4}=y_1$$

whence $c_0=y_0$; $c_1=\dfrac{y_1-y_{-1}}{b-a}$; and $c_2=\dfrac{2(y_{-1}-2y_0+y_1)}{(b-a)^2}$

and the required integral

$$=\text{approximately}\int_{-\frac{b-a}{2}}^{\frac{b-a}{2}}(c_0+c_1x+c_2x^2)\,dx$$

$$=c_0(b-a)+\frac{c_2}{12}(b-a)^3=(b-a)\frac{y_{-1}+4y_0+y_1}{6}$$

The geometrical interpretation of this result is that the area representing the required integral is approximately equal to the rectangle contained by the base $(b-a)$ and the mean of the two end ordinates and four times the central ordinate. This would, in general, be too rough an approximation to be of any practical use. Better results may be obtained by giving a larger value to n (*i.e.*, by making the substituted curve coincide with the true curve at a larger number of points), but if n be taken large enough to give a good result, the values of the constants would become very complicated. It is more usual, therefore, to subdivide the whole range of integration into comparatively short sections, and to add the results obtained by approximately integrating over each short section by a simple formula such as that given above. Thus, let the integral $\int_a^b \phi(x)dx$ be represented by the area $MABN$ in the annexed diagram. Suppose AB to be divided into $2n$ equal

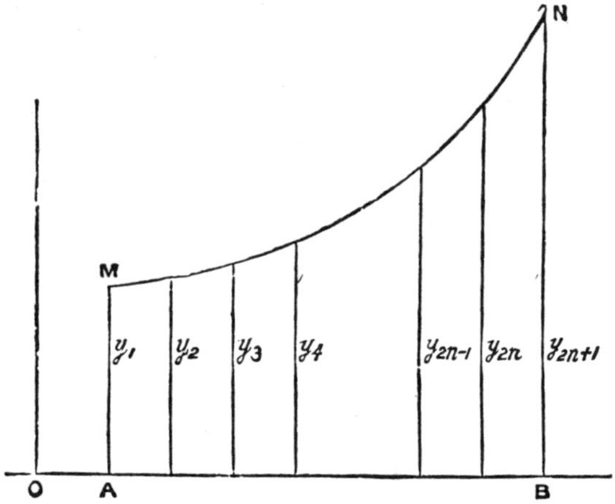

parts, and let the successive ordinates be denoted by $y_1, y_2, y_3, \ldots y_{2n+1}$. Then the area between the 1st and 3rd ordinates is approximately $\frac{b-a}{n} \cdot \frac{y_1+4y_2+y_3}{6}$, the area between the 3rd and 5th is approximately $\frac{b-a}{n} \cdot \frac{y_3+4y_4+y_5}{6}$, and so on.

Hence, approximately,

$$\int_b^a \phi(x)dx = \frac{b-a}{6n}\left[(y_1+4y_2+y_3)+(y_3+4y_4+y_5)+\ldots + (y_{2n-1}+4y_{2n}+y_{2n+1})\right]$$

$$= \frac{b-a}{6n}\left[y_1+2(y_3+y_5+\ldots+y_{2n-1}) + 4(y_2+y_4+y_6+\ldots+y_{2n})+y_{2n+1}\right]$$

An analytical proof of this formula will be found, with other formulas of a similar nature, in the *Text-Book*, Part II, ch. xxiv, Arts. 49–56.

37. The object of the *second* of the methods of approximate integration mentioned in Art. 35 is to establish a relation between the

Definite Integral $\int_a^b \phi(x)dx$ and the Finite Sum $h[\phi(a)+\phi(a+h)+\ldots+\phi(b-h)]$.

For convenience, let u_x be written for $\phi(x)$. Then

$$h[u_a+u_{a+h}+\ \ldots\ +u_{b-h}]$$
$$=h[1+(1+\Delta)^h+\ \ldots\ +(1+\Delta)^{b-a-h}]u_a$$

(where $\Delta u_x=u_{x+1}-u_x$, in accordance with the ordinary notation of the Calculus of Finite Differences)

$$=\frac{h[(1+\Delta)^{b-a}-1]}{(1+\Delta)^h-1}u_a=\frac{h}{(1+\Delta)^h-1}(u_b-u_a).$$

But $(1+\Delta)^h u_x=u_{x+h}=$ (by Taylor's Theroem)

$$u_x+h\frac{du_x}{dx}+\frac{h^2}{2!}\frac{d^2u_x}{dx^2}+\ldots$$
$$=\left(1+h\frac{d}{dx}+\frac{h^2}{2!}\frac{d^2}{dx^2}+\ldots\right)u_x.$$

Hence
$$\frac{h}{(1+\Delta)^h-1}u_b=\frac{1}{\frac{d}{db}+\frac{h}{2}\frac{d^2}{db^2}+\frac{h^2}{6}\frac{d^3}{db^3}+\ldots}u_b$$
$$=\left[\left(\frac{d}{db}\right)^{-1}-\frac{h}{2}+\frac{h^2}{12}\frac{d}{db}-\frac{h^4}{720}\frac{d^3}{db^3}+\ldots\right]u_b$$

Similarly,
$$\frac{h}{(1+\Delta)^h-1}u_a=\left[\left(\frac{d}{da}\right)^{-1}-\frac{h}{2}+\frac{h^2}{12}\frac{d}{da}-\frac{h^4}{720}\frac{d^3}{da^3}+\ldots\right]u_a$$

$$\therefore\ h[u_a+u_{a+h}+\ \ldots\ +u_{b-h}]$$
$$=\left(\frac{d}{db}\right)^{-1}u_b-\left(\frac{d}{da}\right)^{-1}u_a-\frac{h}{2}(u_b-u_a)+\frac{h^2}{12}\left(\frac{du_b}{db}-\frac{du_a}{da}\right)$$
$$-\frac{h^4}{720}\left(\frac{d^3u_b}{db^3}-\frac{d^3u_a}{da^3}\right).$$

Now, when h is indefinitely diminished, $h[u_a+u_{a+h}+\ldots+u_{b-h}]$ assumes the limiting value $\int_a^b u_x dx$, and the third and subsequent terms on the right-hand side of the equation vanish, provided the series be convergent. Hence the symbolical expression $\left(\frac{d}{db}\right)^{-1}u_b-\left(\frac{d}{da}\right)^{-1}u_a$

must be interpreted as denoting $\int_a^b u_x dx$, and the equation becomes

$$h[u_a+u_{a+h}+\ldots u_{b-h}]=\int_a^b u_x dx-\frac{h}{2}(u_b-u_a)+\frac{h^2}{12}\left(\frac{du_b}{db}-\frac{du_a}{da}\right)$$
$$-\frac{h^4}{720}\left(\frac{d^3u_b}{db^3}-\frac{d^3u_a}{da^3}\right)+\ldots$$

or

$$\int_a^b u_x dx=h[u_a+u_{a+h}+\ldots+u_{b-h}]+\frac{h}{2}(u_b-u_a)-\frac{h^2}{12}\left(\frac{du_b}{db}-\frac{du_a}{da}\right)$$
$$+\frac{h^4}{720}\left(\frac{d^3u_b}{db^3}-\frac{d^3u_a}{da^3}\right)+\ldots,$$

If the lower limit be taken as 0, and the function vanish at the upper limit, then

$$\int_0^\infty u_x dx=h[u_0+u_h+u_{2h}+\ldots]-\frac{h}{2}u_0+\frac{h^2}{12}u'_0-\frac{h^4}{720}u'''_0+\ldots$$

where u'_0 and u'''_0 denote the results of putting $x=0$ in the first and third differential coefficients of u_x.

If h be put $=\frac{1}{m}$, then

$$\int_0^\infty u_x dx=\frac{1}{m}(u_{\frac{1}{m}}+u_{\frac{2}{m}}+\ldots)+\frac{1}{2m}u_0+\frac{1}{12m^2}u'_0-\frac{1}{720m^4}u'''_0+\ldots$$

A similar demonstration of the formula for the case in which $h=1$, and an alternative demonstration of the general formula, will be found in the *Text-Book*, Part II.

It will be noted that the validity of all the formulas depends on the assumption that $h[u_a+u_{a+h}+\ldots+u_{b-h}]$ can be expanded in a *convergent* series in powers of h.

CHAPTER X.

Applications of the Calculus of Finite Differences and the Infinitesimal Calculus.

1. For the purposes of the present chapter it will be convenient to follow the general arrangement of the earlier part of the book, and to take up in order such of the subjects therein discussed, as may, with advantage, be further investigated with the aid of Finite Differences or the Differential and Integral Calculus.

2. In some problems in which interest is involved, either alone or in conjunction with some other factor such as mortality, it is found convenient to deal with *infinitely short intervals of time.* The word *continuous* is used in this connection. Thus, an annuity payable by infinitely small instalments at infinitely short intervals is called a *continuous* annuity, and a Conversion Table giving the Single Premium, or Premium per annum payable momently, corresponding to a given continuous annuity-value, is said to be constructed according to the *Continuous Method.* The nominal rate of interest, convertible momently, or *force of interest,* corresponding to a given effective rate might, in a similar sense, be described as a *continuous* rate of interest. Although such conceptions as those of a Force of Interest or a Continuous Annuity do not admit of actual realization, approximations to them may be found in practical finance. Consider, for instance, the case of a company possessing large funds invested in numerous securities upon which the interest becomes due at various dates through the year, receiving income from various sources in daily instalments, and frequently making new investments. In such a case, the income taken as a whole approximates to a continuous varying annuity and, similarly, the fund as a whole may be regarded as accumulating continuously at a continuous varying rate of interest.

The continuous method of analysis naturally suggests the use of the Infinitesimal Calculus.

3. Suppose a unit of money to accumulate under the operation of a force of interest—this force not being necessarily constant. Let $f(t)$ be the amount of the unit at the end of any time t, and let δ_t be the force of interest operating at that precise moment. Then the amount of the unit in $(t+h)$ years will be $f(t+h)$, and since δ_t is the nominal rate of interest per unit per annum convertible momently, or, in other words, the *instantaneous* rate of interest per unit per annum, at the precise moment under consideration, it follows that in the limit when $h=0$

$$f(t+h)=f(t)+hf(t)\delta_t$$

or

$$\delta_t=\mathrm{Lt}_{h=0}\frac{f(t+h)-f(t)}{hf(t)}.$$

Hence, if $f(t)$ be a continuous function of t (in the sense defined in Chapter IX, Art. 7),

$$\delta_t=\frac{1}{f(t)}\frac{df(t)}{dt}=\frac{d\log_e f(t)}{dt} \quad . \quad . \quad . \quad . \quad (1)$$

This result expresses the fact that if the amount of 1 in t years can be represented by a continuous function of t for all values of t within given limits, then the force of interest operating at any time t within these limits is equal to the differential coefficient of the Napierian logarithm of the function.

In the form $\delta_t=\frac{1}{f(t)}\frac{df(t)}{dt}$ the relation may be deduced directly from the definitions of a force of interest and a differential coefficient. For, if $f(t)$ be the amount of 1 in t years, then $\frac{df(t)}{dt}$ represents the instantaneous rate of increase of $f(t)$ as the independent variable passes through the precise value t. Hence the force of interest δ_t—which represents the instantaneous rate of increase of $f(t)$ *per unit*—is equal to $\frac{1}{f(t)}\cdot\frac{df(t)}{dt}$.

In general, δ_t will be a continuous function of t.

4. Since $f(t)=1$ and $\log_e f(t)=0$ when $t=0$, it follows from equation (1) that

$$\log_e f(t)=\int_0^t \delta_t dt.$$

whence

$$f(t)=e^{\int_0^t \delta_t dt} \quad . \quad . \quad . \quad . \quad . \quad . \quad . \quad . \quad (2)$$

This equation expresses the fact that if the force of interest operating at any time t within given limits can be represented by a continuous function of t, δ_t say, then the amount of a unit in any time t within those limits will be $e^{\int_0^t \delta_t dt}$.

Whether the rate of interest be constant or variable, the present value of 1 due t years hence is, on the ordinary, assumptions of finance, the reciprocal of the amount of 1 in t years. Hence, the present value of 1 due t years hence will be given by the equation

$$[f(t)]^{-1}=e^{-\int_0^t \delta_t dt} \quad . \quad . \quad . \quad . \quad . \quad (3)$$

5. By means of formulas (2) and (3) the amount and present value of 1 may be accurately calculated in any case in which δ_t is an integrable function of t. It will be convenient to take a few examples.

(*a*) Let δ_t be a constant, δ say.

Then, since $\int_0^t \delta dt=\delta t$, it follows that $f(t)=e^{\delta t}$ and $[f(t)]^{-1}=e^{-\delta t}$

Also $$f(1)=e^{\delta} \text{ and } [f(1)]^{-1}=e^{-\delta}$$

whence $$f(t)=[f(1)]^t \text{ and } [f(t)]^{-1}=[f(1)]^{-t}.$$

If $f(1)$, the amount of 1 in a year, be denoted by $(1+i)$, the above results take the form $f(t)=(1+i)^t$; $[f(t)]^{-1}=(1+i)^{-t}$. In fact, the general formulas reproduce, as they should of course do, the results obtained by ordinary algebraical methods for a uniform rate of interest.

(*b*) Let $\delta_t=\delta_0 r^t$, where δ_0 and r are constants, δ_0 being the value of δ_t when $t=0$. Then, since

$$\int_0^t \delta_0 r^t dt=\frac{\delta_0}{\log_e r}(r^t-1)$$

$$f(t)=e^{\frac{\delta_0}{\log_e r}(r^t-1)}; \quad [f(t)]^{-1}=e^{\frac{\delta_0}{\log_e r}(1-r^t)}$$

o

These results give the amount and present value of 1 under the operation of a force of interest commencing at δ_0 and continuously increasing or decreasing (according as r is greater or less than 1) in such a ratio that its values at successive equidistant times are in geometric progression. The corresponding *effective* rates of interest for successive years will be as follows:—

$$\text{1st year} \ldots f(1)-1 \quad \text{or} \quad e^{\frac{\delta_0(r-1)}{\log_e r}}-1$$

$$\text{2nd} \quad ,, \quad \ldots \frac{f(2)}{f(1)}-1 \quad ,, \quad e^{\frac{\delta_0 r(r-1)}{\log_e r}}-1$$

$$\text{3rd} \quad ,, \quad \ldots \frac{f(3)}{f(2)}-1 \quad ,, \quad e^{\frac{\delta_0 r^2(r-1)}{\log_e r}}-1$$

and so on.

(*c*) Let $\delta_t=\delta_0-rt$ for all values of t up to n, and remain constant and $=\delta_n$ for all values of t greater than n.

For values of t *less* than n

$$f(t)=e^{\int_0^t(\delta_0-rt)dt}=e^{\delta_0 t-\frac{rt^2}{2}}; \quad [f(t)]^{-1}=e^{-\delta_0 t+\frac{rt^2}{2}}.$$

For values of t *greater* than n, the integration must be divided into two parts, since δ_t is not represented by a single continuous function. Thus

$$f(t)=e^{\int_0^n(\delta_0-rt)dt+\int_n^t\delta_n dt}=e^{\delta_0 n-\frac{rn^2}{2}+(t-n)\delta_n}$$

and, similarly,

$$[f(t)]^{-1}=e^{-\delta_0 n+\frac{rn^2}{2}-(t-n)\delta_n}$$

Since $\delta_0-rn=\delta_n$, whence $r=\dfrac{\delta_0-\delta_n}{n}$, the above results may be written in the form

$$t<n \qquad f(t)=e^{\delta_0 t-\frac{1}{2n}(\delta_0-\delta_n)t^2}; \quad [f(t)]^{-1}=e^{-\delta_0 t+\frac{1}{2n}(\delta_0-\delta_n)t^2}$$

$$t>n \qquad f(t)=e^{\frac{n}{2}(\delta_0-\delta_n)+t\delta_n}; \quad [f(t)]^{-1}=e^{-\frac{n}{2}(\delta_0-\delta_n)-t\delta_n}.$$

These formulas give the amount and present value of 1 under the operation of a force of interest commencing at δ_0, decreasing by equal decrements in equal times to δ_n, and thereafter remaining constant.

If $i_1, i_2, i_3, \ldots$ be the corresponding effective rates of interest for the 1st, 2nd, 3rd, &c., years, and m be $<n$, then

$$1+i_1=f(1)=e^{\delta_0-\frac{1}{2n}(\delta_0-\delta_n)}$$

$$1+i_2=\frac{f(2)}{f(1)}=e^{\delta_0-\frac{3}{2n}(\delta_0-\delta_n)}$$

$$\vdots$$

$$1+i_{m-1}=\frac{f(m-1)}{f(m-2)}=e^{\delta_0-\frac{2m-3}{2n}(\delta_0-\delta_n)}$$

$$1+i_m=\frac{f(m)}{f(m-1)}=e^{\delta_0-\frac{2m-1}{2n}(\delta_0-\delta_n)}$$

whence $1+i_2=e^{-\frac{1}{n}(\delta_0-\delta_n)}(1+i_1)$, and generally, if m be $< n$

$$1+i_m=e^{-\frac{1}{n}(\delta_0-\delta_n)}(1+i_{m-1})$$

that is, since $e^{-\frac{1}{n}(\delta_0-\delta_n)}$ is independent of t,

$$(1+i_m)=(1-k)(1+i_{m-1}) \text{ where } k=1-e^{-\frac{1}{n}(\delta_0-\delta_n)}$$

It appears, therefore, that the assumption that δ_t is of the form (δ_0-rt) leads to a relation between the effective rates of successive years similar to that assumed in the second paragraph of Art. 33, Chap. I, and that if this relation is such that the amount of 1 for a year in any one year is $(1-k)$ times the amount of 1 for a year in the preceding year, then the corresponding force of interest at any time t will be $\delta_0+t\log_e(1-k)$, where, if i_1 be the effective rate for the first year, $1+i_1=e^{\delta_0+\frac{1}{2}\log_e(1-k)}=(1-k)^{\frac{1}{2}}e^{\delta_0}$, or $\delta_0=\log_e(1+i_1)-\frac{1}{2}\log_e(1-k)$.

As an example of the application of the formulas, let it be required to find the amounts of 1 in 10 and 40 years respectively, on the assumption that the force of interest falls by equal decrements in 20 years from the force corresponding to an effective rate of 3 per-cent to that corresponding to 2 per-cent, and thereafter remains constant.

The amount of 1 in 10 years

$$=f(10)=e^{10\delta_0-\frac{1}{40}(\delta_0-\delta_{20})\times 100}=e^{7\frac{1}{2}\delta_0+2\frac{1}{2}\delta_{20}}$$

$$=(1\cdot03)^{7\frac{1}{2}}.(1\cdot02)^{2\frac{1}{2}}=1\cdot31153.$$

The amount of 1 in 40 years

$$=f(40)=e^{10(\delta_0-\delta_{20})+40\delta_{20}}=(1\cdot03)^{10}.(1\cdot02)^{30}$$

$$=2\cdot43432.$$

6. If the amount of 1 in t years be denoted, for all values of t from 0 to m, by $f(t)$, then

$$s_{\overline{m}|}=1+\frac{f(m)}{f(m-1)}+\frac{f(m)}{f(m-2)}+\ldots+\frac{f(m)}{f(1)}$$

$$a_{\overline{m}|}=[f(1)]^{-1}+[f(2)]^{-1}+\ldots+[f(m)]^{-1}$$

$$s_{\overline{m}|}^{(p)}=\sum_{r=1}^{r=mp}\frac{1}{p}\frac{f(m)}{f\left(\frac{r}{p}\right)}$$

and
$$a_{\overline{m}|}^{(p)}=\sum_{r=1}^{r=mp}\frac{1}{p}\left[f\left(\frac{r}{p}\right)\right]^{-1}$$

Hence, if p be made infinitely great,

$$\bar{s}_{\overline{m}|}=\int_0^m f(m)\,.\,[f(t)]^{-1}dt \quad . \quad . \quad . \quad . \quad . \quad (4)$$

and
$$\bar{a}_{\overline{m}|}=\int_0^m [f(t)]^{-1}dt. \quad . \quad . \quad . \quad . \quad . \quad . \quad . \quad . \quad (5)$$

These definite integrals give, in general terms, the amount and present value of a continuous annuity of 1 per annum; but, in order that they may be exactly evaluated, $[f(t)]^{-1}$—that is, $e^{-\int_0^t \delta_t dt}$—must be an integrable function of t. Their application may be illustrated by an investigation of the cases in which δ_t has the special values assigned to it in the examples of Art. 5. Since $\bar{s}_{\overline{m}|}=f(m)\,.\,\bar{a}_{\overline{m}|}$, it will be sufficient to consider the values of $\bar{a}_{\overline{m}|}$.

(a) Let δ_t be a constant, δ say.

Then $[f(t)]^{-1}=e^{-\delta t}$, and

$$\bar{a}_{\overline{m}|}=\int^m e^{-\delta t}dt=\frac{1-e^{-m\delta}}{\delta},$$

a result which agrees, as it should do, with that obtained by ordinary algebra, on the assumption of a uniform rate of interest.

(b) Let $\delta_t=\delta_0 r^t$.

Then
$$[f(t)]^{-1}=e^{-\frac{\delta_0}{\log_e r}(r^t-1)}$$

and
$$\bar{a}_{\overline{m}}=\int_0^m e^{-\frac{\delta_0}{\log_e r}(r^t-1)}dt$$

The definite integral thus obtained for $\bar{a}_{\overline{m}|}$ cannot be evaluated in a finite form, but by expansion of the exponential and integration of the successive terms its value may be expressed in the infinite series

$$\frac{e^{\frac{\delta_0}{\log_e r}}}{\log_e r}\left[m \log_e r - \frac{\delta_0}{\log_e r}(r^m-1) + \left(\frac{\delta_0}{\log_e r}\right)^2 \frac{r^{2m}-1}{2.2\,!} \right.$$
$$\left. - \left(\frac{\delta_0}{\log_e r}\right)^3 \frac{r^{3m}-1}{3.3\,!} + \ldots\right]$$

or, if k be written for $-\dfrac{\delta_0}{\log_e r}$,

$$\frac{ke^{-k}}{\delta_0}\left[\frac{m\delta_0}{k} + k(1-r^m) + \frac{k^2}{2.2\,!}(1-r^{2m}) + \frac{k^3}{3.3\,!}(1-r^{3m}) + \ldots\right]$$

In a practical case δ_0 might be the force of interest corresponding to $i = {\cdot}035$, and r might be $= {\cdot}995$, which would give $k = 6{\cdot}87$; $\dfrac{\delta_0}{k} = {\cdot}00501$; and $\dfrac{ke^{-k}}{\delta_0} = {\cdot}207$. It will be seen, therefore, that although the series given above is in all cases ultimately convergent the number of terms that would have to be calculated in any practical case would be so large as to be prohibitive. It would be necessary, therefore, to employ some formula of approximate integration such as that given in Art. 36 of Chap. IX—the range of integration being divided into sections selected in any given case with reference to the actual numerical value of m.

(*c*) Let $\delta_t = \delta_0 - rt$ for all values of t up to n, and remain constant, and $= \delta_n$ for all greater values of t.

Then, if m be $< n$,

$$\bar{a}_{\overline{m}|} = \int_0^m e^{-\delta_0 t + \frac{rt^2}{2}}\,dt.$$

The definite integral may be expressed in the ultimately convergent series

$$e^{-k}\left[m + \frac{k}{3}\cdot\frac{\delta_0}{r}\left(1 - \overline{1 - \frac{mr}{\delta_0}}^{\,3}\right) + \frac{k^2}{5}\cdot\frac{\delta_0}{r}\left(1 - \overline{1 - \frac{mr}{\delta_0}}^{\,5}\right) + \ldots\right]$$

where $k = \dfrac{\delta_0^2}{2r}$, but, in this case, as in that of the series obtained in (*b*), the number of terms to be calculated would, for practical values of δ_0 and r, be prohibitive. Hence, in this case also, it would be necessary to employ a formula of approximate integration.

If m be $>n$, then obviously

$$\bar{a}_{\overline{m}|}=\int_0^n e^{-\delta_0 t+\frac{rt^2}{2}}dt+e^{-\delta_0 n+\frac{rn^2}{2}}\cdot\frac{1-e^{-(m-n)\delta_n}}{\delta_n}$$

and

$$\bar{s}_{\overline{m}|}=e^{\delta_0 n-\frac{rn^2}{2}+(m-n)\delta_n}\cdot\int_0^n e^{-\delta_0 t+\frac{rt^2}{2}}+\frac{e^{(m-n)\delta_n}-1}{\delta_n}.$$

7. The foregoing investigations with reference to varying rates of interest might, of course, be extended to any problem in Compound Interest, but the subject is not of sufficient practical importance to call for further exemplification. In the remainder of the chapter the rate of interest involved in any given problem will be assumed to be constant.

8. The Calculus of Finite Differences may be conveniently employed, as stated in Chap. III, Art. 35, to obtain general formulas for the amount and present value of a varying annuity.

Let $u_1, u_2, u_3 \ldots u_n$ be the successive payments of a varying annuity payable annually for n years. Then, with the ordinary notation of the Calculus of Finite Differences, the payments of the annuity may be exhibited in the following form:—

1st payment $=u_1$

2nd " $=u_1+\Delta u_1$

3rd " $=u_1+2\Delta u_1+\Delta^2 u_1$

4th " $=u_1+3\Delta u_1+3\Delta^2 u_1+\Delta^3 u_1$

⋮ ⋮

nth " $=u_1+(n-1)\Delta u_1+\dfrac{(n-1)(n-2)}{2!}\Delta^2 u_1+\ldots+\Delta^{n-1}u_1$

Now the successive coefficients of each difference in this series of expressions are the successive figurate numbers of the next higher order. Consequently, the given annuity is equivalent to the sum of an annuity of u_1 of the first order, an annuity of Δu_1 of the second order, an annuity of $\Delta^2 u_1$ of the third order, &c. . . . and, finally, an annuity of $\Delta^{n-1}u_1$ of the nth order. Hence, if $(\mathrm{v}s)_{\overline{n}|}$ and $(\mathrm{v}a)_{\overline{n}|}$ denote the amount and present value respectively of the given annuity

$$(\mathrm{v}s)_{\overline{n}|}=u_1 s_{\overline{n}|}+\Delta u_1 s_{\overline{n}|\overline{2}|}+\Delta^2 u_1 s_{\overline{n}|\overline{3}|}+\ldots+\Delta^{n-1}u_1 s_{\overline{n}|\overline{n}|} \quad . \quad . \quad . \quad (6)$$

and

$$(\mathrm{v}a)_{\overline{n}|}=u_1 a_{\overline{n}|}+\Delta u_1 a_{\overline{n}|\overline{2}|}+\Delta^2 u_1 a_{\overline{n}|\overline{3}|}+\ldots+\Delta^{n-1}u_1 a_{\overline{n}|\overline{n}|} \quad . \quad . \quad . \quad (7)$$

In the case of a *varying perpetuity*, since $a_{\overline{\infty}|\overline{r}|}=\frac{1}{i^r}$,

$$(\mathrm{v}a)_{\infty}=\frac{u_1}{i}+\frac{\Delta u_1}{i^2}+\frac{\Delta^2 u_1}{i^3}+\ldots \quad . \quad . \quad . \quad . \quad . \qquad (8)$$

Since by the result just obtained

$$u_1v+u_2v^2+u_3v^3+\ldots \textit{ ad inf.}=\frac{u_1}{i}+\frac{\Delta u_1}{i^2}+\frac{\Delta^2 u_1}{i^3}+\ldots$$

and $\quad u_{n+1}v^{n+1}+u_{n+2}v^{n+2}+u_{n+3}v^{n+3}+\ldots \textit{ ad inf.}$

$$=v^n\left(\frac{u_{n+1}}{i}+\frac{\Delta u_{n+1}}{i^2}+\frac{\Delta^2 u_{n+1}}{i^3}+\ldots\right)$$

it follows, by subtraction, that

$$(\mathrm{v}a)_{\overline{n}|}=\frac{u_1-v^n u_{n+1}}{i}+\frac{\Delta u_1-v^n\Delta u_{n+1}}{i^2}+\ldots \quad . \quad . \quad . \qquad (9)$$

an alternative formula which may sometimes be more convenient than formula (7).

9. The utility of formulas (6)—(9) is practically limited to those cases in which the differences of the successive payments vanish after the first few orders, that is, to those cases in which u_t is a rational algebraic function of t of a *low* order. In other cases (unless the series for $(\mathrm{v}a)_{\overline{n}|}$ could be summed algebraically, as, for example, in the case of an annuity of which the successive payments are in Geometric Progression), it would be best to calculate the separate values of the payments and to add the results. Even if the higher differences of the payments were very small, it would not necessarily be safe to neglect them for the purpose of obtaining an approximate result, because the values of the successive annuities of the various orders increase very rapidly.

10. The following examples illustrate the application of the formulas of Art. 8:—

(*a*) Required the present value at rate i of an annuity of which the payments increase in arithmetic progression. Let p be the first payment, q the annual increment, and a the present value of the first n payments. Here $u_1=p$; $\Delta u_1=q$; the higher differences vanish; and by formula (7)

$$a=pa_{\overline{n}|}+qa_{\overline{n}|\overline{2}|}=pa_{\overline{n}|}+q\frac{a_{\overline{n}|}-nv^n}{i}$$

or, by formula (9), since $u_{n+1}=p+nq$, and $\Delta u_{n+1}=q$,

$$a=\frac{p-(p+nq)v^n}{i}+\frac{q-qv^n}{i^2}$$

which $=pa_{\overline{n}|}+q\frac{a_{\overline{n}|}-nv^n}{i}$.

The present value of the perpetuity is, by formula (8), $\frac{p}{i}+\frac{q}{i^2}$.

The results have already been obtained by ordinary algebraical methods (Chap. III, Art. 28).

(*b*) Required the present value at rate i of an n-year annuity of which the successive annual payments are $1^3, 2^3, 3^3 \ldots n^3$.

Here
$$\Delta u_n=(n+1)^3-n^3=3n^2+3n+1$$
$$\Delta^2 u_n=3(\overline{n+1}^2-n^2)+3(\overline{n+1}-n)=6(n+1)$$
$$\Delta^3 u_n=6(n+2)-6(n+1)=6$$
$$\Delta^4 u_n=0$$

whence, if n be put $=1$,

$$\Delta u_1=7;\ \Delta^2 u_1=12;\ \Delta^3 u_1=6.$$

Hence
$$a=a_{\overline{n}|}+7a_{\overline{n}|\overline{2}|}+12a_{\overline{n}|\overline{3}|}+6a_{\overline{n}|\overline{4}|}$$

or, by formula (9),

$$a=\frac{1-(n+1)^3v^n}{i}+\frac{7-(3n^2+9n+7)v^n}{i^2}+\frac{12-6(n+2)v^n}{i^3}+\frac{6(1-v^n)}{i^4}.$$

(*c*) The first three payments of an n-year annuity are 18, 28, 40. On the assumption that the tth payment is a rational algebraic function of t of the 2nd degree, find the present value of the annuity at rate i.

Formula (7) gives at once

$$a=18a_{\overline{n}|}+10a_{\overline{n}|\overline{2}|}+2a_{\overline{n}|\overline{3}|}.$$

To employ formula (9) it would be necessary to determine, in the first instance, u_{n+1}, Δu_{n+1}, and $\Delta^2 u_{n+1}$. This can readily be done; for

$$u_{n+1}=u_1+n\Delta u_1+\frac{n(n-1)}{2}\Delta^2 u_1$$
$$=18+10n+n(n-1)=n^2+9n+18$$
$$\Delta u_{n+1}=u_{n+2}-u_{n+1}=2n+10$$
$$\Delta^2 u_{n+1}=\Delta u_{n+2}-\Delta u_{n+1}=2$$

Hence $a=\frac{18-(n^2+9n+18)v^n}{i}+\frac{10-(2n+10)v^n}{i^2}+\frac{2(1-v^n)}{i^3}$.

11. If B denote the present value at rate i of any series of annual payments, u_1, u_2, u_3 . . . u_n, and (IB) denote the present value at the same rate of the series u_1, $2u_2$, $3u_3$ . . . nu_n, then the value of (IB) can be very simply deduced from that of B by means of the Differential Calculus.

For, since
$$\frac{d}{di}=\frac{dv}{di}\cdot\frac{d}{dv}=-v^2\frac{d}{dv},$$

$$\frac{dB}{di}=-v^2\frac{d}{dv}\{u_1v+u_2v^2+\ldots+u_nv^n\}$$
$$=-v^2\{u_1+2u_2v+\ldots+nu_nv^{n-1}\}$$
$$=-v.(IB).$$

Hence
$$(IB)=-(1+i)\frac{dB}{di} \quad \ldots\ldots\ldots \quad (10)$$

For example, since the successive payments of the ordinary increasing annuity are 1, 2, 3 . . .

$$(Ia)_{\overline{n}|}=-(1+i)\frac{da_{\overline{n}|}}{di}$$
$$=-(1+i)\frac{n(1+i)^{-\overline{n+1}}.i+(1+i)^{-n}-1}{i^2}$$
$$=a_{\overline{n}|}+\frac{a_{\overline{n}|}-nv^n}{i}$$

and
$$(Ia)_\infty=-(1+i)\frac{d}{di}\cdot\frac{1}{i}$$
$$=\frac{1+i}{i^2}=\frac{1}{i}+\frac{1}{i^2}$$

as in Chap. III, Art. 29.

12. In the case of a continuous series of payments, if $\overline{B}$ denote the value of $\int_0^n v^t u_t dt$ and $(I\overline{B})$ that of $\int_0^n v^t t u_t dt$, then, as in the case of the annuity payable annually, since

$$\frac{dv^t}{di}=-v^2\frac{dv^t}{dv}=-v.tv^t,$$

$$(I\overline{B})=-(1+i)\frac{d\overline{B}}{di}$$

or, since

$$\frac{d}{di}=\frac{d\delta}{di}\cdot\frac{d}{d\delta}=\frac{1}{1+i}\frac{d}{d\delta},$$

$$(\mathrm{I}\bar{\mathrm{B}})=-\frac{d\bar{\mathrm{B}}}{d\delta} \quad . \quad . \quad . \quad . \quad . \quad . \quad . \quad . \quad . \quad . \quad (11)$$

in which form the relation might have been deduced directly from the definite integrals for $\bar{\mathrm{B}}$ and $(\mathrm{I}\bar{\mathrm{B}})$, since $v^t=e^{-\delta t}$.

As an example of the application of formula (11), let it be required to find, on the assumption of a uniform distribution of deaths, the value at the beginning of the year of death of the proportion payable at the moment of death under a complete annuity.

The required value, being $=\int_0^1 tv^t dt$,

$$=-\frac{d}{d\delta}\int_0^1 v^t dt=-\frac{d\bar{a}_{\overline{1}|}}{d\delta}=-\frac{d}{d\delta}\cdot\frac{1-e^{-\delta}}{\delta}=\frac{-\delta e^{-\delta}-e^{-\delta}+1}{\delta^2}$$

$$=e^{-\delta}\frac{e^{\delta}-1-\delta}{\delta^2} \text{ or } v\,\frac{i-\delta}{\delta^2}$$

as in Text-Book, Part II, Chap. XI, Art. 5.

This result could, of course, have been obtained directly by integration by parts.

13. A somewhat similar relation to that established in Art. 11 exists between the values of the annuities of the successive figurate orders.

For, since $\quad a_{\overline{n}|\overline{r}|}=v^r+rv^{r+1}+\ldots+\frac{\overline{n-1}\,!}{\overline{n-r}\,!\;\overline{r-1}\,!}v^n,$

$$\frac{da_{\overline{n}|\overline{r}|}}{di}=-v^2\frac{da_{\overline{n}|\overline{r}|}}{dv}=-v^2\left[rv^{r-1}+r\,\overline{r+1}\,v^r+\ldots+\frac{n\,!}{\overline{n-r}\,!\;\overline{r-1}\,!}v^{n-1}\right]$$

$$=-r\left[v^{r+1}+\overline{r+1}\,v^{r+2}+\ldots+\frac{n\,!}{\overline{n-r}\,!\;r\,!}v^{n+1}\right]$$

But $\quad a_{\overline{n+1}|\overline{r+1}|}=v^{r+1}+\overline{r+1}\,v^{r+2}+\ldots+\frac{n\,!}{\overline{n-r}\,!\;r\,!}v^{n+1}.$

Hence $$a_{\overline{n+1}|\overline{r+1}|}=-\frac{1}{r}\frac{da_{\overline{n}|\overline{r}|}}{di} \quad . \quad . \quad . \quad . \quad . \quad . \quad . \quad (12)$$

By means of this relation, the values of the annuities of the successive orders may be deduced. Thus

$$a_{\overline{n+1}|\overline{2}|} = -\frac{da_{\overline{n}|}}{di} = \frac{-niv^{n+1}+1-v^n}{i^2}$$

$$= \frac{a_{\overline{n}|} - nv^{n+1}}{i} = \frac{a_{\overline{n+1}|} - \overline{n+1}v^{n+1}}{i}$$

whence
$$a_{\overline{n}|\overline{2}|} = \frac{a_{\overline{n}|} - nv^n}{i}.$$

Since
$$a_{\overline{n}|\overline{r}|} = -\frac{1}{r-1}\frac{da_{\overline{n-1}|\overline{r-1}|}}{di};\quad a_{\overline{n-1}|\overline{r-1}|} = -\frac{1}{r-2}\frac{da_{\overline{n-2}|\overline{r-2}|}}{di};$$

and so on; it follows that

$$a_{\overline{n}|\overline{r}|} = (-1)^{r-1}\frac{1}{\overline{r-1}\,!}\frac{d^{r-1}a_{\overline{n-r+1}|}}{di^{r-1}} \quad . \quad . \quad . \quad . \quad . \quad (13).$$

14. Formula (13) suggests an interesting generalization of the investigation of Chap. VI, Art. 8, in regard to the rate of interest yielded by an annuity.

For let a be the present value and n the term of the annuity, and i the unknown rate of interest; and suppose that at rate i' $a_{\overline{n}|} = a'$ —a value differing from a by a small quantity only—and that $i = i' + \rho$, so that a is a function of $(i' + \rho)$. Then, by Taylor's Theorem,

$$a = a' + \rho\frac{da'}{di'} + \frac{\rho^2}{2\,!}\frac{d^2a'}{di'^2} + \frac{\rho^3}{3\,!}\frac{d^3a'}{di'^3} + \ldots$$

But by formula (13) $\dfrac{1}{r\,!}\dfrac{d^r a_{\overline{n}|}}{di^r} = (-1)^r a_{\overline{n+r}|\overline{r+1}|}$

Hence
$$a = a' - \rho a'_{\overline{n+1}|\overline{2}|} + \rho^2 a'_{\overline{n+2}|\overline{3}|}$$
$$\ldots + (-1)^r \rho^r a'_{\overline{n+r}|\overline{r+1}|} + \quad . \quad . \quad . \quad (14)$$

The successive approximations to the value of ρ may, therefore, be exhibited in the form

1st approximation $\rho = \dfrac{a' - a}{a'_{\overline{n+1}|\overline{2}|}}$

2nd " $\rho = \dfrac{a' - a}{a'_{\overline{n+1}|\overline{2}|} - a'_{\overline{n+2}|\overline{3}|}\dfrac{a'-a}{a'_{\overline{n+1}|\overline{2}|}}}$

&c.

The method of the present article may obviously be extended to the determination of the rate of interest involved in any financial transaction, but the resulting formulas would not appear to be of much practical use.

15. With the aid of the Calculus of Finite Differences, several approximate and comparatively simple formulas can be obtained for the unknown rate of interest involved in a given transaction. The method employed in obtaining these formulas will be seen to be a further development of the method of first-difference interpolation discussed in Arts. 14–17 of Chap. VI.

Let u be the given present value or amount of any given series of payments, and suppose it to have been found by trial (or by reference to the Tables, if the given series be one of which the present value or amount has been tabulated), that u lies between u_0 and u_1, where u_0 and u_1 are the present values or amounts, as the case may be, of the given series at rates i_0 and i_0+h respectively; let u_{-2}, u_{-1}, u_2, &c., be the corresponding present values or amounts at rates i_0-2h, i_0-h, i_0+2h, &c.: and let i (the rate to be found) $=i_0+\rho$.

Then, if Δ, Δ^2, &c., denote the successive differences of u_0, corresponding to a difference of h in the variable,

$$u=u_0+\frac{\rho}{h}\Delta+\frac{\rho}{h}\left(\frac{\rho}{h}-1\right)\frac{\Delta^2}{2!}+\ldots$$

and, if the higher differences be neglected,

$$u=u_0+\frac{\rho}{h}(\Delta-\tfrac{1}{2}\Delta^2)+\frac{\rho^2}{h^2}\cdot\frac{\Delta^2}{2}\cdot$$

Hence, as a first approximation,

$$\rho=h\frac{u-u_0}{\Delta-\frac{1}{2}\Delta^2}\quad\ldots\ldots\ldots\ldots\quad(15)$$

and, as a second approximation, by substitution of $\frac{\rho}{h}\cdot\frac{u-u_0}{\Delta-\frac{1}{2}\Delta^2}$ for $\frac{\rho^2}{h^2}$ in the original equation,

$$\rho=h\cdot\frac{u-u_0}{\Delta-\frac{1}{2}\Delta^2+\dfrac{u-u_0}{\Delta-\frac{1}{2}\Delta^2}\cdot\dfrac{\Delta^2}{2}}$$

$$=h\cdot\frac{1}{\dfrac{\Delta}{u-u_0}\left(1-\frac{1}{2}\dfrac{\Delta^2}{\Delta}\right)+\frac{1}{2}\dfrac{\Delta^2}{\Delta}\left(1-\frac{1}{2}\dfrac{\Delta^2}{\Delta}\right)^{-1}}$$

$$=h\frac{\left(1-\frac{1}{2}\dfrac{\Delta^2}{\Delta}\right)^{-1}}{\dfrac{\Delta}{u-u_0}+\frac{1}{2}\dfrac{\Delta^2}{\Delta}\left(1-\frac{1}{2}\dfrac{\Delta^2}{\Delta}\right)^{-2}}$$

or, say, approximately, if powers of $\frac{\Delta^2}{2\Delta}$ above the first be neglected,

$$\rho=h\cdot\frac{1+\frac{1}{2}\frac{\Delta^2}{\Delta}}{\frac{\Delta}{u-u_0}+\frac{1}{2}\frac{\Delta^2}{\Delta}} \quad . \quad . \quad . \quad . \quad . \quad . \quad . \quad . \quad . \quad . \quad (16)$$

16. Again, with the notation of ordinary *central* differences,

$$u=u_0+\left(a_0-\frac{c_0}{6}\right)\frac{\rho}{h}+\left(\frac{b_0}{2}-\frac{d_0}{24}\right)\frac{\rho^2}{h^2}+\ldots$$

Hence, as a first approximation,

$$\rho=h\frac{u-u_0}{a_0-\frac{c_0}{6}} \quad . \quad . \quad . \quad . \quad . \quad . \quad . \quad . \quad . \quad . \quad . \quad . \quad . \quad (17)$$

and, as a second approximation,

$$\rho=h\frac{u-u_0}{a_0-\frac{1}{6}c_0+(u-u_0)\frac{\frac{1}{2}b_0-\frac{1}{24}d_0}{a_0-\frac{1}{6}c_0}} \quad . \quad . \quad . \quad . \quad . \quad (18)$$

This formula, although of a sufficiently simple form, involves the *fourth* central difference, and if u were not a function of which the values are tabulated, this would involve the calculation of five values of u, namely, u_{-2}, u_{-1}, u_0, u, and u_2. For most practical purposes, however, the terms $\frac{1}{6}c_0$ and $\frac{1}{24}d_0$ may be neglected, and the formula then reduces to

$$\rho=h\frac{1}{\frac{a_0}{u-u_0}+\frac{b_0}{2a_0}} \quad . \quad . \quad . \quad . \quad . \quad . \quad (19)$$

17. Yet another series of approximations may obviously be obtained by reference to the central differences relative to the interval between u_0 and u_1, instead of to u_0. If α_0, β_0, γ_0, δ_0 . . . denote the successive differences, so that $\alpha_0=\Delta u_0$; $\beta_0=\frac{1}{2}\Delta^2(u_{-1}+u_0)$; $\gamma_0=\Delta^3 u_{-1}$; $\delta_0=\frac{1}{2}\Delta^4(u_{-2}+u_{-1})$, &c., then

$$u=u_0+(\alpha_0-\tfrac{1}{2}\beta_0+\tfrac{1}{12}\gamma_0+\tfrac{1}{12}\delta_0\ldots)\frac{\rho}{h}$$

$$+(\tfrac{1}{2}\beta_0-\tfrac{1}{4}\gamma_0-\tfrac{1}{24}\delta_0\ldots)\frac{\rho^2}{h^2}+\ldots$$

If the differences above β_0 (which involves the four values u_{-1}, u_0, u_1, u_2) be neglected, then, as a first approximation,

$$\rho = h \frac{u - u_0}{a_0 - \frac{1}{2}\beta_0} \quad . \quad . \quad . \quad . \quad . \quad . \quad . \quad . \quad (20)$$

and as a second approximation

$$\rho = h \frac{u - u_0}{a_0 - \frac{1}{2}\beta_0 + \frac{1}{2}\beta_0 \dfrac{u - u_0}{a_0 - \frac{1}{2}\beta_0}} \quad . \quad . \quad . \quad . \quad (21)$$

18. Formulas (15) to (21) may, of course, be applied to determine the approximate yield on any description of financial transaction. They are, in fact, perfectly general formulas for the approximate determination of that value of the variable which will give an assigned value to the function $f(x)$. For purposes of comparison, it will be useful to apply them to find the rate of interest in the cases of the annuity and redeemable security taken as examples in Chap. VI.

(*a*) In the case of the annuity, the given value of a is 20 (n being 30), and, since this is considerably nearer to the $2\frac{7}{8}$ per-cent value than to the $2\frac{3}{4}$ per-cent value, it will be better to take i as $\cdot 02875 - \rho$, than as $\cdot 0275 + \rho$. Hence the annuity-values and their differences required for the purposes of interpolation will be as follows:

i	a	Δ	Δ^2	Δ^3	Δ^4
·03125	19·28749				
		·31295			
·03	19·60044		·00758		
		·32053		·00022	
·02875	19·92097		·00780		·00001
		·32833		·00023	
·0275	20·24930		·00803		
		·33636			
·02625	20·58566				

Here $h = -\cdot 00125$; $u = 20$; $u_0 = 19\cdot 92097$;

$\Delta u_0 = \cdot 32833$; $\Delta^2 u_0 = \cdot 00803$

$a_0 = \frac{1}{2}\Delta(u_{-1} + u_0) = \cdot 32443$; $b_0 = \Delta^2 u_{-1} = \cdot 00780$

$c_0 = \frac{1}{2}\Delta^3(u_{-2} + u_{-1}) = \cdot 000225$; $d_0 = \Delta^4 u_{-2} = \cdot 00001$

$\alpha_0 = \Delta u_0 = \cdot 32833$; $\beta_0 = \frac{1}{2}\Delta^2(u_{-1} + u_{-0}) = \cdot 007915$

Hence by Formula (15)

$$i = \cdot 02875 - \cdot 00125 \frac{\cdot 07903}{\cdot 324315} = \cdot 0284454$$

By Formula (16)

$$i = \cdot 02875 - \cdot 00125 \frac{1 + \frac{\cdot 00803}{\cdot 65666}}{\frac{\cdot 32833}{\cdot 07903} + \frac{\cdot 00803}{\cdot 65666}} = \cdot 0284463$$

By Formula (17)

$$i = \cdot 02875 - \cdot 00125 \frac{\cdot 07903}{\cdot 32443 - \cdot 00004} = \cdot 0284455$$

By Formula (18)

$$i = \cdot 02875 - \cdot 00125 \frac{\cdot 07903}{\cdot 32439 + \cdot 07903 \frac{\cdot 0039}{\cdot 32439}} = \cdot 0284464$$

By Formula (19)

$$i = \cdot 02875 - \cdot 00125 \frac{1}{\frac{\cdot 32443}{\cdot 07903} + \frac{\cdot 0039}{\cdot 32443}} = \cdot 0284464$$

By Formula (20)

$$i = \cdot 02875 - \cdot 00125 \frac{\cdot 07903}{\cdot 32833 - \cdot 00396} = \cdot 0284454$$

And finally, by Formula (21)

$$i = \cdot 02875 - \cdot 00125 \frac{\cdot 07903}{\cdot 32437 + \cdot 07903 \frac{\cdot 00396}{\cdot 32437}} = \cdot 0284463$$

The true value of i, to seven places of decimals, being ·0284464, it will be seen that any of the formulas gives a result sufficiently accurate for most practical purposes. Of the simpler formulas, involving three annuity-values only, No. (19) is perhaps the best.

(*b*) In the case of the $4\frac{1}{2}$ per-cent debenture redeemable in 25 years at $112\frac{1}{2}$, the given value is 120, and the values of the debenture calculated at $1\frac{5}{8}$, $1\frac{3}{4}$, $1\frac{7}{8}$ and 2 per-cent half-yearly from the expression $(112\frac{1}{2}v^{50} + 2\frac{1}{4}a_{\overline{50}|})$ are, with their successive differences, as follows:—

i	A	Δ	Δ^2
·01625	126·866		
		−5·045	
·0175	121·821		·261
		−4·784	
·01875	117·037		·247
		−4·537	
·02	112·500		

Here $h = \cdot 00125$; $u_0 = 121\cdot 821$; $u = 120$;

$$\Delta u_0 = -4\cdot 784 \qquad \Delta^2 u_0 = \cdot 247$$

$$a_0 = -4\cdot 915 \qquad b_0 = \cdot 261$$

$$\alpha_0 = -4\cdot 784 \qquad \beta_0 = \cdot 254$$

Hence by Formula (16)

$$i = \cdot 0175 + \cdot 00125 \frac{1 - \dfrac{\cdot 247}{9 \cdot 568}}{\dfrac{4 \cdot 784}{1 \cdot 821} - \dfrac{\cdot 247}{9 \cdot 568}} = \cdot 017968$$

By Formula (19)

$$i = \cdot 0175 + \cdot 00125 \frac{1}{\dfrac{4 \cdot 915}{1 \cdot 821} - \dfrac{\cdot 261}{9 \cdot 830}} = \cdot 017968$$

And by Formula (21)

$$i = \cdot 0175 + 00125 \frac{1}{\dfrac{4 \cdot 911}{1 \cdot 821} - \dfrac{\cdot 127}{4 \cdot 911}} = \cdot 017968$$

It will be seen that all three formulas give the value correctly to the sixth place of decimals.

TABLE I.

Amount of 1 : *viz.*, $(1+i)^n$.

n	2½%	3%	3½%	4%	4½%	5%	n
1	1·02500	1·03000	1·03500	1·04000	1·04500	1·05000	1
2	1·05063	1·06090	1·07123	1·08160	1·09203	1·10250	2
3	1·07689	1·09273	1·10872	1·12486	1·14117	1·15763	3
4	1·10381	1·12551	1·14752	1·16986	1·19252	1·21551	4
5	1·13141	1·15927	1·18769	1·21665	1·24618	1·27628	5
6	1·15969	1·19405	1·22926	1·26532	1·30226	1·34010	6
7	1·18869	1·22987	1·27228	1·31593	1·36086	1·40710	7
8	1·21840	1·26677	1·31681	1·36857	1·42210	1·47746	8
9	1·24886	1·30477	1·36290	1·42331	1·48610	1·55133	9
10	1·28008	1·34392	1·41060	1·48024	1·55297	1·62889	10
11	1·31209	1·38423	1·45997	1·53945	1·62285	1·71034	11
12	1·34489	1·42576	1·51107	1·60103	1·69588	1·79586	12
13	1·37851	1·46853	1·56396	1·66507	1·77220	1·88565	13
14	1·41297	1·51259	1·61869	1·73168	1·85194	1·97993	14
15	1·44830	1·55797	1·67535	1·80094	1·93528	2·07893	15
16	1·48451	1·60471	1·73399	1·87298	2·02237	2·18287	16
17	1·52162	1·65285	1·79468	1·94790	2·11338	2·29202	17
18	1·55966	1·70243	1·85749	2·02582	2·20848	2·40662	18
19	1·59865	1·75351	1·92250	2·10685	2·30786	2·52695	19
20	1·63862	1·80611	1·98979	2·19112	2·41171	2·65330	20
21	1·67958	1·86029	2·05943	2·27877	2·52024	2·78596	21
22	1·72157	1·91610	2·13151	2·36992	2·63365	2·92526	22
23	1·76461	1·97359	2·20611	2·46472	2·75217	3·07152	23
24	1·80873	2·03279	2·28333	2·56330	2·87601	3·22510	24
25	1·85394	2·09378	2·36324	2·66584	3·00543	3·38635	25
26	1·90029	2·15659	2·44596	2·77247	3·14068	3·55567	26
27	1·94780	2·22129	2·53157	2·88337	3·28201	3·73346	27
28	1·99650	2·28793	2·62017	2·99870	3·42970	3·92013	28
29	2·04641	2·35657	2·71188	3·11865	3·58404	4·11614	29
30	2·09757	2·42726	2·80679	3·24340	3·74532	4·32194	30
31	2·15001	2·50008	2·90503	3·37313	3·91386	4·53804	31
32	2·20376	2·57508	3·00671	3·50806	4·08998	4·76494	32
33	2·25885	2·65234	3·11194	3·64838	4·27403	5·00319	33
34	2·31532	2·73191	3·22086	3·79432	4·46636	5·25335	34
35	2·37321	2·81386	3·33359	3·94609	4·66735	5·51602	35
36	2·43254	2·89828	3·45027	4·10393	4·87738	5·79182	36
37	2·49335	2·98523	3·57103	4·26809	5·09686	6·08141	37
38	2·55568	3·07478	3·69601	4·43881	5·32622	6·38548	38
39	2·61957	3·16703	3·82537	4·61637	5·56590	6·70475	39
40	2·68506	3·26204	3·95926	4·80102	5·81636	7·03999	40
41	2·75219	3·35990	4·09783	4·99306	6·07810	7·39199	41
42	2·82100	3·46070	4·24126	5·19278	6·35162	7·76159	42
43	2·89152	3·56452	4·38970	5·40050	6·63744	8·14967	43
44	2·96381	3·67145	4·54334	5·61652	6·93612	8·55715	44
45	3·03790	3·78160	4·70236	5·84118	7·24825	8·98501	45
46	3·11385	3·89504	4·86694	6·07482	7·57442	9·43426	46
47	3·19170	4·01190	5·03728	6·31782	7·91527	9·90597	47
48	3·27149	4·13225	5·21359	6·57053	8·27146	10·40127	48
49	3·35328	4·25622	5·39606	6·83335	8·64367	10·92133	49
50	3·43711	4·38391	5·58493	7·10668	9·03264	11·46740	50

Table II.

Present Value of 1: *viz.*, v^n.

n	$2\frac{1}{2}$%	3%	$3\frac{1}{2}$%	4%	$4\frac{1}{2}$%	5%	n
1	·97561	·97087	·96618	·96154	·95694	·95238	1
2	·95181	·94260	·93351	·92456	·91573	·90703	2
3	·92860	·91514	·90194	·88900	·87630	·86384	3
4	·90595	·88849	·87144	·85480	·83856	·82270	4
5	·88385	·86261	·84197	·82193	·80245	·78353	5
6	·86230	·83748	·81350	·79031	·76790	·74622	6
7	·84127	·81309	·78599	·75992	·73483	·71068	7
8	·82075	·78941	·75941	·73069	·70319	·67684	8
9	·80073	·76642	·73373	·70259	·67290	·64461	9
10	·78120	·74409	·70892	·67556	·64393	·61391	10
11	·76214	·72242	·68495	·64958	·61620	·58468	11
12	·74356	·70138	·66178	·62460	·58966	·55684	12
13	·72542	·68095	·63940	·60057	·56427	·53032	13
14	·70773	·66112	·61778	·57748	·53997	·50507	14
15	·69047	·64186	·59689	·55526	·51672	·48102	15
16	·67362	·62317	·57671	·53391	·49447	·45811	16
17	·65720	·60502	·55720	·51337	·47318	·43630	17
18	·64117	·58739	·53836	·49363	·45280	·41552	18
19	·62553	·57029	·52016	·47464	·43330	·39573	19
20	·61027	·55368	·50257	·45639	·41464	·37689	20
21	·59539	·53755	·48557	·43883	·39679	·35894	21
22	·58086	·52189	·46915	·42196	·37970	·34185	22
23	·56670	·50669	·45329	·40573	·36335	·32557	23
24	·55288	·49193	·43796	·39012	·34770	·31007	24
25	·53939	·47761	·42315	·37512	·33273	·29530	25
26	·52623	·46369	·40884	·36069	·31840	·28124	26
27	·51340	·45019	·39501	·34682	·30469	·26785	27
28	·50088	·43708	·38165	·33348	·29157	·25509	28
29	·48866	·42435	·36875	·32065	·27902	·24295	29
30	·47674	·41199	·35628	·30832	·26700	·23138	30
31	·46511	·39999	·34423	·29646	·25550	·22036	31
32	·45377	·38834	·33259	·28506	·24450	·20987	32
33	·44270	·37703	·32134	·27409	·23397	·19987	33
34	·43191	·36604	·31048	·26355	·22390	·19035	34
35	·42137	·35538	·29998	·25342	·21425	·18129	35
36	·41109	·34503	·28983	·24367	·20503	·17266	36
37	·40107	·33498	·28003	·23430	·19620	·16444	37
38	·39128	·32523	·27056	·22529	·18775	·15661	38
39	·38174	·31575	·26141	·21662	·17967	·14915	39
40	·37243	·30656	·25257	·20829	·17193	·14205	40
41	·36335	·29763	·24403	·20028	·16453	·13528	41
42	·35448	·28896	·23578	·19257	·15744	·12884	42
43	·34584	·28054	·22781	·18517	·15066	·12270	43
44	·33740	·27237	·22010	·17805	·14417	·11686	44
45	·32917	·26444	·21266	·17120	·13796	·11130	45
46	·32115	·25674	·20547	·16461	·13202	·10600	46
47	·31331	·24926	·19852	·15828	·12634	·10095	47
48	·30567	·24200	·19181	·15219	·12090	·09614	48
49	·29822	·23495	·18532	·14634	·11569	·09156	49
50	·29094	·22811	·17905	·14071	·11071	·08720	50

Table III.

Amount of 1 *per Annum: viz.*, $s_{\overline{n}|}$.

n	2½ %	3 %	3½ %	4 %	4½ %	5 %	n
1	1·0000	1·0000	1·0000	1·0000	1·0000	1·0000	1
2	2·0250	2·0300	2·0350	2·0400	2·0450	2·0500	2
3	3·0756	3·0909	3·1062	3·1216	3·1370	3·1525	3
4	4·1525	4·1836	4·2149	4·2465	4·2782	4·3101	4
5	5·2563	5·3091	5·3625	5·4163	5·4707	5·5256	5
6	6·3877	6·4684	6·5502	6·6330	6·7169	6·8019	6
7	7·5474	7·6625	7·7794	7·8983	8·0192	8·1420	7
8	8·7361	8·8923	9·0517	9·2142	9·3800	9·5491	8
9	9·9545	10·1591	10·3685	10·5828	10·8021	11·0266	9
10	11·2034	11·4639	11·7314	12·0061	12·2882	12·5779	10
11	12·4835	12·8078	13·1420	13·4864	13·8412	14·2068	11
12	13·7956	14·1920	14·6020	15·0258	15·4640	15·9171	12
13	15·1404	15·6178	16·1130	16·6268	17·1599	17·7130	13
14	16·5190	17·0863	17·6770	18·2919	18·9321	19·5986	14
15	17·9319	18·5989	19·2957	20·0236	20·7841	21·5786	15
16	19·3802	20·1569	20·9710	21·8245	22·7193	23·6575	16
17	20·8647	21·7616	22·7050	23·6975	24·7417	25·8404	17
18	22·3863	23·4144	24·4997	25·6454	26·8551	28·1324	18
19	23·9460	25·1169	26·3572	27·6712	29·0636	30·5390	19
20	25·5447	26·8704	28·2797	29·7781	31·3714	33·0660	20
21	27·1833	28·6765	30·2695	31·9692	33·7831	35·7193	21
22	28·8629	30·5368	32·3289	34·2480	36·3034	38·5052	22
23	30·5844	32·4529	34·4604	36·6179	38·9370	41·4305	23
24	32·3490	34·4265	36·6665	39·0826	41·6892	44·5020	24
25	34·1578	36·4593	38·9499	41·6459	44·5652	47·7271	25
26	36·0117	38·5530	41·3131	44·3117	47·5706	51·1135	26
27	37·9120	40·7096	43·7591	47·0842	50·7113	54·6691	27
28	39·8598	42·9309	46·2906	49·9676	53·9933	58·4026	28
29	41·8563	45·2189	48·9108	52·9663	57·4230	62·3227	29
30	43·9027	47·5754	51·6227	56·0849	61·0071	66·4388	30
31	46·0003	50·0027	54·4295	59·3283	64·7524	70·7608	31
32	48·1503	52·5028	57·3345	62·7015	68·6662	75·2988	32
33	50·3540	55·0778	60·3412	66·2095	72·7562	80·0638	33
34	52·6129	57·7302	63·4532	69·8579	77·0303	85·0670	34
35	54·9282	60·4621	66·6740	73·6522	81·4966	90·3203	35
36	57·3014	63·2759	70·0076	77·5983	86·1640	95·8363	36
37	59·7339	66·1742	73·4579	81·7022	91·0413	101·6281	37
38	62·2273	69·1594	77·0289	85·9703	96·1382	107·7095	38
39	64·7830	72·2342	80·7249	90·4091	101·4644	114·0950	39
40	67·4026	75·4013	84·5503	95·0255	107·0303	120·7998	40
41	70·0876	78·6633	88·5095	99·8265	112·8467	127·8398	41
42	72·8398	82·0232	92·6074	104·8196	118·9248	135·2318	42
43	75·6608	85·4839	96·8486	110·0124	125·2764	142·9933	43
44	78·5523	89·0484	101·2383	115·4129	131·9138	151·1430	44
45	81·5161	92·7199	105·7817	121·0294	138·8500	159·7002	45
46	84·5540	96·5015	110·4840	126·8706	146·0982	168·6852	46
47	87·6679	100·3965	115·3510	132·9454	153·6726	178·1194	47
48	90·8596	104·4084	120·3883	139·2632	161·5879	188·0254	48
49	94·1311	108·5406	125·6018	145·8337	169·8594	198·4267	49
50	97·4843	112·7969	130·9979	152·6671	178·5030	209·3480	50

TABLE IV.

Present Value of 1 *per Annum: viz.*, $a_{\overline{n}|}$.

n	$2\frac{1}{2}$%	3%	$3\frac{1}{2}$%	4%	$4\frac{1}{2}$%	5%	n
1	0.9756	0.9709	0.9662	0.9615	0.9569	0.9524	1
2	1.9274	1.9135	1.8997	1.8861	1.8727	1.8594	2
3	2.8560	2.8286	2.8016	2.7751	2.7490	2.7232	3
4	3.7620	3.7171	3.6731	3.6299	3.5875	3.5460	4
5	4.6458	4.5797	4.5151	4.4518	4.3900	4.3295	5
6	5.5081	5.4172	5.3286	5.2421	5.1579	5.0757	6
7	6.3494	6.2303	6.1145	6.0021	5.8927	5.7864	7
8	7.1701	7.0197	6.8740	6.7327	6.5959	6.4632	8
9	7.9709	7.7861	7.6077	7.4353	7.2688	7.1078	9
10	8.7521	8.5302	8.3166	8.1109	7.9127	7.7217	10
11	9.5142	9.2526	9.0016	8.7605	8.5289	8.3064	11
12	10.2578	9.9540	9.6633	9.3851	9.1186	8.8633	12
13	10.9832	10.6350	10.3027	9.9856	9.6829	9.3936	13
14	11.6909	11.2961	10.9205	10.5631	10.2228	9.8986	14
15	12.3814	11.9379	11.5174	11.1184	10.7395	10.3797	15
16	13.0550	12.5611	12.0941	11.6523	11.2340	10.8378	16
17	13.7122	13.1661	12.6513	12.1657	11.7072	11.2741	17
18	14.3534	13.7535	13.1897	12.6593	12.1600	11.6896	18
19	14.9789	14.3238	13.7098	13.1339	12.5933	12.0853	19
20	15.5892	14.8775	14.2124	13.5903	13.0079	12.4622	20
21	16.1845	15.4150	14.6980	14.0292	13.4047	12.8212	21
22	16.7654	15.9369	15.1671	14.4511	13.7844	13.1630	22
23	17.3321	16.4436	15.6204	14.8568	14.1478	13.4886	23
24	17.8850	16.9355	16.0584	15.2470	14.4955	13.7986	24
25	18.4244	17.4131	16.4815	15.6221	14.8282	14.0939	25
26	18.9506	17.8768	16.8904	15.9828	15.1466	14.3752	26
27	19.4640	18.3270	17.2854	16.3296	15.4513	14.6430	27
28	19.9649	18.7641	17.6670	16.6631	15.7429	14.8981	28
29	20.4535	19.1885	18.0358	16.9837	16.0219	15.1411	29
30	20.9303	19.6004	18.3920	17.2920	16.2889	15.3725	30
31	21.3954	20.0004	18.7363	17.5885	16.5444	15.5928	31
32	21.8492	20.3888	19.0689	17.8736	16.7889	15.8027	32
33	22.2919	20.7658	19.3902	18.1476	17.0229	16.0025	33
34	22.7238	21.1318	19.7007	18.4112	17.2468	16.1929	34
35	23.1452	21.4872	20.0007	18.6646	17.4610	16.3742	35
36	23.5563	21.8323	20.2905	18.9083	17.6660	16.5469	36
37	23.9573	22.1672	20.5705	19.1426	17.8622	16.7113	37
38	24.3486	22.4925	20.8411	19.3679	18.0500	16.8679	38
39	24.7303	22.8082	21.1025	19.5845	18.2297	17.0170	39
40	25.1028	23.1148	21.3551	19.7928	18.4016	17.1591	40
41	25.4661	23.4124	21.5991	19.9931	18.5661	17.2944	41
42	25.8206	23.7014	21.8349	20.1856	18.7235	17.4232	42
43	26.1664	23.9819	22.0627	20.3708	18.8742	17.5459	43
44	26.5038	24.2543	22.2828	20.5488	19.0184	17.6628	44
45	26.8330	24.5187	22.4955	20.7200	19.1563	17.7741	45
46	27.1542	24.7754	22.7009	20.8847	19.2884	17.8801	46
47	27.4675	25.0247	22.8994	21.0429	19.4147	17.9810	47
48	27.7732	25.2667	23.0912	21.1951	19.5356	18.0772	48
49	28.0714	25.5017	23.2766	21.3415	19.6513	18.1687	49
50	28.3623	25.7298	23.4556	21.4822	19.7620	18.2559	50

Table V.

Annuity that 1 *will purchase: viz.*, $(a_{\overline{n}|})^{-1}$.

n	$2\frac{1}{2}$%	3%	$3\frac{1}{2}$%	4%	$4\frac{1}{2}$%	5%	n
1	1·025000	1·030000	1·035000	1·040000	1·045000	1·050000	1
2	0·518827	0·522611	0·526400	0·530196	0·533998	0·537805	2
3	·350137	·353530	·356934	·360349	·363773	·367209	3
4	·265818	·269027	·272251	·275490	·278744	·282012	4
5	·215247	·218355	·221481	·224627	·227792	·230975	5
6	·181550	·184598	·187668	·190762	·193878	·197017	6
7	·157495	·160506	·163544	·166610	·169701	·172820	7
8	·139467	·142456	·145477	·148528	·151610	·154722	8
9	·125457	·128434	·131446	·134493	·137574	·140690	9
10	·114259	·117231	·120241	·123291	·126379	·129505	10
11	·105106	·108077	·111092	·114149	·117248	·120389	11
12	·097487	·100462	·103484	·106552	·109666	·112825	12
13	·091048	·094030	·097062	·100144	·103275	·106456	13
14	·085537	·088526	·091571	·094669	·097820	·101024	14
15	·080766	·083767	·086825	·089941	·093114	·096342	15
16	·076599	·079611	·082685	·085820	·089015	·092270	16
17	·072928	·075953	·079043	·082199	·085418	·088699	17
18	·069670	·072709	·075817	·078993	·082237	·085546	18
19	·066761	·069814	·072940	·076139	·079407	·082745	19
20	·064147	·067216	·070361	·073582	·076876	·080243	20
21	·061787	·064872	·068037	·071280	·074601	·077996	21
22	·059647	·062747	·065932	·069199	·072546	·075971	22
23	·057696	·060814	·064019	·067309	·070682	·074137	23
24	·055913	·059047	·062273	·065587	·068987	·072471	24
25	·054276	·057428	·060674	·064012	·067439	·070952	25
26	·052769	·055938	·059205	·062567	·066021	·069564	26
27	·051377	·054564	·057852	·061239	·064719	·068292	27
28	·050088	·053293	·056603	·060013	·063521	·067123	28
29	·048891	·052115	·055445	·058880	·062415	·066046	29
30	·047778	·051019	·054371	·057830	·061392	·065051	30
31	·046739	·049999	·053372	·056855	·060443	·064132	31
32	·045768	·049047	·052442	·055949	·059563	·063280	32
33	·044859	·048156	·051572	·055104	·058745	·062490	33
34	·044007	·047322	·050760	·054315	·057982	·061755	34
35	·043206	·046539	·049998	·053577	·057270	·061072	35
36	·042452	·045804	·049284	·052887	·056606	·060434	36
37	·041741	·045112	·048613	·052240	·055984	·059840	37
38	·041070	·044459	·047982	·051632	·055402	·059284	38
39	·040436	·043844	·047388	·051061	·054856	·058765	39
40	·039836	·043262	·046827	·050523	·054343	·058278	40
41	·039268	·042712	·046298	·050017	·053862	·057822	41
42	·038729	·042192	·045798	·049540	·053409	·057395	42
43	·038217	·041698	·045325	·049090	·052982	·056993	43
44	·037730	·041230	·044878	·048665	·052581	·056616	44
45	·037268	·040785	·044453	·048262	·052202	·056262	45
46	·036827	·040363	·044051	·047882	·051845	·055928	46
47	·036407	·039961	·043669	·047522	·051507	·055614	47
48	·036006	·039578	·043306	·047181	·051189	·055318	48
49	·035623	·039213	·042962	·046857	·050887	·055040	49
50	·035258	·038865	·042634	·046550	·050602	·054777	50

Table VI.

Values of d, v, $j_{(2)}$, $j_{(4)}$, δ, and $\log_{10}(1+i)$ corresponding to given values of i.

i	d	v	$j_{(2)}$	$j_{(4)}$	δ	$\log_{10}(1+i)$
·025	·024390	·975610	·024846	·024769	·024693	·0107239
·030	·029126	·970874	·029778	·029668	·029559	·0128372
·035	·033816	·966184	·034699	·034550	·034401	·0149403
·040	·038462	·961538	·039608	·039414	·039221	·0170333
·045	·043062	·956938	·044505	·044260	·044017	·0191163
·050	·047619	·952381	·049390	·049089	·048790	·0211893

Table VII.

Values of i corresponding to given values of $j_{(p)}$.

p	$j=$·025	$j=$·03	$j=$·035	$j=$·04	$j=$·045	$j=$·05
2	·025156	·030225	·035306	·040400	·045506	·050625
4	·025235	·030339	·035462	·040604	·045765	·050945

Table VIII.

Values of $\frac{i}{j_{(p)}}$ for given values of i and p.

p	$i=$·025	$i=$·03	$i=$·035	$i=$·04	$i=$·045	$i=$·05
2	1·00621	1·00744	1·00867	1·00990	1·01113	1·01235
4	1·00933	1·01118	1·01303	1·01488	1·01672	1·01856
12	1·01141	1·01368	1·01594	1·01820	1·02046	1·02271
∞	1·01245	1·01493	1·01740	1·01987	1·02233	1·02480

DIMENSIONS OF ACCOUNTING THEORY AND PRACTICE

An Arno Press Collection

The American Association of University Instructors in Accounting. **Papers and Proceedings of the American Association of University Instructors in Accounting.** 1916-1925

Baily, Francis. **The Doctrine of Interest and Annuities.** 1808

Beckett, Thomas. **The Accountant's Assistant.** 1901

Blough, Carman G. **Practical Applications of Accounting Standards.** 1957

Bray, F[rank] Sewell. **Precision and Design in Accountancy.** 1947

Brief, Richard P., editor. **Dicksee's Contribution to Accounting Theory and Practice.** 1980

Brinton, Willard C. **Graphic Methods For Presenting Facts.** 1914

Brooks, Collin, editor. **The Royal Mail Case.** 1933

Burns, Thomas J. and Edward N. Coffman, editors. **Ohio State Institute of Accounting Conferences: Collected Papers, 1938-1963.** 1980

By a Chartered Accountant and William A. Vawter Foundation on Business Ethics. **The Etiquette of the Accountancy Profession and The Ethical Problems of Modern Accountancy.** 1927/1933

Carey, John L. **Professional Ethics of Public Accounting.** 1946

Cerboni, Giuseppe. **Primi Saggi Di Logismografia Presentati All' XI Congresso Degli Scienziati Italiani In Roma.** 1873

Cleveland, Frederick A. **Chapters on Municipal Administration and Accounting.** 1909

Cocke, Sir Hugh. **A Summary of the Principal Legal Decisions Affecting Auditors.** 1946

Cotter, Arundel. **Fool's Profits.** 1940

Courcelle-Seneuil, J.G. **Traité Élémentaire de Comptabilité.** 1869

Daniels, Mortimer B. **Corporation Financial Statements.** 1934

DeMond, C.W. **Price, Waterhouse & Company in America.** 1951

Devine, Carl Thomas. **Inventory Valuation and Periodic Income.** 1942

Dicksee, Lawrence Robert. **Business Methods and the War** with **The Fundamentals of Manufacturing Costs;** and **Published Balance Sheets and Window Dressing.** 1916/1927, 1928

Dicksee, Lawrence Robert. **Business Organisation.** 1910

Dicksee, Lawrence Robert and Editor of the Accountant's Library. **Fraudulent Accounting** and **Fraud in Accounts.** 1909/1924, 1925

Edwards, J.R., editor. **British Company Legislation and Company Accounts, 1844-1976.** 1980

Ficker, Nicholas Thiel. **Shop Expense.** 1917

Goldberg, Louis. **An Inquiry Into the Nature of Accounting.** 1965

Green, David, Jr. **Accounting for Corporate Retained Earnings.** 1980

Greene, Catharine De Motte. **The Dynamic Balance Sheet.** 1980

Hain, Hans Peter. **Uniformity and Diversity.** 1980

Hawawini, Gabriel A., and Ashok Vora, editors. **The History of Interest Approximations.** 1980

Hepworth, Samuel Richard. **Reporting Foreign Operations.** 1956

The Herwood Library of Accountancy. 1938

The Institute of Chartered Accountants in England and Wales *Library Catalogue, 1913.* 1913

The Institute of Chartered Accountants in England and Wales **Library Catalogue, 1937.** 1937

Het Internationaal Accountantscongres, Amsterdam 1926. 1927

Johnson, H. Thomas, editor. **System and Profits: Early Management Accounting at DuPont and General Motors.** 1980

King, George. **The Theory of Finance.** 1882

Langenderfer, Harold Q. **The Federal Income Tax: 1861-1872.** 1980

Leake, P.D. **Commercial Goodwill.** 1921

Leautey, Eugene and Adolfe Guilbaut. **La Science Des Comptes Mise A La Portée De Tous.** 1889

Levy, Saul. **Accountants' Legal Responsibility.** 1954

Lubell, Myron Samuel. **The Significance of Organizational Conflict on the Legislative Evolution of the Accounting Profession in the United States.** 1980

Marchi, Francesco. **I Cinquecontisti.** 1867

Merino, Barbara, editor. **Business Income and Price Levels.** 1980

Norris, Harry. **Accounting Theory.** 1946

O'Neill, Michael T., editor. **A.P. Richardson: The Ethics of a Humanist.** 1980

Parker, R.H., editor. **Bibliographies for Accounting Historians.** 1980

Parker, R.H., editor. **British Accountants: A Biographical Sourcebook.** 1980

Perera, M.H.B. **Accounting for State Industrial and Commercial Enterprises in a Developing Country.** 1980

Previts, Gary John. **A Critical Evaluation of Comparative Financial Accounting Thought in America 1900 to 1920.** 1980

Rich, Wiley Daniel. **Legal Responsibilities and Rights of Public Accountants.** 1935

Richardson, A[lphyon] P[erry], editor. **The Influence of Accountants' Certificates on Commercial Credit.** 1913

Roberts, Alfred R., editor. **Selected Papers of Earle C. King.** 1980

Saliers, Earl A. **Principles of Depreciation.** 1915

Schiff, Michael, editor. **The Hayden Stone Accounting Forums 1962-1967.** 1980

Schmalenbach, Eugen. **Dynamic Accounting.** 1959

Scovell, Clinton H. **Cost Accounting and Burden Application.** 1916

Sprague, T[homas] B[ond]. **A Treatis on Life Insurance Accounts** and **A Treatise on Insurance Companies' Accounts** 1874/1911

Stacey, Nicholas A.H., **English Accountancy 1800-1954.** 1954

Stamp, Edward, G.W. Dean, and P.W. Wolnizer, editors. **Notable Financial Causes Célèbres.** 1980

Staubus, George J. **An Accounting Concept of Revenue.** 1980

Taylor, R. Emmett. **No Royal Road.** 1942

Todhunter, Ralph. **Institute of Actuaries' Text-Book of the Principles of Interest, Life Annuities, and Assurances, and Their Practical Application.** 1901

Wells, Murry C., editor. **Controversies on the Theory of the Firm, Overhead Allocation and Transfer Pricing.** 1980

Wildman, John R. and Weldon Powell. **Capital Stock Without Par Value.** 1928